"The state of Connecticut [...] convene a grand [...] Mr. Fuhrman is right [...] that Connecticut should 'Do what the legal system allows. . . .' We think everyone can agree that so far, justice has been lacking in the Moxley murder."

—*Greenwich Time*, May 13, 1998

"In a highly unusual legal move in Connecticut, a one-man grand jury has been appointed to investigate the unsolved 1975 slaying of 15-year-old Martha Moxley, state officials announced yesterday. . . ."

—*Boston Globe*, June 18, 1998

Lies of Silence

The people of Greenwich are living a lie. They think that by moving out to an exclusive suburb and sheltering themselves with money, and all the things and people money can buy, they can avoid, or at least ignore, human depravity. They are wrong. Greenwich may be richer, prettier, and safer than most other places on earth, but it is not immune to evil. In fact, the massive state of denial under which the town seems to operate is a form of evil itself.

In the fall of 1975, Belle Haven was the richest neighborhood in the richest town in the richest country in the world. With all of the guard booths and security patrols and off-duty policemen working on the side, Belle Haven residents couldn't protect themselves from murder.

"Fuhrman presents a detailed, straightforward piece of work—notably not splashy or sensational—in which he convincingly identifies the person he believes is responsible for the murder."
—*Milwaukee Sentinel*

Also by Mark Fuhrman

Murder in Brentwood

MURDER
IN
GREENWICH

Who Killed
Martha Moxley?

MARK FUHRMAN

With a new afterword by the Author

Foreword by
DOMINICK DUNNE

HarperPaperbacks
A Division of HarperCollins*Publishers*

HarperPaperbacks
A Division of HarperCollins*Publishers*
10 East 53rd Street, New York, NY 10022-5299

ISBN 0-06-109692-X

HarperCollins®, 📖®, and HarperPaperbacks™ are trademarks of HarperCollins Publishers, Inc.

Cover design © 1998 by Rick Pracher/
Cover photograph courtesy of the Moxley family

A hardcover edition of this book was published in 1998 by Cliff Street Books, an Imprint of HarperCollins*Publishers.*

First paperback printing: February 1999

Printed in the United States of America

❖ 10 9 8 7 6 5 4 3

For Martha

CONTENTS

PART V: ANATOMY OF A MURDER INVESTIGATION

ACKNOWLEDGMENTS

The author would like to thank the following:

Stephen Weeks—He was on the case from the beginning. Without Steve's extraordinary investigative and literary skills, this book would not have been possible.

Dominick Dunne—He gave me the inspiration and information I needed to get started. His friendship, generosity, and passion for justice kept me going.

Dorthy and John Moxley—Two brave and resilient people who gave me full support and cooperation. There is no way I can bring Martha back, but I hope this book helps in some way.

Steve Carroll—A good man, a good cop, and a good friend. If the Greenwich police were filled with Steve Carrolls, they would have solved the case.

Bernice and Suzanne Carroll—Thanks for your hospitality and support. Sorry things aren't so exciting around there anymore.

Len Levitt—Without his diligent reporting skills, the Moxley case might have been forgotten.

Joe Johnson—His journalism was indispensable, and I consider him a friend.

Vin Cannato—His research assistance was extremely useful. Vin has a brilliant career ahead of him.

Jerry Oppenheimer—He gave me useful tips, and

his own work helped contribute to my understanding of the case.

Dr. Michael Baden—His help on the autopsy was crucial, and his analysis was both detailed and concise.

Theresa Carroll, her family and staff at the Homestead Inn—They made my visit as comfortable and pleasant as any trip to Greenwich could possibly be.

Carnes—Thanks for the company and the doctor's expertise.

Sheila—Thanks for the pie.

Arthur Gorton—Thanks for all your help. Please get to work on time.

Andy Goodman—A living oxymoron, an ethical attorney.

Lucianne Goldberg—She went above and beyond the duties of a literary agent. Her generosity and faith helped see me through the toughest times.

Diane Reverand—She believed in the project and gave me incredible support and superb editorial guidance. It was a pleasure to work with a real publisher.

The many people at HarperCollins whose hard work made this book possible.

Finally, I would like to thank my family for tolerating me, the stress of doing two books in less than one year, the traveling, and the anxiety over dealing with the business world after so many years of working in civil service.

FOREWORD

For some reason, the 1975 unsolved murder of Martha Moxley in Greenwich, Connecticut, never really became a national story, although it had all the elements that usually fascinate the public: a beautiful fifteen-year-old victim from a prosperous family named Martha Moxley and a handsome young suspect from an even more prosperous family, with connections that reached all the way to the White House, named Thomas Skakel. After a few days in the *New York Times*, the story dropped out of the national news and became a local story in the Greenwich papers. Being from Connecticut myself, I was always interested in the case and from time to time over the years heard updates, but no arrest was ever made. Once I suggested to Tina Brown, the then-editor of *Vanity Fair*, that I write a piece about it, but she said it was an old story by then with no developments of consequence and no arrest, and she declined.

Later, I went to Palm Beach to cover the rape trial of William Kennedy Smith. During the trial, a bit of misleading gossip was circulated that Smith had been a guest in the Skakel house on the night of the Moxley murder. It turned out not to be true, but again I became interested in the unsolved case. I made myself known to Dorthy Moxley, the mother of the slain Martha, and told her I wanted to write a novel based on the case. She gave me her blessing. The book, *A Season in Purgatory*, became a national best-seller. Dan Rather did a segment on the

CBS Nightly News about how my novel put a spotlight back on the long dormant Moxley case. Time passed. Nothing happened. Then came the miniseries of my book. It was highly publicized as being based on a famous unsolved murder in Greenwich, Connecticut, involving an illustrious family. The spotlight was on it again. Nothing happened. But the name Skakel was spoken in louder and louder tones. Tommy Skakel. Michael Skakel.

I was not unfamiliar with the Skakel family. In 1950, when I was a young man in New York, a year out of Williams College, a girlfriend of mine invited me to take her—on the yacht of a friend of hers—to a fancy wedding in Greenwich, Connecticut.

"Whose wedding?" I asked.

"One of those Kennedys from Boston and a girl I went to Sacred Heart Convent with, Ethel Skakel," she answered.

These days, the words "estate" and "mansion" have lost their meaning, so frequently and inappropriately are they thrown about. O. J. Simpson did not live in a mansion or on an estate, as was widely reported. He lived in a large house on a large plot. But the Skakels lived on an estate: I remember a long, winding white-pebbled driveway, lush green grounds in all directions, fountains spouting water in the air, and a stone mansion of monumental proportions. I was impressed. I mean, my mouth was hanging open.

"Who the hell are the Skakels?" I asked.

"Richer than the Kennedys," my girlfriend answered.

During the reception, I discovered a further connection. Ethel's brother, Rushton, the father of the two suspects in the Martha Moxley murder, had been a couple of years ahead of me at Canterbury, a Catholic boarding school in Connecticut, although I hadn't known him there. It happens frequently in my life that I interact in the very world I write about. At the William Kennedy Smith trial, I sat directly across the aisle in the courtroom from three Kennedy sisters and Ethel Skakel Kennedy. We all dropped our eyes when we passed each other in the corridors.

In both fiction and reportage, I have made no secret of the fact that I hate killers who get away with murder, and I am utterly without respect for the kind of lawyers who cheat and lie to win an acquittal for a guilty man. Consequently, I am the recipient each week of a great many requests to look into unreported murder and crime in grand families and high places. Shortly before I left New York to cover the O. J. Simpson civil trial, I received a message at my magazine that interested me. "I have information about the Moxley murder," the message said. We met in a midtown restaurant. He was a recent college graduate and future writer who had been hired by a private detective agency in New York to write in an orderly flow the findings and discoveries of the agency concerning a murder that had taken place in Greenwich, Connecticut, in 1975. It was the Moxley murder. The agency had been hired by Rushton Skakel nearly four years earlier, at the time my book came out, to clear the name of Tommy Skakel, who lived under constant suspicion of being a murderer and whose powerful family was able to keep the police at bay. The agency, known as Sutton Associates, had access to the Skakel family in a way that the Greenwich police never had. The findings from the Sutton investigation were such a shock to Rushton Skakel that he terminated the contract between them and paid up. All of the detectives on the case had signed confidentiality oaths, except the young writer who contacted me and gave me a copy of the Sutton files. I read it that night. I told Dorthy Moxley, who had become a friend over the years, that I had something astonishing. I swore her to secrecy until I could decide how to handle it, but, in her excitement, she told a few people. The word spread. I started receiving hostile calls. Someone tipped off the Sutton agency that I had been given their files. My informant felt he was in jeopardy, and I felt responsible. I was due to leave for the O. J. Simpson civil trial in Santa Monica. I returned the Sutton files. I told everyone I didn't have them anymore. But, of course, I kept a copy. I asked my secretary to hide it and not tell me where it was.

When the civil trial was over and I returned to New York, I gave a copy of the files to a detective who had been working on the Moxley case from almost the night of the murder. Time went by. Nothing happened. I began to think that nothing was ever going to happen. Then along came Mark Fuhrman, whom I grew to admire after the fiasco of the Simpson trial. I had loved his book, *Murder in Brentwood*, and was impressed with how well he conducted himself on television. Say what you want, the guy is a great detective. He was looking for an unsolved murder to write about. I said, "Hey, Mark, I've got just the one for you, and I have a private detective report that's going to knock you on your ass."

This book is the result.

—DOMINICK DUNNE

PART I
Background

1

A Murder in Greenwich

*At my funeral I want everybody to be happy
and remember all the good times we had.*
—Martha Moxley

Although she had lived in Greenwich for only
a little more than a year, Martha Moxley had
made many friends. At least five hundred of
them attended her funeral. All the pews in the nave
and the balcony of the First Lutheran Church were
filled, along with rows of folding chairs set up in
the back. Many more young people stood behind
the folding chairs and spilled out the church door.
Greenwich High School had excused students from
classes in order to attend the service, and students
from the local private schools attended as well.

The funeral was held on Tuesday, November 4,
1975. Martha had been dead for five days. During
this time, Greenwich had been overwhelmed by
Martha's death. Earlier in the week, students had
thrown rocks at the television crews who came to
Greenwich High School to report on the reaction to the
murder. Martha's classmates were starting a scholar-

ship fund in her name, and there were plans to plant a tree in her memory. Before the previous Friday's football game, there had been a moment of silence.

The children of Greenwich were the sons and daughters of some of the wealthiest and most prominent families in the country. Their parents were corporate executives, lawyers, Wall Street bankers, socialites, and polo players. They led a comfortable and sheltered existence—until Martha Moxley was beaten to death with a golf club on her family's estate in the exclusive neighborhood of Belle Haven.

At her funeral the Reverend Richard Manus read a eulogy that a group of her friends had written: "Martha Moxley loved life. Every day was something special. After only a short time here, she made more friends than most people make in a lifetime.

"She was always the first to come around and she was fun to be around—it was an education to be with her.

"She made everyone she met feel as though he were her friend. It was an adventure to be with her, and we will always reminisce about the experiences we shared."

Martha's closed coffin stood in front of a church window, the autumn sun filtering through the stained glass and shining onto the casket. Nine of Martha's closest friends walked up and each placed a single yellow rose on the casket as a sign of affection. They all broke into tears during the ritual.

Reverend Manus said that "family came first in Martha's life." The Moxley family "were very close, they did everything together. They were the perfect foursome." Her mother Dorthy, father David, and brother John stood in the front pew. They were still in shock. A business transfer had required their recent move from California, and they chose Greenwich because it was pretty and safe.

Reverend Manus read a poem by Edgar Guest: "No Friend Who Loves Will Ever Die." Then he closed the service with a recitation of the Lord's Prayer.

The mourners filed quietly from the church, past a gauntlet of onlookers outside. Television cameras and news photographers took pictures of the crowd as they exited the church. Several of the fifteen Greenwich police detectives assigned to investigate the murder stood on the sidewalk, closely observing the mourners. Across the street captain of detectives Tom Keegan hid behind a row of parked cars, snapping photos with a camera equipped with a telephoto lens.

Dorothy Moxley was one of the last to leave the church. Outside she saw seventeen-year-old Thomas Skakel. He was standing alone, looking sad and somewhat aloof while his fifteen-year-old brother Michael was talking with his other brothers and friends. Dorothy knew that Martha had been with Thomas the night she died, and he was the last person to be seen with her. Dorothy felt sorry for the boy, so she went up to Thomas and hugged him. She didn't know he was already a suspect in the murder.

At the time, Dorothy didn't believe that Thomas, or anyone else from Belle Haven, could have mur-

dered her daughter. She assumed, like everyone else
in Greenwich, that the killer must have been an outsider.

Several youths broke down crying as Martha's
coffin was carried into the hearse and driven to the
Putnam Hills cemetery. Accompanied by David and
John, Dorthy Moxley stepped into the first of a long
line of black limousines. A single Greenwich police
car with its lights silently flashing led the funeral
procession. They drove to the Putnam Hills cemetery
to bury a beautiful young girl.

Martha Moxley was murdered on October 30, 1975,
the night before Halloween. Earlier that evening, she
planned to celebrate Hacker's Night by going out
with her friends and engaging in harmless mis-
chief—throwing eggs at cars and decorating trees
with toilet paper. There was no school the next day. It
was the beginning of a three-day weekend. And there
was a party at the Skakels. Mr. Rushton Skakel was
out of town. Whenever he went away, the kids had
free run of the house.

Martha Moxley was a pretty, popular fifteen-
year-old. Outgoing, even flirtatious, Martha had no
problem making friends. She had moved to
Greenwich from northern California and had already
been voted the girl with the best personality in her
junior-high-school class that first year. During the
summer, Martha had become even more attractive.
She finally got her braces off and lost the last traces of

her baby fat. She was beginning to mature into a beautiful, self-assured young woman.

On October 30, her father, David Moxley, was in Atlanta for a partners' meeting of Touche Ross, the Big Eight accounting firm for which he worked as partner in charge of the New York office. David often worked late and traveled on business, but Dorthy almost always cooked a full sit-down dinner for the children. That evening John Moxley had already gone out to hang around with his friends. Since Martha was eager to get going herself, Dorthy cooked her a grilled cheese sandwich for dinner.

The Moxleys did not have an established curfew for Martha. Instead, it was a judgment call. Martha was expected home at a reasonable hour, and she was expected to know what was reasonable and what was not. The previous week Martha had stayed out until two or three in the morning at a party given by her neighborhood friends, Holly and Tory Fuchs. She was supposed to be grounded as punishment, but Martha convinced her mother to allow her to go out for Hacker's Night. Martha was throwing a party herself the next night and was busy with preparations. Dorthy figured she wouldn't stay out too late.

Martha's friends, Helen Ix and Geoffrey Byrne soon showed up at the Moxley house. Martha called her friend Margie Walker, but Margie's mother didn't want her daughter going out on Hacker's Night.

Outside it was freezing, one of the first really cold evenings of the fall. Martha's favorite coat was a shearling jacket. Since she knew there would be shaving cream and eggs flying around, she decided to wear her blue down parka over a white flower-print turtleneck and blue jeans.

Martha, Helen, and Geoffrey left the Moxley house, walked across the back of the property, through a hole in the fence, across the McGuire property, and over to Field Point Road, where the Wetenhalls lived. They picked up Jackie Wetenhall, then cut over to Otter Rock Drive to get Marie Coomoraswamy. From there, the five kids crossed back over Otter Rock Drive to the Mouakad house. Mrs. Odette Mouakad, recently widowed with several young children, did not want her kids attending a party at the Skakel house. The Skakels had a reputation of being wild. Mrs. Mouakad wanted no part of them.

Even by Greenwich standards, the Skakels were very wealthy. The family business was Great Lakes Carbon, one of the largest privately held companies in the world. They were related to the Kennedys, as Rushton Skakel's sister, Ethel Skakel, had married Bobby Kennedy in 1950. Like the Kennedys, it was a large Catholic family. Rushton Skakel had six boys and one girl: Rushton Jr. (nineteen), Julie (eighteen), Thomas (seventeen), John (sixteen), Michael (fifteen), David (twelve), and Steven (nine). Since their mother Ann Reynolds Skakel had died of cancer in 1973, the children were being raised by their father, along with a team of household help. That night the help included Ken Littleton, a live-in tutor Rushton had just hired to look after the children.

Since the Skakel children all went to private schools and Martha attended Greenwich High, she didn't know them very well. In fact, she has just gotten to be friendly with Thomas and Michael Skakel. Martha had started to write about the two boys in her diary. Both brothers were interested in her. Martha, like most adolescent girls, enjoyed boys and their attention.

Early in the evening, some dozen kids were hanging around the chain at the end of Walsh Lane facing Otter Rock Drive. Around 7:00 P.M. one of them threw an egg at a passing car and they all ran away. A few minutes later a police car arrived. When the car departed, the kids regrouped back at the chain.

Belle Haven was a very exclusive and close-knit neighborhood of forty homes on a hundred-acre peninsula jutting into Long Island Sound. The Belle Haven private security force patrolled the streets around the clock and manned guard posts at every public access.

People moved to Belle Haven—literally "beautiful shelter"—because it was private, secure, and exclusive. Residents enjoyed their own private beach club. Everybody knew each other. Houses were left unlocked. Keys were left in cars. Children cut through residents' backyards on the way to each other's houses. It was not uncommon for large groups of teenagers to be seen hanging out. On Hacker's Night, the Belle Haven security force put extra officers on duty, anticipating increased youth activity. The Belle Haven security officers were mostly there to keep outsiders away, not to discipline the local youngsters, sons and daughters of some of Greenwich's wealthiest families. Martha's friends that night included: Helen Ix, whose father was the president of Cadbury/Schweppes; and Jackie Wetenhall, whose father was the former chairman of the American Dairy Association.

At 7:30 P.M. Martha, Helen, Jackie, and Geoffrey Byrne arrived at the Skakel house. Franz Wittine, the Skakel gardener, told them that the boys were down at the Belle Haven Club eating dinner. Martha and her friends returned to the Mouakads', where Mrs. Mouakad gave them ice cream.

Sometime around 8:30 Martha and her friends went back to the Skakel house. The girls sent Geoffrey Byrne to ask Wittine again if the boys were back yet, but they still had not returned from dinner. When the Skakels came back from the club at 8:45, Martha and her friends were walking Jackie Wetenhall back home to make her 9:00 P.M. curfew.

After dropping Jackie off, they returned to the Skakel house, where they met up with Michael Skakel. The four kids sat together listening to music in the Skakel Lincoln, which was parked in the driveway. Martha sat next to Michael in the front seat, while Helen and Geoff sat in the back. At 9:15 Thomas Skakel came out of the house wearing a big red cowboy hat. He went to the Lincoln and said he wanted to get a music tape from the car. Instead of just taking the tape and leaving, he got into the car, sitting in the front seat.

Martha was between the two Skakel boys. Thomas started flirting with Martha. He put his hand on her leg and she loudly told him, "Get your hand off." Thomas removed his hand, but he continued to joke and flirt with her. Michael watched as his older brother put the moves on a girl they both were interested in. Thomas was bigger and stronger than his younger brother. He had had a few beers and a couple scotches at the Belle Haven Club and had continued drinking once he got home.

Sometime around 9:30 the party began breaking up. Julie Skakel and her friend Andrea Shakespeare came out of the house, where they had been watching television. Julie was going to take Andrea home. Also inside the house were Rush Skakel Jr. and John Skakel, along with their cousin Jim Terrien. They came outside and told everybody to get out of the Lincoln because they wanted to drive to the Terrien house in the north part of town.

Everyone got out of the car. Michael asked Martha if she wanted to go to the Terriens' with him. She said no, she had to go home. Thomas decided he didn't want to go to the Terriens' either. Michael got in the car with his brothers and cousin and the Lincoln drove away. Left alone, Thomas and Martha walked near the shed off the driveway, where they began flirting, roughhousing, and eventually kissing.

Helen Ix and Geoffrey Byrne were a little bit disgusted with Martha's behavior and decided to go home. As they walked together across the Skakel backyard, they saw Thomas and Martha falling together behind the fence near the Skakel pool. This was the last time they saw their friend Martha Moxley.

The Moxley house at 38 Walsh Lane was a large, stucco English-style mansion on three acres with extensive but run-down formal gardens in the back. The house was old and in disrepair when the Moxleys bought it. Dorthy liked fixing up old houses and had been successful with similar projects. Still, the house on Walsh Lane needed a lot of work.

Around 9:30, Dorthy Moxley was upstairs painting the mullions around the windows of her second-floor bedroom. Martha's room was directly above on the third floor. Outside, the night was so cold that Dorthy had to close the windows, even though she was painting with enamel and would have preferred to let the fresh air in. After she had been painting for a while, she heard a commotion on the side of the house—the sound of voices so loud that she could hear them through the closed windows. She clearly heard the voices of male youths, or at least one male youth. She was accustomed to hearing kids on the property, since they often cut through her yard. But these voices didn't sound friendly or innocent, so she thought she'd better check and see what was going on.

The nearest window Dorthy could see from was in her bathroom, where she went. She turned on the light but couldn't see anything outside. The light shone down onto the screened-in porch where Martha kept her brand-new yellow Schwinn bicycle. Dorthy thought that if she left the light on, someone might see Martha's bicycle and take it. So she turned the light off.

Around the same time—approximately 9:30 to 9:45—several dogs in the neighborhood started barking loudly. Many families in Belle Haven had dogs and they often barked, but the barking at this time was so loud and sustained that several residents noted the disturbance. The Ixes' dog Socks went to the edge of their property on Walsh Lane. The Bjorks' springer spaniel went over to the edge of their property nearest the Moxleys'. Several neighbors were startled enough to go out and check on the commotion. Nanny Sweeney, the Skakels' live-in housekeeper, asked Ken Littleton to go outside and see who was there. He stepped out for a few minutes and heard some noises, but didn't investigate. Somehow, in the midst of all this racket, the Skakels' dog Max was uncharacteristically quiet.

Around 10:00 P.M., Dorthy Moxley decided to stop painting for the evening. She wrapped her brushes up and put them away, then took a quick shower. Dressed in a nightgown and bathrobe she went downstairs and started watching the 11:00 news in a little room on the first floor where, if there had been more commotion, she probably would not have heard it.

That night John Moxley had gone out with his

friends John Harvey and Vincent Cortese. They bought eggs at the grocery store and went to the high school, where they lobbed the eggs at some cheerleaders preparing for a pep rally. Running away from the scene, John and his friends got separated. They met up later at Dairy Queen and then went to a couple of parties. Around 11:20 John Moxley returned home.

"You know, Martha isn't home yet," Dorthy said when John walked in. "It's really funny, I don't know where she is."

Dorthy was annoyed because Martha had stayed out too late twice in a week. John was secretly a little pleased. For once it was his perfect sister and not he who was in trouble. John said he would go out and look for Martha. He got in his car and cruised around the Belle Haven neighborhood for a half hour. He only saw one person—a drunk kid trying to sleep it off outside the Ferguson house. When he came back, he told his mother he didn't see Martha.

Dorthy fell asleep in front of the television. When she woke up sometime after midnight, she went upstairs and checked Martha's bedroom. Her daughter still wasn't home. Dorthy went back downstairs. She didn't think to go outside and look for Martha there. Instead she began making phone calls to Martha's friends. First she called Helen Ix, who told her that she last saw Martha with Thomas Skakel and gave her the Skakels' phone number.

When Dorthy called the Skakel house, Julie Skakel answered. Dorthy asked if anyone there had seen Martha. Julie went upstairs and asked Thomas when he had last seen Martha. Without getting out of bed or turning on the light, Thomas said he last saw her at the back door at 9:30 when he had to go inside and study for a test. Julie relayed this information to Mrs. Moxley.

As the hours passed and there was still no sign of Martha, Dorthy called the Skakels several more times. Every time she called, Julie answered.

"I'm very concerned," Dorthy told Julie during one phone call. "Would you please go upstairs and ask Thomas again if he had seen Martha, what the circumstances were, when he last saw her?"

Julie went back upstairs and asked Thomas again. He told her the same story—he had last seen her at 9:30 at the back door, when they said good-bye and he went in to study for a test.

At one point, Dorthy insisted on speaking to Thomas himself. Julie got him out of bed and he came to the phone.

"Do you know where Martha could be?" Dorthy asked.

"I have no idea where she is," Thomas replied.

On Julie's suggestion, Dorthy called the Terriens. Georgeann Terrien, Rushton Skakel and Ethel Kennedy's sister, said that her son Jim wasn't home. She checked the entire house and a guest house on the property but couldn't find him.

Dorthy also called Jackie Wetenhall and Peter Ziluca. Jackie didn't have any idea where Martha could be. Peter's mother said that Peter had been home the entire night. He was also grounded for staying out late the previous week. Dorthy called Jackie Wetenhall again at 3:15 A.M. Twenty minutes later, Dorthy woke John up and asked him to go out and look for Martha. This time John was truly concerned. He drove all over Greenwich until dawn, looking for his sister.

Dorthy called her closest friends, Jean Wold, Marilyn Robertson, and Jean Walker, in the middle of the night to tell them she couldn't find Martha and was very worried. Dorthy knew that Martha wouldn't run away and she hadn't spent the night with any of her friends because she had called all her friends.

At 3:48 A.M. Dorthy called the Greenwich Police Department and reported Martha missing. Patrolman Daniel Merchant proceeded to the Moxley residence to interview Dorthy, who told him that she had no reason to suspect that Martha could have run away and it was not like her to stay out this late. Together they searched the Moxley house and a small cottage just a short distance behind the main house. They didn't find Martha or any clue that could lead to her whereabouts.

Two Greenwich police cars made a visual search of the Belle Haven area for Martha Moxley. They drove around the neighborhood shining their flashlights, hoping to see her walking down the street or through somebody's yard.

At 6:35 A.M. Patrolman Merchant called Dorthy to see if there had been any sign of Martha. She still hadn't come home. Dorthy called Peter Ziluca's house again. This time Peter's mother woke him and asked if he knew where Martha was. Peter said he hadn't seen or talked to her the night before.

At some point early in the morning, Dorthy fell asleep in the window seat in the library where she had been making the calls.

After waking up around 10:00 A.M. and still no sign of Martha, Dorthy decided to go to the Skakels'. She walked out the front door, down the driveway, and across Walsh Lane toward the Skakels' back sunporch. Although she had lived in the neighborhood for more than a year, and Rushton Skakel had sponsored their membership in the Belle Haven Club, this was the first time that Dorthy had ever been to the Skakel house. Their German shepherd Max barked ferociously at her, frightening her half to death. She got past Max and knocked on the door of the rear sunporch. Michael Skakel answered the door.

"Hi, Michael, I'm Martha Moxley's mother and Martha didn't come home," Dorthy said. "Do you know where she might be?"

"No," Michael answered.

Michael looked very pale and disheveled, as if he were hungover and hadn't slept all night, but he was helpful to Mrs. Moxley, who had never spoken to him before.

"Is Martha there?" Dorthy asked.

"No," Michael answered without looking or asking anyone inside.

"Could she be in the camper?" Dorthy knew that

her daughter liked beer; maybe she had drunk too much and passed out in the camper.

Franz Wittine, the Skakel gardener, showed up. Wittine told Dorthy that he had already checked the camper that morning, but he did so again. No sign of Martha there. Dorthy thanked Michael and Franz, then went back home.

At 9:15 A.M. juvenile officer Dan Hickman had called Dorthy Moxley to inform her that her daughter's case was being handled by the Youth Division Office. Dorthy told Officer Hickman that she had contacted all of Martha's friends and no one had any idea where she was. Hickman and his partner, juvenile officer Millard Jones, conducted a motorized search of the Belle Haven area. At this point, the police were not terribly concerned; teenagers were always staying out late and worrying their parents. It happened all the time.

If the police weren't concerned yet, Dorthy and her friends were. In the late morning, her friends began to arrive at the house: Marilyn Robertson, a close friend whose husband, Lowell, was a business associate of David Moxley; Jean Wold, an elderly woman with severe health problems who was a close friend of Dorthy's; and Jean Walker, a friend of Dorthy's whose daughter Marjorie was one of Martha's closest friends. Dorthy sat with Marilyn, Jean Walker, and Jean Wold in the living room. Marilyn Robertson called Atlanta to contact David Moxley. She left a message that Martha was missing and for David to come home as soon as possible. They called other friends and neighbors, hoping to find someone who might know what happened to Martha.

Around 12:15 P.M., Sheila McGuire, a fifteen-year-old girl who lived nearby, was walking from her house through a wooded section of the Moxley property. It was common for neighborhood children to pass through that area, particularly if they were going to Walsh Lane or the Moxley house. Sheila was a Belle Haven neighbor, but she wasn't one of Martha's close friends. She later said that she was on her way to the Moxleys' to see if Martha wanted to go downtown. Although the entire neighborhood was abuzz with the news, Sheila apparently hadn't heard that Martha was missing.

Walking across the Moxley yard, Sheila noticed something beneath a large pine tree about two hundred feet away from the house. At first she thought it was a sleeping bag on top of a foam mattress. Then she stepped closer and saw the partially clothed body of her friend Martha. She ran to the Moxley house and rang the doorbell. Jean Walker answered the door. Dorthy Moxley followed closely behind.

"I found Martha," Sheila said, crying.

"Where?" Dorthy asked.

"Out under the tree."

"Is she okay?" Dorthy asked.

"I don't think so," Sheila sobbed.

Dorthy was stunned. She started to go outside, but Jean Walker stopped her.

"I'd better go look." Jean Walker took Sheila's hand and went outside with her.

At the time, Jean Walker thought that it all must have been some kind of accident or a prank. They walked down the sloping lawn to the large pine tree. Sheila stopped and pointed toward the tree but wouldn't go any closer. Jean Walker went on ahead. As she approached the tree, she saw the body partially hidden under the low, overhanging boughs that reached almost to the ground. Martha was face-down. Her head was covered with dried blood. Her blue jeans and panties were pulled down below her knees. Jean Walker touched the small of Martha's back. She was ice cold.

When she realized what must have happened, Jean Walker's first reaction was fear. Standing under the tree next to Martha's lifeless body, she felt as if she were being watched. She dashed back to the house, taking Sheila with her. When they returned, Dorthy asked, "Is Martha okay?"

Jean Walker paused a moment before telling Dorthy that her daughter was dead.

Dorthy collapsed into a chair in the living room. She started crying hysterically. Her friends tried to comfort her, but there was nothing they could do or say. They tried to help, but little could be done except to notify the police. Thinking of her own daughter, Jean Walker quickly left to collect Marjorie and her friends at a field hockey game at Rye Country Day School.

Minutes later officers Hickman and Jones arrived at the Moxley house. Sheila McGuire was outside. She pointed them toward the body but wouldn't go near the tree herself. The officers ran toward the body. When Jones saw the body and established that she was dead, he went to the Moxley house to notify police headquarters by phone so the word wouldn't get out over police scanner, which was routinely monitored by many journalists and civilians. He told Hickman to stay with the body. When Jones came out of the Moxley house, he saw Hickman frantically calling on the police radio in their squad car. Soon Walsh Lane and nearby Otter Rock Drive were crowded with detectives, uniformed officers, emergency personnel, journalists, curious neighbors, and other onlookers.

Meanwhile, John Moxley was at an early football practice. While he was getting dressed in the locker room, the coach took John aside and told him that something had happened at home. John was concerned when he left home that morning, and once the coach told him to go back there, he knew something terrible had happened. Feeling a chilling premonition, John drove home like a madman. When he arrived at Walsh Lane, he saw what looked like a police convention. Cops and reporters and civilians were everywhere.

He left his car at the end of the driveway and ran up to the house, where Lowell Robertson stopped him. Robertson had come to the Moxley house to be with Dorthy and his wife, Marilyn. The police had asked Robertson to formally identify the body. Once he did so, he waited in the driveway for John to come back. He didn't want John to hear the bad news from someone else.

When Robertson told John that his sister was dead, John took a swing at him. Understanding the boy's frustration and anger, Robertson stepped back and avoided the blow. John collected himself and apologized.

Robertson tried to stop John from going inside, but John pushed past him, yelling, "It's my sister!"

When John ran into the house, his mother told him that Martha has been murdered. John asked, "How did she get killed? What happened?"

"I don't know," Dorthy said. "They found her out by the tree."

They hugged, and Dorthy held tightly on to John. He was now her only child.

David Moxley called from the Atlanta airport. He had received Marilyn Robertson's message and was on his way home. Marilyn told him that Martha's body had been found and she was dead. Dorthy wished that David didn't have to learn this while he was alone at an airport.

While the police began their investigation and her friends did their best to comfort her, Dorthy sat on a chair in the living room.

"I have to keep control of myself," Dorthy thought. "The only thing I can do is just sit down and just stay right in one spot and not just completely fall apart." She didn't move for the rest of the afternoon, trying to keep herself together as the police asked her questions and her friends hovered around.

Dorthy tried desperately to maintain control, but every so often she would break down. She couldn't help thinking about the daughter she would never see again. "Martha was my very favorite person in the world."

2

The Official Story

*This is either a case of the most inept police work in history or
a rich and powerful family holding the police at bay.*
—Dominick Dunne

The investigation into the death of Martha
Moxley began sometime after noon on October
31, 1975, and continues to this day. Based on
public records and published accounts, this is the
official story of that investigation.

At 12:30 P.M. youth officers Hickman and Jones
responded to the Moxley residence. There they
encountered Sheila McGuire, who directed them to a
large pine tree on the west side of the property.
Martha Moxley's body was beneath the tree. Her blue
jeans and panties were pulled down to her knees. Her
head was a bloody mess. She was obviously dead.

News traveled quickly, and soon the neighborhood was filled with police and emergency personnel,
as well as reporters, neighbors, and onlookers. Since
the Greenwich Police Department did not have the

resources or experience to process a violent crime scene, the Connecticut State Police Mobile Crime Lab was called in.

The Greenwich police detectives fanned out into the surrounding houses, interviewing any neighbors who happened to be home. "It was very disorganized at the beginning," retired detective Steve Carroll said years later. "Individual teams of detectives began canvassing the neighborhood. Everyone was out to make a collar."

None of the detectives on the scene had ever investigated a homicide before. "We haven't had anything like this as far as I can remember," Greenwich police chief Stephen Baran told the *New York Times* that first day. Baran had been on the department for thirty years.

Greenwich residents were shocked that a local girl had been murdered, particularly since she lived in the exclusive and well-guarded community of Belle Haven.

"I've never been scared before," Linda Skovron, a twelve-year-old Greenwich resident told a reporter. "I never thought of it happening in Belle Haven. It's so rich."

The people of Greenwich immediately focused their suspicions outside the community. They couldn't believe that the killer was one of their own; it must have been an outsider. They speculated that some transient had wandered into Belle Haven from the nearby Connecticut Turnpike and killed Martha Moxley.

Sixteen-year-old Nick Bernard echoed the town's sentiments, or hopes, when he said, "It had to be some crazy person. I don't think anybody who knew her would hurt her."

Shortly after Martha's body was discovered, police found several pieces of a broken golf club on the Moxley lawn. The golf club head and two pieces of shaft measuring eight and eleven inches were laying on the ground near the crime scene. The police immediately assumed that the handle and a portion of the shaft had been part of the murder weapon and were missing from the scene.

Beginning the next morning, much of the Greenwich Police Department's investigative resources were directed toward finding the golf club handle. The neighborhood was searched with metal detectors, the trees on the Moxley property were checked by men in cherry pickers, catch basins were searched, ponds and pools were drained, the nearby Long Island Sound was searched, every outbuilding, bomb shelter, and storage basement in the neighborhood was examined.

Two days after Martha's body was found, the Greenwich police issued a Teletype and press release describing the missing piece of the weapon and its importance to the investigation. Through the course of the investigation, dozens of citizens and law-enforcement officials responded to the bulletins, turning in scores of broken golf clubs. None of them matched the pieces found at the crime scene.

On October 31, detectives had already determined that the golf club was a rare Toney Penna model. That same day, they discovered a set of similar Toney Penna clubs in the Skakel house. After extensive investigation, the detectives could find no one else in the area who owned a set of Toney Penna clubs. The Skakel clubs once belonged to Ann Skakel, who had died of cancer in 1973. The police and the press already knew that Thomas Skakel was the last person reported seen with Martha Moxley.

That first afternoon of the investigation, detectives Ted Brosko and Jim Lunney went to the Skakel residence to interview the family. Because Thomas was not home at the time, they spoke to Julie and Michael Skakel first. Being the second oldest and the only female in the family, Julie was something of a den mother to her brothers. She told the police that her father was away and Ken Littleton was staying there to keep an eye on the family. She related the events of the previous evening, saying that they had all gone to the club for dinner and then come back home around 9:00 P.M.

Michael Skakel told officers that at approximately 9:10 P.M. Martha, Helen Ix, and Geoffrey Byrne came over. He said that they went to the family car, where they listened to music. They were in the car when his brother Thomas came out of the house and started talking to them. Michael was two years younger than Thomas, was romantically involved with, or at least interested in, Martha Moxley, and had a reputation for reckless and violent behavior. Greenwich police did not suspect

Michael, since they believed the murder occurred between 9:30 and 10:00 P.M. and Michael had an alibi covering that time. Michael had reportedly gone to the Terriens' with Rush Jr., John, and Jim Terrien. Since they left at 9:30 and did not return until at least 11:20, the police concluded there was no way Michael could have killed Martha.

On October 31, Thomas Skakel returned home sometime around 5:30 P.M. The police interviewed him, and he said that at approximately 9:15 the night before he had left the house to get a music tape from the Lincoln. When he reached the car, he saw the other kids there and joined them. About ten minutes later, his brothers Rush and John and his cousin, Jim Terrien, came out of the house. They needed the Lincoln to drive Jim home, so everyone got out of the car. Thomas said that Helen Ix and Geoff Byrne headed home, while the Lincoln pulled out of the driveway. He talked to Martha for a few minutes, then said good-night and went back into the house to do homework. This was around 9:30 P.M. He last saw Martha walking out of the driveway toward the backyard. As he walked back into the house, the doorbell rang. It was Andrea Shakespeare—she needed the keys to the other Skakel car so Julie could drive her home. Thomas said he gave Andrea the keys and then went upstairs.

Since he was the last person reported to see Martha alive, the police took Thomas down to headquarters for a formal statement. His statement matched the story told by his younger brother

Michael, who said he last saw Thomas with Martha at 9:30.

From October 31, Thomas Skakel was a suspect in the murder of Martha Moxley, but he was not the only suspect. Ed Hammond was a twenty-six-year-old graduate student at Columbia Business School who lived next door to the Moxleys'. He also came under suspicion that first day after neighbors reported that he sometimes acted odd. Around 3:00 P.M. on October 31, the police brought Hammond down to the station for questioning while detectives searched the Hammond residence under a consent-to-search form that Mrs. Hammond reportedly signed. Despite the fact that he passed a polygraph and no evidence connected him to the crime or the victim, Ed Hammond remained a prime suspect for several months.

On November 1, Dr. Elliot Gross, Connecticut chief medical examiner, conducted an autopsy of Martha Moxley. While a few details were leaked, such as the cause of death—multiple head wounds caused by a golf club—and the fact that Martha was not sexually molested or under the influence of drugs, the autopsy was never publicly released.

During the early phase of the investigation, the police focused on Ed Hammond, and also tracked down every lead they received concerning suspects from outside the community. At the same time, suspicion began to focus more closely on Thomas Skakel.

On Monday, November 3, 1975, detectives

asked Rushton Skakel if Thomas would take a polygraph test. Mr. Skakel and Thomas agreed to the procedure. They were taken to the Connecticut State Police polygraph examiners in Bethany. After three separate tests, the results were inconclusive. Thomas hadn't been sleeping. He was too exhausted and anxious for an accurate polygraph reading.

Two days later, Thomas agreed to take another examination. On November 9, 1975, he took a second polygraph, which he passed. Although the police admitted that Thomas passed the second test, they never released any documents concerning the examination and did not eliminate him as a suspect.

Suspicion quickly arose that Thomas Skakel was the killer, but official Greenwich dismissed these claims as gossip. In a press conference soon after the murder, Chief Stephen Baran complained about the "irresponsible and groundless rumors" that were flying around the case. A *Greenwich Time* editorial echoed the chief's concerns, asking the public to "cool the Perry Mason bit and stop trying to pin guilt on anyone." The editorial mentioned "a very young man" who was the subject of these rumors.

At first the Skakel family, particularly Rushton Skakel, was cooperative with the police. The Greenwich detectives didn't feel they needed a search warrant for the Skakel house, because Rushton allowed them to examine it whenever they wished. He also gave them a set of keys so they could search his ski lodge in Windham, New York.

As the months dragged on and no other suspects

emerged, police began increasingly to focus on
Thomas Skakel. When a December 11, 1975, reinterview with Helen Ix and Geoffrey Byrne revealed
that they saw flirtatious horseplay between Thomas
and Martha, including pushing and shoving at the
back door of the Skakel residence around 9:30 P.M.
the night of her murder, a new theory began to
emerge. Perhaps Martha had spurned Thomas's sexual advances; then he became enraged and killed her.

On December 13, Thomas Skakel appeared at
the detective bureau and was reinterviewed by detectives Steve Carroll and Jim Lunney. The content of
that interview was not made public, but Thomas was
asked if he would allow investigators to take hair
samples. He agreed, and Detective Lunney cut several strands of hair from his head.

A month later, Greenwich detectives asked for
and received written authorization from Rushton
Skakel to obtain Thomas's medical and school
records. The detectives contacted several medical and
educational professionals who held such records.

On January 20, 1976, Chris Roosevelt, a former
Justice Department lawyer who served as counsel and
board member for the Whitby School, where
Thomas had been a student, called Carroll and
Lunney at police headquarters. Roosevelt advised the
detectives that he would personally contact Rushton
and Thomas Skakel to obtain their oral permission to
release the records the detectives had requested.
During the conversation, Roosevelt became highly
agitated. He seemed to think that an arrest had either

occurred or was imminent. He told the detectives that if Thomas was in fact arrested, he would be defended by a battery of lawyers claiming that the boy had been temporarily insane.

The detectives informed Roosevelt that Thomas had not been arrested or even accused at that point. They told him that their obtaining his records was just another part of the investigation. Roosevelt said that he would not release any records until he spoke with Thomas and his father.

Two days later Rushton Skakel appeared at the complaint desk of the Greenwich Police Department and turned over a letter that he asked be delivered immediately to Chief Stephen Baran. In the letter, Skakel withdrew his authorization for the Greenwich Police Department to obtain Thomas's records.

A half hour later, a Greenwich police ambulance was dispatched to the Ix residence, next door to the Skakels' and across the street from the Moxleys'. Someone at the Ixes' was in need of medical attention. The injured person turned out to be Rushton Skakel, who had collapsed complaining of chest pains. He was taken to Greenwich Hospital and admitted for tests and observation.

Carroll and Lunney immediately went to Walsh Lane and interviewed the Ixes. Mildred Ix told the detectives that shortly before the attack, Rushton Skakel had arrived at her house in the company of Joseph Donovan, an attorney for Great Lakes Carbon, the Skakel family company. They proceeded to the Ixes' study, and Mildred went to get some refreshments. Upon returning to the study, she observed Rushton sitting in the chair holding his chest and complaining of chest pains. He told her that he had received some bad news during a telephone conversation, but she didn't know to whom he had talked or what the bad news was. She further advised that she was aware of a meeting Rushton had attended earlier that day with Paul Czaja, headmaster of the Whitby School, and Chris Roosevelt, a lawyer for the school. According to Mildred Ix, Rushton had been upset after that meeting.

Following their interview with the Ixes, Carroll and Lunney went to Greenwich Hospital to interview Rushton himself. Father Mark Connolly, a Catholic priest and Skakel family advisor, told them that Rushton was under sedation and only a short interview would be possible. The detectives then spoke with Rushton, who told them he had hired a criminal attorney for his son's protection and that he had rescinded his authorization for the detectives' background investigation.

The Skakels had hired Emmanuel "Manny" Margolis, an experienced criminal attorney from nearby Stamford. He immediately made arrangements to represent the entire family, including the household staff: Ken Littleton; Nanny Sweeney; the maid, Amelia Rodriguez; the cook, Ethel Jones; and the gardener, Franz Wittine. Margolis consistently refused to allow the police to reinterview Thomas or any of the other Skakel family members. In addition, he also refused to allow authorities to administer fur-

ther polygraph or other examinations of the suspect.
He did allow the help to be interviewed.

One of the members of the Skakel household
to whom the police kept going back for information was Littleton. On the advice of Brunswick
School, where he worked as a science teacher and
coach, Ken Littleton retained his own attorney,
John Meerbergen, in April 1976. Throughout the
investigation, Littleton cooperated with authorities,
submitting to several interviews, but would not
sign a statement indicating that circumstantial
evidence pointed toward Thomas Skakel as Martha
Moxley's murderer.

Since the police had relied so heavily on the
Skakel family's voluntary cooperation, and since the
investigation had already gone on for so long and
covered so much ground, they didn't know what to
do once the Skakels ceased cooperating. Never having investigated a homicide—much less one in
which the prime suspect was wealthy, well connected, and well represented—the Greenwich police
seemed to run out of options and ideas.

On March 26, 1976, Fairfield County state's
attorney Donald Browne told the Associated Press
that the police were "apparently being frustrated by
the refusal of a particular family which could supply
pertinent information to assist or cooperate" in the
Moxley investigation. Browne would not name the
family. His published comments became the source
of so much speculation that he soon had to "clarify"
his position in another statement to the press.

By then, everybody in Greenwich knew the family to whom Browne was referring, that Thomas Skakel was a suspect, and that the Skakels were no longer cooperating.

During March 1976, Thomas Skakel was repeatedly absent from school and did not attend a memorial mass held for his late mother. It was said he had the flu. In late April 1976, Thomas was admitted to Greenwich Hospital for hemorrhagic gastritis— bleeding from the stomach or intestines, a condition often caused by drug or alcohol abuse. His repeated absences from school and the neighborhood led to rumors that he had been shipped off to Switzerland. In fact, he had gone to Ireland for a few weeks to visit his aunt, Pat Cuffe. While family members claimed that the trip to Ireland had been planned long in advance, it came at a time when Thomas was under increasing scrutiny as a murder suspect.

Ever since Martha's murder, Rushton Skakel had been friendly to the Moxleys, but he had never directly addressed his son's possible involvement. On March 28, 1976, he came to the Moxley house holding a drink and saying that he had just returned from an AA meeting. He told the Moxleys that he was there to set their minds at ease about Thomas. Rushton said that his son had undergone numerous unspecified examinations that proved negative. David Moxley asked whether the Greenwich Police Department had been informed of the results of these examinations, and Rushton said no, his lawyer had advised against that.

The Moxleys told the police about their conversation with Rushton and hired their own attorney to assist them and the police in obtaining the test results Rushton mentioned. Jack Zeldes, the Moxley lawyer, hired a doctor to examine the test results. Although he did not see the results himself, Zeldes told the Moxleys and the police that they indicated Thomas was not the killer.

With no cooperation from the Skakels and no leads pointing to other suspects, the Greenwich police were stymied. The impasse continued through the summer and into the fall of 1976. Then the police got what they thought might be a huge break in the case. After failing a polygraph examination concerning the Moxley homicide, Ken Littleton admitted that he had been arrested in Nantucket that previous summer. Looking deeper into Littleton's life since the murder, the Greenwich police painted a picture of a promising Williams graduate who had turned into a petty thief with apparent emotional problems. Several people in Nantucket told police that Littleton acted in a bizarre and obnoxious manner that summer.

The Greenwich police thought they had found their murderer. They virtually forgot about Thomas Skakel and focused almost entirely on Ken Littleton.

Now a murder suspect, Littleton's behavior became increasingly self-destructive. During the next few years, he was arrested on numerous occasions and hospitalized several times for alcohol dependency and mental illness. Keeping track of his

various difficulties, the Greenwich police appeared
convinced that Littleton had killed Martha. Despite
the fact that they investigated him more thoroughly
than any other suspect (and still consider him a prime
suspect to this day), they could find no evidence linking him to the murder.

While the investigation foundered, the Moxleys
never gave up hope that their daughter's killer would
be caught. David Moxley buried himself in his work,
rising from head of the New York office of Touche
Ross to managing partner of Touche Ross, U.S.A.,
and finally managing partner of Touche Ross
International. Meanwhile, he also worked hard to
assist and oversee the investigation. He brought on
John McCreight, a friend and Touche Ross partner
who had extensive consulting experience with police
departments and other law-enforcement agencies.
McCreight convinced the Greenwich Police Department to seek outside help and initiated contacts
between Greenwich and the Detroit Police Department. At the time, Detroit was the murder capital of
America and its homicide detectives were considered
among the country's best. Greenwich detectives
Steve Carroll and Jim Lunney first flew to Michigan
to brief the Detroit police and ask their advice. Then
two Detroit detectives came out to Greenwich to
assist them in the investigation.

Detectives from the Nassau County homicide
squad were also briefed on the investigation and
asked for their comments. Cooperation from the two
departments gave Greenwich some new perspectives

on the investigation but did not stimulate any real break in the case.

The Moxleys had moved from Greenwich to New York City. David Moxley still kept in close touch with the Greenwich police and the Connecticut state's attorney office, but the investigation seemed to have run into a ditch. For years virtually nothing happened.

In 1988, David Moxley died of a heart attack. Dorthy Moxley moved to Annapolis where they had bought a waterfront condo on David's retirement. While her husband was alive, Dorthy had not been directly involved with the investigation. With David gone, Dorthy realized that she would have to take responsibility for her daughter's case.

But what could she do? David Moxley was a successful management consultant with connections in the worlds of business, politics, and law enforcement. Dorthy was a housewife who, in her own words, was "probably too nice a person." At least Dorthy could make sure that Martha wasn't forgotten. So she talked to every person interested in the case.

Len Levitt was the first journalist to speak with Dorthy at length. During his research, Levitt discovered that there was virtually no public record on the Moxley investigation. Along with *Greenwich Time,* Levitt sued the Greenwich Police Department for release of the police records concerning the Moxley investigation. In May 1983, the Connecticut Freedom of Information Commission decided that then–police chief Tom Keegan would conduct an examination of the Moxley file to determine which documents might be disclosed, and then release the redacted documents to the public. Forced to release the documents of a case he personally supervised, Keegan requested that he and Detective Jim Lunney be allowed to review and edit the article prior to publication. That request was denied.

Keegan redacted much of the police record before he released it to Levitt. Even in its redacted form, the record was extremely useful. Most journalists and outside investigators looking into the Moxley case have used it as their primary documentary source.

Unfortunately, Len Levitt's efforts were largely wasted for years, as Connecticut Newspapers, which owned and operated *Greenwich Time* and the *Stamford Advocate,* refused to publish the story he wrote on the Moxley murder in 1983. Levitt went on to head the investigative team at the *New York Post* and then become a columnist specializing on the NYPD for *Newsday.* Meanwhile, his story went unpublished and the Moxley case languished.

In the spring of 1991 William Kennedy Smith was charged with rape in Palm Beach, Florida. As the case and trial attracted much publicity, reporters looked for related stories. The connection was quickly made between the Kennedys and the Skakels, and the unsolved murder of Martha Moxley was seen as possibly another Kennedy cover-up. Rumors were rampant; there was even gossip that William Kennedy Smith was at the Skakel house on the evening of October 30, 1975, and could be the killer, although there was no evidence that he was at the house.

As a result of the renewed publicity about the Moxley case, Levitt's article was finally published by *Greenwich Time* and the *Stamford Advocate* on June 21, 1991. The article, headlined "Moxley Murder Still Haunts Greenwich," was the first comprehensive news account of the murder and investigation.

The public attention generated by the Palm Beach rape trial and Levitt's article forced authorities officially to reopen the case. The Moxley family had been urging renewed action for years, and now the officials were finally complying.

At an August 9, 1991, press conference at Greenwich police headquarters, state and local officials announced that the Moxley case would be formally reinvestigated. Greenwich detective Frank Garr, who was police dispatcher the night Martha was murdered, and state's attorney inspector Jack Solomon, who was on the crime scene the first day, were given the case to reinvestigate from the beginning. Henry Lee of the Connecticut State Police Crime Lab would review the forensic evidence in the case. Dorthy and John Moxley, who attended the press conference, announced that they would personally increase the standing $20,000 reward offered by the state to $50,000. They would also pay for a toll-free tip line that would ring in the investigators' office at the police administration building in Bridgeport.

"The Palm Beach case may have created some renewed interest," Don Browne said, "but I would have to say there is no connection between the two."

While Garr and Solomon reinvestigated the murder, media attention increased. *CBS News, Hard Copy, A Current Affair,* and other television news programs ran pieces on the case, often running updates as new information became available. Dorthy Moxley sat for countless interviews with television, newspaper, and magazine reporters. Jerry Oppenheimer's book on Ethel Skakel Kennedy, *The Other Mrs. Kennedy,* included a chapter on Martha's murder.

Enter Dominick Dunne. The popular author, celebrated journalist, and society fixture has a burning passion for justice, a passion inspired by the brutal murder of his own daughter Dominique, whose killer was convicted but served only two and a half years on a manslaughter charge. Dominick's specialty has been taking true crime stories about the rich getting away with murder and turning them into novels. He met Dorthy Moxley, and she told her story. After that, Dominick conducted his own investigation, talking to many of the principals in the investigation and some people who had never previously come forward.

The result was *A Season in Purgatory,* a novel that resembles the Moxley murder in a few specific details but also takes a novelist's license with the facts. Dunne's 1993 novel and a subsequent television movie based on the book stirred even more interest in the case.

Meanwhile, the official reinvestigation had attracted some media attention but never seemed to

go anywhere. Don Browne made several vague statements on television but did not proceed with a prosecution. Frank Garr and Jack Solomon kept promising
the Moxley family that progress was being made, but
still there were no significant breakthroughs in terms
of evidence—no arrests, no indictments, no grand
juries. Nothing.

On January 21, 1994, Henry Lee said that his lab
had done everything they could with the remaining
evidence and still didn't have anything. Along with
six scientists from the State Police Forensic Science
Laboratory in Meriden, Connecticut, Lee said he spent
two years studying the physical evidence and com-
piled a six-inch-thick report to the Greenwich police
in October 1993. The results of this report were kept
secret, but were said to include Lee's reconstruction of
the crime, using the autopsy and police reports.
Despite all his effort, Lee's analysis had gone nowhere.

By October of that year, the Greenwich Police
Department had apparently given up. Chief Kenneth
Moughty said that the Moxley investigation was
entirely in the hands of the state's attorney office.
"The reinvestigation has gone a long way," Moughty
said. "It wouldn't make any sense to bring anyone
new into it."

A year later, Frank Garr was forced to admit that
no arrest was expected. He stated that "nothing in
the way of investigation has been done probably in
the last year." Jack Solomon described their investigative strategy by saying, "A confession would certainly clear it up."

Once again, the Connecticut investigators were at a standstill. And again, they blamed the Skakel family.

Soon after the official reinvestigation had been announced, the Skakel family decided to investigate the murder themselves. They hired Sutton Associates, a private investigation firm headquartered in Jericho, New York. Comprising former law enforcement officers and headed by fifteen-year FBI veteran Jim Murphy, Sutton Associates' official mandate was to investigate the Moxley murder from the beginning and to see if the evidence pointed to anybody outside the Skakel family. If they were convinced that one of the Skakels was in fact involved, then Sutton was to work with the Skakel attorneys in building a credible defense in the event of prosecution.

Rushton Skakel met with Jim Murphy at the Belle Haven Club in July 1992. During that meeting, Rushton reportedly told the investigator, "If my kids didn't do it, I want my family's name cleared publicly. If they did do it, I want to prepare the best possible defense."

Sutton Associates performed a lengthy and expensive investigation, taking several years and costing, according to some estimates, upwards of a million dollars. They soon found out that the evidence against the Skakel boys was even more damaging than previously thought. Their own investigation uncovered new information that could only lead to more suspicion.

Chief among these revelations was the fact that

during interviews conducted by Sutton Associates investigators and attended by Skakel family lawyers, Thomas and Michael significantly changed their alibis for the night of Martha's murder.

Thomas had originally stated that at approximately 9:30 P.M. he had talked to Martha by the back door and then gone inside to do homework. On the face of it, the homework alibi was questionable. Thomas was not a very good student. It was late on a nonschool night and he had been drinking and fooling around with Martha. While he said that the subject of his homework was the Puritans, Abraham Lincoln, and log cabins, his teachers at Brunswick, along with the Skakels' live-in tutor, Ken Littleton, stated that no such assignment had been given.

During interviews with Sutton, Thomas changed his story. Instead of going back inside the house to do homework, he stated that he and Martha kissed and fondled each other in the backyard of the Skakel property. This encounter lasted about twenty minutes, from 9:30 until 9:50, and concluded in mutual masturbation to orgasm. This statement placed Thomas with Martha right around the time police had assumed she was murdered. It also raised the question: Why did he lie about his actions in statements to the police?

Michael Skakel also changed his story during interviews with the private investigators. Although he still maintained that he went to the Terrien home at 9:30, he stated that once he returned home around 11:30, he went out again to peep in windows.

Eventually he came to the Moxley house, where he climbed a tree and threw pebbles at a window he thought was Martha's. Unable to summon her, Michael climbed down from the tree and went into the side yard where the attack occurred. Finally, he ran home. His activities outside lasted from approximately 11:40 P.M. to 12:30 A.M.

These revelations were first reported by Len Levitt in *Newsday*. Those who closely followed the case understood the significance of the two boys' changing their stories. Why was Thomas expanding the time and extent of his contact with Martha? Why was Michael admitting to being on the crime scene after the murder supposedly occurred?

Now it appeared that at least Thomas Skakel was more involved than he said. For the first time since the investigation had begun years earlier, Michael emerged as a suspect.

Connecticut authorities appeared to react optimistically to the Sutton revelations. Frank Garr was charged with verifying the Sutton Associates accounts, but no progress on the case was publicly reported.

Documents and interviews collected by Sutton Associates were assembled into a series of draft chapters for a planned report that Sutton intended to submit to the Skakel family. When the Skakels were informed of this pending report, they told Sutton Associates it was not necessary. The report was never completed, but the draft chapters were given to Dominick Dunne by a freelance employee of Sutton

Associates, who had been fashioning the information into a coherent and flowing document. The draft chapters came to be known as the Sutton files. Dominick Dunne secretly slipped a copy of the files to Frank Garr while saying publicly that he would not give the documents to police. Len Levitt had not seen the files. He went out and got the story by interviewing the Sutton investigators, sources he had developed when the agency was first hired by the Skakels.

Jim Murphy told Levitt that if he were subpoenaed, he would tell all that he knew. He was evidently hoping that some form of prosecution or an investigative grand jury would force him to break his investigator-client privilege with the Skakels and make the leak from within his organization less damaging to his professional reputation.

Unfortunately, nothing came of the Sutton Associates files. In conversations with the Moxleys, Frank Garr first denied that he had the files, then said they were mere "scenarios" with little evidentiary value. Donald Browne continued to give excuses as to why there was no prosecution or investigative legal proceeding. Nobody subpoenaed Jim Murphy, even though he was literally asking to be called to court. Once again, it seemed as if the Moxley case was going nowhere.

Frustrated by this lack of action, Dominick Dunne now sought to give the Sutton Associates files to somebody who might be able to do something with them. That's when I came into the story.

PART II

Taking on the Case

3

A Cold Case

Death investigation constitutes a heavy responsibility and as
such let no person deter you from the truth and your own
personal commitment to see that justice is done—not only for
the deceased, but for the surviving family as well.
—Vernon J. Geberth,
Practical Homicide Investigation

By the summer of 1997, my first book, *Murder in Brentwood*, was a best-seller. The book helped to set the record straight about the kind of detective and person I am.

With the book out and the media tour finished, I found myself at a professional crossroads. I still wanted to investigate homicides, but circumstances prevented me from doing that for any law-enforcement agency or private investigative firm. Since I basically reinvestigated the Simpson murder in *Murder in Brentwood*, I already had experience conducting a homicide investigation as a nonfiction author. I realized that although I might not be able to carry a gun or arrest anybody while writing a book about a murder, I also had a certain amount of independence and control that a working detective does not. Writing about homicide investigations seemed to be the perfect way to use my detective experience and passion for investigative work while still being able to enjoy a new life with my family in Idaho.

The only question I faced was what case I should write about. While I was fishing around for an idea, I got a call from my friend Dominick Dunne. Dominick and I met as a result of the Simpson trial and have been in contact ever since. We often discuss the case and the people involved in it, but we have common interests outside of the O. J. travesty. I told Dominick that I enjoyed the investigative part of *Murder in Brentwood* and was looking for another project on which I could do similar detective work. I explained the sort of crime book I wanted to write, basically treating the book project like a homicide case by focusing on the investigation of clues and analysis of evidence.

Dominick suggested that I write a book about an unsolved homicide. He knew the perfect case—the murder of fifteen-year-old Martha Moxley in Greenwich, Connecticut. Since I was not familiar with the case, Dominick described the circumstances of the crime and the subsequent investigation. He told me about *A Season in Purgatory,* which I hadn't read. Dominick said he would send me a copy. Then we talked about the case for nearly an hour. The more I heard of Martha's tragic and unnecessary death, the more interested I became.

Unable to wait for Dominick's book to arrive in the mail, I went to the local library and took out its well-read copy of *A Season in Purgatory*. Although *A*

Season in Purgatory is a novel, there was much food for thought. I saw how Dominick used themes he is interested in—crime, justice, the rich getting away with murder—in a fictional format. While it was an entertaining read, the book also angered me. Money, power, celebrity, deceit, corruption. It was the Simpson case all over again.

So I began to do my own research into the Moxley case. First I started with published newspaper reports from the time of the murder and the initial investigation.

Reading the first newspaper accounts in the *New York Times* and *Greenwich Time,* I thought that the murder did not make much sense. Martha Moxley was bludgeoned to death within one hundred feet of her home in one of the wealthiest and most secure residential communities in the country.

"In a case as serious as this, no information which relates to any aspect of the case can be made public. . . . Criminals read newspapers too," Greenwich police chief Stephen Baran said days after the murder. Meanwhile, according to the newspaper reports I read, the following information had already been released: the estimated time of death; the cause of death; the method and place of death; the murder weapon; the clothing the victim was wearing; the condition of the victim's body; people known to be with the victim the night of her murder; who was last seen with her, where and when; the victim's actions and movements that night.

The police had identified a golf club as the murder weapon. Meanwhile, Chief Baran tried to belittle the importance of finding the set from which it came. "The owner of the set of clubs would not necessarily be the murderer," Baran told *Greenwich Time*. "Kids are always leaving bicycles, tennis racquets, and golf clubs outdoors, after playing with them on the lawn."

I could not understand why the police chief in charge of a department investigating a homicide would make such statements. His words sounded more like the opening arguments of a defense attorney in a murder trial than the public statements of a police chief who wants to solve a murder.

On November 2, 1975, *Greenwich Time* described how the police had issued a nationwide Teletype for the missing grip and shaft of a stainless-steel golf club that was believed to be the murder weapon. The club head as well as "pieces" of the club had all apparently been found at the crime scene. Within the first week of the investigation, the newspapers revealed that the police were searching for the portion of the golf club shaft with the handle grip. Police described the missing pieces of golf club as being sixteen to twenty-four inches in length.

The police had already said they had only found the golf club head and "pieces" of the shaft. The police must have had larger portions of the club shaft to be this specific about the length of the missing piece. How did the police know that the murder weapon had been a complete golf club, as the pieces they found at the scene were sufficient to cause the wounds on the victim?

This and other questions—Why did the police think the murderer was a transient? Why weren't they focusing on the children who were with Martha? Why were so many details of the crime made public?—continued to bother me the more I thought about the Moxley murder.

Newspapers only tell part of the story. I wanted to learn all I could about this case. When I was east on other business, I visited Greenwich to take a look at the police report. My associate, Stephen Weeks, had made an appointment with the general services secretary of the Greenwich Police Department to see the released documents on the Moxley murder. Steve told the secretary that he would be bringing along an associate, though he did not give her my name. When the day of our appointment arrived, we approached the general services desk. Steve introduced himself and then said, "And here is my associate, Mark Fuhrman."

From the first instant I stepped into the Greenwich Police Department, I knew my presence was not welcome. I sat down in the waiting room outside the chief's office while his secretary gave me some five hundred pages of police reports. They did not provide me with a desk or working area, almost as if they wanted me to be as uncomfortable and inconvenienced as possible.

The secretary who gave me the reports said, "There's nothing in here. A whole bunch of people have been through these. Journalists. Lawyers. Private investigators. There's nothing new."

I told her that I would see for myself.

While I studied the reports, I could hear the buzz around the office and out in the hall. Officers and clerical personnel stopped by and looked in the open doorway. The only person to greet me was a police captain, who introduced himself and then asked what I was doing here.

"I'm looking into the Moxley case," I told him.

"Why?"

"Oh, you know, money, power, murder."

"It happens everywhere," the captain said as he walked away.

As I read the reports, I realized that the Moxley case was unique in a lot of ways. Greenwich is a very wealthy town. Belle Haven is the most exclusive and secure neighborhood in that town. Martha Moxley was a pretty, popular girl who came from a high-powered family. Thomas Skakel also came from a prominent family, one with a history of unstable behavior as well as a connection to the Kennedys. The police were obviously intimidated by the Skakel family and their Kennedy cousins. To make matters worse, the Greenwich police were woefully inexperienced in homicide investigations. Wealth, power, incompetence, fear. This case had all the right ingredients for a botched investigation, perhaps even a cover-up.

The next step was to contact the victim's family. Dominick Dunne had given me the number of Martha's mother, Dorthy Moxley. He said she was a wonderful person who really wanted the case solved, or at least to achieve some kind of closure. Martha had to walk only a few hundred feet from the Skakel backyard to her own front door. She never made it home and Dorthy doesn't know why.

Never having met her, I felt deeply for Dorthy Moxley. In the course of my police career, I had made too many death notifications and interviewed too many families of murder victims. It is always awkward and uncomfortable, because you want to do everything you can for them. Even if you solve the case, you will never bring their loved ones back. I never know what to say to the families of murder victims, and I hope I never get good at it.

I met with Dorthy and received her full support and cooperation. She is an incredibly brave and resilient lady. She is also very warm, and I felt an instant friendship with her. I wanted to help her. I hoped I could bring her daughter's murderer to justice, or at least be able to tell her who I think did it and how. I still didn't know if there was enough information to write a book. I called Dominick and expressed my concern to him.

The pause on the phone seemed long, almost deliberate. Then Dominick finally spoke: "I've got something I want to send you that might help make the decision to write a book. Tell me what you think when you get it."

Late in the afternoon the next day I received a Federal Express package from New York. The thick envelope contained typewritten reports. There was no accompanying letter, but the return address was Dominick's.

I sat down immediately and began reading what we now know as the Sutton Associates files. As I read, I realized the importance of the documents in front of me. The files contained firsthand statements from the suspects and important witnesses in the case. The sources for all these interviews and analyses were the Skakel family attorneys and their private investigators. The material was explosive—it clearly indicated that the Skakel boys had a great deal to hide, quite possibly their role in the murder of Martha Moxley. The Sutton Associates files changed everything. Now I knew I had the information necessary to reinvestigate the murder and possibly solve this twenty-two-year-old mystery.

Newsday columnist Len Levitt had written extensively about Sutton Associates and their involvement in the Moxley case. I called Len, who was very pleased to hear that I was writing a book about the case. He was eager to help.

Len shared with me a report written by Detroit homicide detective Gerald Hale on May 10, 1976, that basically summarized the initial investigation. Hale had been brought in to evaluate and offer advice on the investigation conducted by the Greenwich police. Hale's memo was released as part of Len's Freedom of Information Act request that made the police reports public.

The Hale memo is concise and informative, obviously written by a seasoned detective. Since many of the details about the crime scene were redacted in the police reports, this document enabled me for the first time to actually learn many of the pertinent facts in the case.

The memo goes into greater detail about the actions of Thomas and Martha around 9:30 P.M., including witness reports from Helen Ix and Geoffrey Byrne. "Geoff and Helen stated that it appeared as if Martha and Thomas were making out. This, after careful questioning, consisted of Martha pushing Thomas and Thomas pushing Martha. At one point, Thomas pushed Martha down and either fell or got down on her. This point is not clear as it happened partly out of view of Helen and Geoff behind a brick wall."

From the Sutton Associates files, I already knew that Martha and Thomas were engaged in sexual activity. The Hale memo makes it clear that this activity at least started as roughhousing.

Details of the crime scene were even more revealing. According to the memo, Martha's body was found approximately two hundred feet southwest of the Moxley home. "The body was lying facedown partially under a large evergreen bough that is part of a clump of evergreens. The head was facing easterly."

Hale stated that the initial assault "most likely took place approximately forty feet into the west exit driveway of the Moxley home, south of Walsh Lane. A small amount of blood was found in that location." Forty feet to the southwest, according to Hale, two large pools of blood were found. "It is felt that the main part of the assault took place here." From the two blood pools was a zig-zagged drag path of blood through the grass to beneath the tree where the body was found.

So there were actually three separate crime scenes and three distinct assaults. The initial attack probably occurred in the driveway where the small amount of blood was found. The second and perhaps fatal assault commenced where the two large pools of blood were discovered. Then she was dragged through the leaves to her final resting place.

To me, the movement of Martha's body to a hiding place away from her house and the street indicated that the killer lived in the area and did not want the body to be discovered until later. The fact that there was little blood at the first crime scene told me that the attack was probably unintentional at first or, at least, Martha's assailant did not initially intend to kill her. After the first blow or blows, she was moved to the second attack site. That area was probably well lit, near the driveway or perhaps on a path where someone could come upon the body easily. That is why the killer dragged her farther away beneath the evergreen boughs.

I did not understand why the police could possibly have thought that the suspect was some transient who wandered in from the turnpike. For a transient to get through Belle Haven security and walk all the way to Walsh Lane undetected, find a golf club, bludgeon Martha to death with it, walk back through Belle Haven, again undetected, get back on the turnpike covered in blood, and hitch another ride was an implausible scenario.

The memo's discussion of the murder weapon was equally revealing. "An eleven-inch piece of golf club shaft is found near the two large pools of blood." The head of a six-iron Toney Penna golf club and an eight-inch piece of shaft were found approximately sixty to seventy feet northeast of the site of the initial attack in the driveway. "It is felt that the pieces of club were thrown to where they were found."

The Moxley house was southeast of the initial attack site. Why would the killer throw pieces of the murder weapon in the direction of the victim's house? If he threw these items, why weren't fingerprints recovered?

Probably repeating the assumptions of the Greenwich police, Hale wrote: "The handle portion and a small part of the shaft is missing. . . ." This statement seemed to assume that an unbroken and complete golf club was used in the attack. How could anyone make that conclusion? The nineteen inches of the recovered shaft and the club head could have caused all the injuries to the victim. Why did the police perform such an intensive search for the golf club handle? It almost appeared as if the police knew that the club had been complete before the attack on Martha Moxley. How could they know that?

Even without taking the security and inaccessibility of Belle Haven into consideration, an initial observation of the crime scene and the victim would direct any experienced homicide investigator to conclude that the victim knew her attacker. There were no defensive wounds, meaning the attack came as a surprise. The suspect was able to intercept the victim within a few hundred feet of her house. This shows that the crime was probably not the result of a chance encounter. The killer knew she would be there, possibly because he followed her or was walking with her. The suspect felt comfortable enough in the neighborhood to attack Martha, showing that he did not fear being seen in the area, let alone in her front yard. There was no doubt in my mind that the suspect knew Martha and was most probably a Belle Haven neighbor.

In this setting, a golf club is a weapon of opportunity, not choice. It also shows that the attack was spontaneous and not planned. The golf club was simply available to the suspect. He would have used a bottle, a branch, or a shovel, whatever had been at hand. And there was a good possibility that the suspect would have been seen with the weapon before. The victim was not alarmed to see the suspect with a golf club in his hand.

Martha's pants and panties were pulled down to her knees. Her body was positioned with her face down. But she was not sexually molested. Then why were her clothes pulled down? And why was she rolled over onto her stomach?

This evidence led me to two initial hypotheses. First, the suspect attempted rape but could not complete the act. Either he was unable to perform or he was disturbed by someone and stopped his attack for fear of being caught. Or the suspect staged the victim in this manner to humiliate her. This theory is somewhat corroborated by the vicious and rage-based attack that was definitely a personal statement by the attacker and further indicates that the victim was known to him and quite possibly they had some kind of intimate relationship.

The crime scene was compact and easily contained, yet the police were disorganized and confused. The day after the murder police knew that Martha was last seen in the company of Thomas Skakel at the Skakel house. Within two days it was established that the golf club was the murder weapon and came from the Skakel house. Still, no search warrant was ever served on the Skakel residence.

The police claimed that they had a signed consent-to-search form from Rushton Skakel and didn't want to lose voluntary access to the house. A consent to search can be revoked at any time, and, in fact, eventually was, while a search warrant cannot. The consent form is actually more work with less yield than a formal search warrant. If someone from the Skakel household had committed the murder, there would have been significant trace evidence in the showers, sinks, and clothes hamper in that house the next day. Several days, weeks, or even months later hair, blood, or fiber evidence could still be recovered.

Why didn't the Greenwich police issue a search warrant for the Skakel house once they knew that Thomas was the last person seen with Martha and the golf club belonged to a set owned by the Skakels? That was just one of many questions I had from my initial look into the case. Instead of answering those questions, my research only led to more questions, questions that people close to the case could not or would not answer.

There were many conditions that made the Moxley investigation difficult. The Greenwich Police Department did not have much experience handling violent homicides. The high-profile nature of the Moxley case, with intensive media coverage, political connections, wealth, power, and celebrity, only added more pressure on the already strained resources of the Greenwich police. I knew from hard experience how a high-profile murder investigation could go sideways.

Still, there was enough evidence to link the suspect with the victim, the murder weapon, and the crime scene. The Sutton Associates report contained even more evidence that at the very least Thomas and Michael knew more than they were telling.

I called Dominick and told him that I was on the case. I explained how the Sutton files changed the whole investigation, answering many questions the police hadn't been able to answer and raising many more. I asked Dominick if the police had the files.

Dominick had known Frank Garr, the lead investigator in the Moxley case, since 1991. When Frank's Greenwich police retirement was up, he went to work as an investigator in Donald Browne's office and took the Moxley case with him. Frank is the one investigator still officially working the Moxley homicide. Since he was the police dispatcher the night Martha was killed, he can say that he has been on the case since the beginning. Dominick had given a copy of the Sutton files to Frank some six months prior. Nothing seemed to have resulted from it.

Dominick felt that Frank Garr was a dedicated cop and a "good guy" and recommended that I speak with him. As I sat down to call Frank, my expectations were reasonable. I was certain that he would have to think about how much he could disclose about an open case. I thought for sure that he would at least be willing to talk to me.

I called Frank and explained that I was writing a book about the Moxley murder and would like some help with the police end of it.

"Well, I don't think I can do that," Frank said. "To tell you the truth, I've been thinking about writing a book about the case."

I tried at least to convince Garr to have lunch with me—I've never known a cop to turn down a free meal—but my efforts were fruitless. Frank wouldn't cooperate with me, wouldn't meet with me, wouldn't have lunch with me, nothing. He said he was too busy, now and in the future.

As I hung up the phone I could only assume that Frank was afraid of something. I didn't believe that he didn't want to cooperate with me because he wanted to write his own book. What could his book be about—How I Didn't Solve a Murder? I sensed that something else was behind Frank's refusal to work with me. Something was starting to smell, but I didn't know what it was.

I'm retired from the force, and now I'm an author

of nonfiction books, but in my heart I'm still a cop. I'm not out to bash police officers or departments. I like cops. I respect cops. Knowing very little about the Greenwich Police Department and the Connecticut state's attorney office, I figured they were good guys, as most cops are. Sure, they didn't have a whole lot of experience investigating homicides, but neither do most smaller departments. The Greenwich police must have known they made mistakes. I was sure they had their reasons for the way they conducted the investigation, and that once they explained those reasons many of my questions would be answered.

I went to Greenwich hoping that the police would cooperate with me the best they could. In return, I would provide them what help and information I had. I figured we were all on the same side. I figured that everybody involved in the case had only one agenda—to solve the murder of Martha Moxley and bring the killer to justice. I figured wrong.

4

Welcome to Greenwich

Money can buy anything in this town.
—A Greenwich resident

When I first arrived in Greenwich in September 1997, it reminded me of Beverly Hills, Bel Air, Carmel, La Jolla—any number of exclusive towns on the West Coast where people have enough money to build an oasis of privilege and comfort, where all the problems of the outside world are absent, or at least ignored.

Driving into downtown Greenwich, one of the first things I saw was a uniformed police officer standing in the middle of the intersection directing traffic. Considering the fact that it was a simple four-way intersection, with one of the streets going only one way and not much car or pedestrian traffic, I didn't understand why they didn't install a traffic light instead of paying a trained law-enforcement officer to tell people when they could walk from Starbucks to the post office. I didn't understand because I didn't know Greenwich or the Greenwich Police Department yet.

My first stop was police headquarters, where I wanted to make an appointment with Peter Robbins, who had just been made chief. Promoted in August 1997, Robbins took charge of a department with a few clouds hanging over it, and the Moxley case was only one of them. Kenneth Moughty, the previous chief, left the department after two separate investigations revealed improprieties in the police department, including Moughty allegedly doing favors for local millionaire Ali Fayed (uncle of the late Dodi Fayed) in return for a free trip to London. Outside auditors brought in to investigate the department discovered numerous improprieties at different levels of the department. The auditors had been told to deliver their final report orally so there wouldn't be any public record.

These scandals might not be such a big deal in a large city, but in Greenwich, which prides itself on being proper—or at least looking proper—the police department troubles were front-page news nearly every day.

Robbins himself had essentially grown up in the Greenwich Police Department. He was a twenty-seven-year veteran, and his father, David Robbins, had been chief. When the Moughty scandals broke, the board of selectmen initially said they would conduct a nationwide search for a new chief. Instead it promoted one of its own, giving Robbins a two-year contract. Since 1904, the town has never gone outside its own department for a new police chief.

Robbins promised to clean up the department, causing one local politician to dub him "Elliot Ness." He also planned to bring it up to professional speed, hiring Vernon Geberth, author of *Practical Homicide Investigation,* to train Greenwich detectives on criminal investigations, particularly homicides. Although Robbins was on the force at the time, the police record does not show him involved in the Moxley investigation. I thought he would be eager to have an experienced homicide detective help him on a cold case.

I called Robbins's office several times. First he was in a meeting. Then he was out of the building. Then he was in a meeting out of the building. So I decided to go to police headquarters and just drop in.

I announced myself at the general services desk and asked to see Chief Robbins. The woman at the desk said he was in the building. After waiting several minutes, his secretary came out and said he was not there. I told her that he really should talk to me. By this time, everybody knew I was working on the Moxley case. His secretary said that she would give him the message.

Since I had already been in the chief's office, I knew his window and desk could be seen from the outside. Walking out of the police headquarters, I asked my associate, Steve Weeks, to look up at Robbins's window.

"There's someone standing at the window," Steve said.

I turned around just in time to see a man scurry over to the other side of his office, out of view from the window.

"Well, I guess Elvis hasn't left the building after all," I said.

The next time I called Robbins he again would not take my phone call. So I went back to headquarters and announced myself at general services. This time they made me wait even longer, but eventually his secretary came out and said that the chief was very busy with visitors from England, but he did have a minute to speak with me.

Chief Robbins greeted me with the polite but cautious manner politicians often have. He is a small, round-shouldered man who looks as if he had spent most of his police career behind a desk. He was visibly uncomfortable when we spoke.

I told him about my book project, that I had a publisher and the full cooperation of the victim's family. I also said that I already had a great deal of information I was sure the police did not possess. Since the Moxley case was still open, I told him that I understood his position about releasing certain information. I told him I was an author, but I was also still a cop and loyal to my brother officers. I knew that the Greenwich police had made a lot of mistakes, but I wasn't interested in slamming them. I told him that once I was finished with the book, I would give him all my files, and while I was writing it, I would funnel information I thought might help him. I wanted to solve the case and get it prosecuted.

For that I needed his help on whatever level he could cooperate.

Chief Robbins took this in. He said that he knew all about the Moxley case and had recently reviewed it before he became chief. Then he told me that he couldn't cooperate. He said that he would be glad to receive any information I had, but, in his words: "This can't be a two-way street. I can't talk to you."

I told him he should think about it. Then the chief said he was very busy with visitors from England and our time was up. The next day I called him, and he was on the phone. When I called again, he was out of the building.

Neither Robbins nor Garr would cooperate. I wondered what they were afraid of.

They were not the only Connecticut officials to give me the stiff-arm. I called Jack Solomon, the former state's attorney investigator who was on the case from day one and had worked with Frank Garr in the reinvestigation. Solomon, who is now police chief of Easton, Connecticut, came highly recommended by the Moxleys. They were sure he would help.

When I called Solomon, he told me that I should talk to state's attorney Donald Browne, his former boss and prosecutor on the case. He said that if Browne advised him to speak with me, then he might consider it. At this point, I had already made calls to Browne. I asked Solomon if he would talk if Browne agreed. Solomon said that at least he would give it some consideration, but he would still be reluctant. He did not want to jeopardize the prosecution.

I talked to Donald Browne, who said as a matter of policy he routinely turned down requests for interviews on this case. After our conversation, I sat down in front of the VCR and watched his television interviews with *Hard Copy, A Current Affair, Unsolved Mysteries,* and several local news programs.

I spoke to the retired detectives who worked the case. Jim Lunney and Ted Brosko wouldn't talk. I spoke with Tom Keegan, who is now a state representative in Myrtle Beach, South Carolina. First, he asked me my home address so he could run a background check. Then, when he realized who I was, he told me to write him a letter and have Dorthy Moxley write him a letter too. I wrote him a letter, Dorthy wrote him a letter, and still he wouldn't talk.

Nearly every public official I spoke to said he did not want to jeopardize the prosecution. What prosecution? There wasn't any prosecution and there hadn't been one for twenty-two years. If they really wanted to prosecute, they would have sat down with me and said, hey, we've got an indictment coming down, we'll give you some information, but please don't disclose X, Y, or Z because it will hurt the case. My main priority was to see justice done. If they had given me a good reason to sit on information, I would have. If they had sat down and given me their side of the story, that would be the story I would have told. Instead, they stonewalled me.

Then I reached Steve Carroll, a retired detective

who worked in the beginning of the Moxley case for
two years. Over the next few weeks Steve spent hours
with me, going over the case, reviewing the police
reports, telling me everything he remembered about
the Moxley murder and investigation. One of the
first things we did was visit the crime scene.

We went to the front door of the former Moxley
house and knocked. A female Caucasian, about forty,
answered the door. She said she worked for the family. We identified ourselves and asked if we could
walk around the old driveway and side yard where
the murder had occurred. She said that would be fine.

Steve Carroll and I walked the scene. Although I
already knew many of the details of this case, being
on the ground where it actually happened gave me a
much clearer picture. Steve's vivid recounting of
what he saw finally made it possible for me to visual-
ize the crime.

Following our first visit to the old Moxley property, we wanted to return. We needed to go over a few
more details, and I was hoping to take some pictures.

On October 3, at approximately 4:00 P.M.
Steve Carroll and I drove down Walsh Lane in
Steve's Isuzu pickup truck. We parked off the
street, well away from the house, walked up the
driveway, and knocked on the front door. I never
go on anybody's property, twenty years ago or
twenty days ago, without asking first. Even when
someone has given you permission, it is a good
idea to let him know you are there. Since we had
only spoken to a household employee the time

before, we wanted to make sure we had the owner's permission.

A young girl, approximately nine or ten years old, answered the door. Steve Carroll and I identified ourselves and said that we had been there before and talked to the housekeeper, who had given us permission to walk on the premises. Then we told the girl that we'd like to take a few pictures in the side yard.

The girl said, "Well, my mom is in the shower."

She went upstairs to speak to her mother. Shortly she returned, telling us, "My mom says, well, today is not a good day."

Steve Carroll told the girl to tell her mom that they had mutual friends.

The girl went back upstairs. When she came down again, she told us, "My mom will be down in a minute."

The girl shut the door and we waited.

Eventually, her mother came downstairs and met us at the door.

"It's too bad that this girl was murdered," she said. "But it's unfair to the people who live here. We've talked to the Ixes and other people in Belle Haven. We want nothing to do with you, nothing to do with the book. What happened to the people who lived in this house before is no concern of ours."

Before I could respond, she spoke again.

"Here comes my husband," the lady said. "He's going to be really pissed."

A man pulled up in a green 700 series BMW. He was about five foot ten, stocky build, short brown hair, eyeglasses. From the moment Robert McAntee stepped out of his car, he was angry and argumentative.

"What are you doing here?" he shouted.

"We're talking to your wife," Steve Carroll explained.

"Who are you?" McAntee shouted at Steve.

"A retired detective," Steve responded calmly. "I worked on the Moxley case."

"I don't care who you were," the man shouted. Then he turned to me.

"I know who you are," McAntee said, wagging his finger.

I tried to explain, but McAntee wouldn't let me get a word in.

"You're on private property," McAntee said. He told his wife, "Call the police."

"This is public access," I explained. "I walked up and knocked on the door and talked to your wife."

"This is private property," McAntee said.

"Then we'll leave," I said.

"Get out!" McAntee screamed.

"Let's go," I told Steve as we started walking away. "These people are rude and insensitive. Doesn't anybody care that a young girl was beaten to death?"

Just as Steve and I were walking down the driveway, a van pulled up and its sliding door opened. A bunch of kids ran out of the car. I wondered how much a neighbor would care if one of their kids was beaten to death.

When I got back to the Homestead Inn, there

was a message from Joe Johnson of *Greenwich Time*.
He said that the police were looking for me. I didn't
see the police anywhere around the Homestead, so I
decided to turn myself in. I called the nonemergency
number of Greenwich Police Department and made
my way through the automated phone menu ("For
the traffic division, including the hiring of off-duty
police officers, press 3, etc.").

I finally got through to Sergeant Marino, who
said there had been a trespassing complaint against
me. I asked him how Joe Johnson had heard about it
before I had. Sergeant Marino told me that a
Greenwich officer had used my name over the scanner.

"That's not a real good idea, is it?" I asked
Marino, who had to agree.

I stood out in the Homestead Inn parking lot and
waited for the police. Greenwich patrol officer Tim
Powell responded. He asked me if I had been down to
38 Walsh Lane, and I told him what had happened.
Powell asked me if I had been advised to stay off Belle
Haven property. I told him that I hadn't. He told me
that from now on, I was forbidden to enter Belle
Haven.

I asked him if Mark Fuhrman was the only person in the state of Connecticut who had been told
that he can't go to Belle Haven. I asked him how they
can keep a citizen with legal business in the neighborhood off public access, even if the roads were privately owned.

Officer Powell didn't have an answer for my
questions. He gave me official notice to stay out of

Belle Haven, even though he wasn't sure what legal authority he had to do so. He said he would get his lieutenant to come and answer my questions.

"I'll try and get you your answer," Powell said. "Where are you going to be?"

"In the Belle Haven Club."

"Huh?"

"No. Just kidding."

When Tim Powell left to get his lieutenant, he was a little perplexed. A few minutes later, Lieutenant Dodson responded. He told me that I was to stay off the properties of 38 Walsh Lane and 71 Otter Rock Drive, the old Skakel house. I told him that if the owners of those properties did not want me, I had no further business there.

Dodson also told me that I was to check in with the Belle Haven security booths anytime I was to go into Belle Haven beyond Field Point Road, which is a public road. I told him that I understood those conditions and didn't want to cause any trouble.

"We don't want to have to arrest you," Lieutenant Dodson said.

"I don't want you to have to try," I responded.

That night I went out to dinner with Steve Carroll and his family. When we got back to their house, the police called to advise Steve to stay away from the two Belle Haven properties.

We were amused by the day's events. It was hard to believe that the Greenwich Police Department had nothing better to do than chase a couple of ex-cops out of Belle Haven. The next morning's newspaper headlines showed how seriously the Greenwich police considered it.

GREENWICH SLAMS DOOR ON FUHRMAN
FUHRMAN FOILED IN BOOK RESEARCH

The Greenwich police made it sound as if I were a fugitive from justice. The newspaper article stated:

> Yesterday [Fuhrman] managed to give Greenwich police the slip after they were called by security guards in the private Belle Haven section of town, where Fuhrman allegedly trespassed at the former Moxley residence.

The account was inaccurate. I had turned myself in as soon as I heard the police were looking for me. Without an initial complaint, it could not have been trespassing. I was asked to leave 38 Walsh Lane, so I left. It could only be alleged trespassing if I ever returned, which I did not. But it gets better:

> Lt. Dodson, while searching unsuccessfully for Fuhrman yesterday, said he did not know whether Fuhrman would be arrested if found.

Of course, Dodson found me that evening, a fact he neglected to tell police reporter Joe Johnson.

Chief Robbins also fed Johnson erroneous information.

> According to Robbins, private guards in
> Belle Haven denied access to Fuhrman twice
> on Thursday, turning him away from a guard
> shack on Field Point Road. The second time,
> he said, the former detective "peeled away"
> in a rented Corvette.

I don't know where Peter Robbins got that. I told
two of his officers that I had no contact with Belle
Haven guards the day before or on any other occasion. The only times I had ever driven into Belle
Haven was either in Steve Carroll's pickup or a Toy-
ota 4Runner with Virginia plates.

Robbins went on: "I don't know his entire background, but I don't consider him an expert homicide
investigator, and I have problems with his credibility
because of his past reputation and think he's here
solely to write a book for financial gain."

When I checked out of the Homestead Inn to go
out of town for a couple of days, the Greenwich police
and Belle Haven Association thought they had gotten
rid of me. One last newspaper article warned that I
might face charges if I ever went back to the former
Moxley or Skakel residences.

I told Steve Carroll that I wasn't close to finished
with this case. What was Peter Robbins so afraid of?
I didn't know, but I intended to find out.

PART III
Examining the Evidence

5

The Crime Scene

*Errors committed during the interrogation and other aspects of
the preliminary investigation can perhaps be corrected,
but errors committed in the protection and examination
of the crime scene can never be rectified.*
—*Barry A. J. Fisher,*
Techniques of Crime Scene Investigation

On October 31, 1975, at approximately 12:15
P.M. the body of Martha Moxley was discovered
beneath the low-hanging boughs of a pine tree
just one hundred feet from her home. Sometime later,
police responded to the scene.

During that first, crucial day of the Moxley
investigation there was no crime scene log to document the arrival and departure of personnel. In
reports filed the next day, times were estimated, if
noted at all. Therefore, all the times I use in this
chapter should be considered approximate.

At 12:30 P.M., juvenile officers Millard Jones and
Dan Hickman were about to get lunch in Riverside.
Jones was waiting in line at a hot dog stand while his
partner, Hickman, sat in the car. Hickman received a
radio dispatch to call the detective division. They
proceeded to a nearby call box on Post Road, where
Hickman contacted the detective division and spoke

with Policewoman Aidinis. The policewoman told Hickman that Mrs. Moxley had information about her missing daughter. Someone had found a body.

Rarely are victims of violent crimes found by the police. That is why all homicide investigations start with some level of crime scene contamination. The goal of the first responding police officers at a homicide scene is to establish order and protect the crime scene from being disturbed.

Hickman and Jones got in the car and sped off with lights flashing and siren blaring. They pulled into the Moxley's circular driveway and parked ten feet away from the house. Jumping from their car, they saw a young girl in the yard frantically pointing to a pine tree in the Moxley side yard. Sobbing uncontrollably, Sheila McGuire said, "She's down there under that tree!"

As Jones wrote in his report dated October 31, 1975: "I advised the girl to 'Wait here,' at which time Officer Hickman and I ran to the pine tree where we observed a body, later identified as Martha Moxley. We immediately checked and found no vital signs of life.

"I then ran up to the Moxley res. and contacted Hdqtrs. via telephone and advised Captain Thomas Keegan of our findings. At this time Officer Hickman remained with the body. After talking with Captain Keegan I immediately rejoined Officer Hickman at the site where the body was found."

That's what the report says. Twenty-two years later, in separate and repeated interviews, Jones and Hickman revealed what actually happened.

Jones went up to the house to phone headquarters because he didn't want the news of a homicide going over the police scanner, where the report could be heard by journalists or police groupies who might then arrive at the fresh crime scene. That's standard procedure and common sense. He told Hickman to remain with the body.

Instead of staying with the body, Hickman panicked and ran back to the car, where he began to make frantic calls over the police radio. Hickman requested more officers and the medical examiner. When Jones came back from the Moxley house, a dog was licking the trail of blood left in the grass and leaves. Hickman was petting the dog.

Captain Keegan arrived and saw Hickman petting a dog who was literally eating evidence. The chief of detectives went ballistic, screaming at the juvenile officer. Hickman was assigned to guard the perimeter, where he stayed for the rest of the afternoon.

"The next thing we knew," Jones said, "the place was crawling with people."

Captain Keegan drove a separate vehicle and by all indications arrived before detectives Steve Carroll and Joe McGlynn. Captain Keegan viewed the body just before them, walking alone down to the pine tree.

When Keegan returned to the driveway, McGlynn and Carroll went down and viewed the body themselves. By this time, several other uniformed officers had arrived, staying up near the driveway along with Keegan and the plainclothes juvenile officers.

Detectives Carroll and McGlynn took a close view of Martha's body. As Carroll remembers, her body was partially hidden under the low-lying branches that were only about a foot off the ground. He had to bend over to get beneath the tree branches so he could look closely. Martha was lying on her right side in a semifetal position. Her arms were pulled up and her hands were clenched. Carroll didn't touch her or check for rigidity, assuming that she was dead due to the massive wounds to her head. Martha still had her blue down jacket on, open over a flower-print turtle-neck. Her blue jeans and panties were pulled down past her knees. Steve noted no scrapes, abrasions, or bruises on the bare skin of her buttocks and thighs. Her eyes were closed and her blood-soaked hair fell over the front of her face. "Her hair was all askew and it was a real bloody mess," Steve said. So much of a mess that later Steve was surprised to learn Martha had blond hair.

At approximately 12:30–12:40 P.M., Dr. Richard Danehower was in the middle of his teaching rounds at Greenwich Hospital when he received an emergency page on his beeper. Danehower was the Moxley family doctor. On this day, he received an unusual request: to determine whether Martha was in fact dead.

Dr. Danehower believes that he viewed the victim's body before detectives Carroll and McGlynn, but the police report and witness statements are unclear as to the exact order of people viewing the body. When Danehower arrived at the Moxley house, Marilyn Robertson led the doctor to the tree where Martha lay.

The doctor could immediately tell that Martha was dead. Nonetheless, he did a brief examination of her wounds and he possibly recalls moving the body to place his stethoscope on her chest. Danehower noted that Martha was lying in an east–west position, head pointing east. The left side of her head was lying on the ground, her face pointed toward the tree trunk. She had a tear in the scalp that went down to the skull on the right side.

Dr. Danehower described Martha's body as being set in a fetal position: "I would think maybe there might have been a little bit of flexion in the legs. If it was called a fetal position, it wouldn't have been a tight fetal."

"Investigators at this point requested Dr. Danehower not make any further examination of the body pending the arrival of the Chief Medical Examiner," according to a police report written on October 31, 1975, by Detective Joe McGlynn. Dr. Danehower walked back to the Moxley house, where he had to inform Dorthy that her daughter was dead. After his involvement that afternoon, Dr. Danehower was never interviewed by the police or any other investigators.

Lowell Robertson, a friend and business associate of the Moxleys', was already in the house when Steve

Carroll entered and asked him to make a positive identification of the body. Robertson agreed to make the ID. As he walked down the sloping lawn, he passed Dr. Danehower coming away from the pine tree. Nearing the homicide scene, Robertson noticed two detectives in close proximity to the body. He didn't recognize the two plainclothes officers, although he knew Steve Carroll and Tom Keegan by sight.

Robertson could clearly see the path the body made as it was dragged from the driveway over the leaf-covered lawn to the pine tree. Martha was lying on her back. Robertson looked at her face. Although he could barely see blond hair through the caked blood, and her face was covered with blood, he knew it was Martha. He noted gravel on the top and back of her hair, intermingled with dried blood.

SCRAPE MARKS ON HIGH POINTS OF VICTIM'S FACE AND SMALL PIECES OF PEBBLE GRAVEL EMBEDDED UNDER SKIN. THESE INJURIES WERE OBSERVED BY DET. STEVE CARROLL FROM COLOR AUTOPSY PHOTOS.
THESE INJURIES ARE CONSISTENT WITH THE VICTIM BEING DRAGGED FACEDOWN THE COLLECTION OF THE VICTIM'S SKIN AND BLOOD FROM THE GRAVEL DRIVEWAY FURTHER CONFIRM THIS THEORY.

Mark Fuhrman

Predominantly all the wounds on the face area were to the left of the face, with the exception of one blow to the back of the head. He described that wound as a large curve-shaped wound to the back of her head, with a big piece of scalp almost completely detached and hanging loose from the rest of the head.

Once Robertson made his identification he was in a hurry to leave. He walked away from the body thinking that he had to tell Martha's brother, John Moxley, before he heard the news from someone else.

When Robertson got back to the house, he noted that from the living-room window in the southwest corner of the house he could see Martha's body even through the branches of the tree. Aside from confirming that the body was in fact Martha, Lowell Robertson was never interviewed by the police.

At some point, Dr. Coleman Kelly, a general practitioner and part-time local medical examiner, arrived and viewed the victim's body. The town's medical examiner duties were handled on a rotating basis. Coleman Kelly was not even on call that afternoon. He heard Hickman's notice on his own police radio and proceeded to the Moxley residence. In 1975, Kelly was in his mid-seventies. Years later, several locals described him as being slightly senile and not very professionally competent at that point in his career. Nonetheless, he served as local medical examiner that afternoon.

It is unclear precisely what Kelly did when he arrived because his name was redacted from many of the early police reports. The first time I saw his name mentioned was in the Sutton Associates files, since he is mentioned in the autopsy, which Sutton somehow obtained. The autopsy has Kelly arriving on the crime scene at 1:15 P.M. Kelly himself probably reported that estimated time to Dr. Elliot Gross when he attended the autopsy the next day.

One of the most important rules of a homicide investigation is that before the body is moved, as much evidence should be recorded from it as possible. As long as the victim is obviously deceased, photographs, videotapes, measurements, sketches, and notes should all be taken before the body is ever touched.

Sometime between 2:00 and 3:00 P.M. detectives Jim Lunney, Dan Pendergast, Ted Brosko, Ronald Timm, and Mike Powell arrived at the crime scene. Detectives Brosko and Lunney approached and viewed the body. Pendergast, Timm, and Powell immediately began a neighborhood canvass to elicit clues.

About the same time, Greenwich police criminalist and photographer Detective Tom Sorenson arrived. He told me that he did not look at the body. Instead, he began taking pictures of the surrounding area. When I interviewed Sorenson, he could not remember taking photos of the body under the tree even though Greenwich detectives have seen pictures of Martha's body.

Carroll also described other officers being on the scene. None of them are named in reports or were ever asked if they viewed or touched the body. One can assume that they at least went over to look.

By 2:00 p.m. at least twelve people had touched or stood over the body of Martha Moxley:

Sheila McGuire
Jean Walker
Millard Jones
Dan Hickman
Tom Keegan
Steve Carroll
Joe McGlynn
Richard Danehower
Lowell Robertson
Coleman Kelly
Ted Brosko
Jim Lunney

Her body had been moved several times—by Millard Jones, Richard Danehower, Lowell Robertson, and probably Coleman Kelly.

In addition to the direct contact by officers and witnesses at the crime scene near the body, many more observers were in the immediate vicinity. Lowell Robertson saw a crowd of several dozen neighbors and reporters on the front lawn and driveway. Even this early into the case, Robertson thought that the police were not experienced enough to handle a crime like this one.

When John Moxley arrived home from football practice, he said that his house looked "like a battle-field." There were so many police officers on the Moxley property that John said later, "It would have been a great day to be out robbing houses, because all the police were right there."

Most of the police personnel were standing in the

circular drive that was part of the crime scene, right where the initial attack took place. Civilian onlookers got as close as twenty feet away from the body and were trampling over the leaf trail and driveway where the blood and other evidence were found. At this point, the only area cordoned off was immediately around the pine tree.

Soon a perimeter was established around what was considered the crime scene. Since the Greenwich Police Department did not have any crime scene tape, uniformed officers used manila rope and traffic barricades to cordon off the scene.

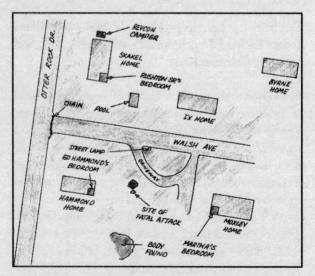

Two hours after Martha Moxley's body was discovered, the crime scene was already chaos. So was the investigation itself.

After viewing the body, detectives Steve Carroll and Joe McGlynn started walking around the crime scene, looking for clues. Quickly, several pieces of evidence were found, including the head of a golf club and two sections of the shaft. From the police records and interviews, I cannot tell who discovered this evidence or when exactly it was discovered. Several officers claim to have found the golf club, but they are either unspecific or unsure about which pieces they discovered. No time of discovery was noted.

The locations of the evidence were recorded. A blood-speckled golf club head and an eight-inch piece of shaft were found in the center of the circular driveway. Drops of blood were on the head of the golf club and some of the leaves nearby. Forty-two feet southwest from the club head, across the pebbled asphalt driveway and next to and just south of a dwarf Japanese elm, was a huge pool of blood approximately three to four feet in diameter. Detectives also found an eleven-inch piece of the golf club shaft at that location.

Carroll described the blood pool as "thick and coagulated, almost jelly." Between the golf club head and the pool of blood detectives saw particles of skin and blood on the pebbled asphalt of the driveway. They also observed drag marks in the leaves and grass leading away in a southerly direction from the pool of blood toward the tree where Martha was finally discovered.

There were no assignments and no control of the

investigation. The officers just fanned out and started knocking on doors. From 1:12 P.M. until at least 3:00 P.M., Captain Keegan was in the Moxley house, interviewing Dorthy Moxley. Meanwhile, the crime scene, which was officially under Keegan's control, was being overrun by journalists and onlookers. The body was left unguarded. Detectives were canvassing the neighborhood when they should have been gathering evidence at the scene.

By 3:00 P.M. detectives Ted Brosko and Jim Lunney were in the Skakel house, interviewing family members there. At 3:40 P.M. Captain Keegan directed detectives Joe McGlynn and Steve Carroll to go to the Hammond house to interview Ed Hammond.

The neighbors would still be there the next day, but the body and much of the evidence would not. It was autumn in New England, and the Moxley lawn was covered with leaves. Many of those leaves had blood or other evidence on them, which was literally vanishing in the wind.

At 4:00 P.M., Tom Sorenson notified the Connecticut State Police Crime Scene Laboratory in Bethany and asked them to report to Walsh Lane, more than an hour's drive away. One report, signed by Mike Powell, has the Connecticut Mobile Crime Scene Lab at the scene at 3:40 P.M., but all the witnesses state that the lab did not arrive until it was nearly dark. On October 31, daylight savings time had just ended. It was dark at about 5:00 P.M.

Whenever the crime lab did arrive, the van

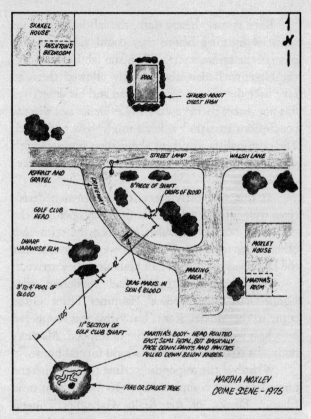

SKAKEL HOUSE

RUSHTON'S BEDROOM

N

POOL

SHRUBS-ABOUT CHEST HIGH

STREET LAMP

WALSH LANE

ASPHALT AND GRAVEL

DRIVEWAY

8" PIECE OF SHAFT

DROPS OF BLOOD

GOLF CLUB HEAD

DWARF JAPANESE ELM

MOXLEY HOUSE

MARTHA'S ROOM

3' TO 4' POOL OF BLOOD

12'

DRAG MARKS IN SKIN & BLOOD

PARKING AREA

105'

11" SECTION OF GOLF CLUB SHAFT

MARTHA'S BODY- HEAD POINTED EAST, SEMI FETAL, BUT BASICALLY FACE DOWN. PANTS AND PANTIES PULLED DOWN BELOW KNEES.

MARTHA MOXLEY CRIME SCENE - 1975

PINE OR SPRUCE TREE

pulled into the circle of the Moxley driveway and drove almost directly on top of the site of the initial attack. Responding with the crime lab was Jack Solomon, a state investigator. When Solomon arrived on the scene, he immediately went to police headquarters to assist in the interrogation of Ed Hammond.

Since it was already dark, the lab had to set up artificial lighting before they could videotape and process the crime scene. When the lab began work, the Greenwich detectives simply allowed them to take over the crime scene. Keegan and his detectives did not direct them toward any evidence nor discuss conclusions that the evidence might have indicated. The criminalists just went about their business with very little interchange between them and the detectives.

At this very early stage, the Greenwich detectives were already relinquishing their control of the case. It is not known what evidence the crime lab observed or recorded, if any. All we do know is that the body was removed a half hour after they arrived.

The Greenwich police had requested that Connecticut chief medical examiner Elliot Gross come to the Moxley scene, but Gross was hampered by a heavy caseload and unable to respond. Martha's body was to be picked up by a local funeral home.

Whatever the responding crime lab did with the crime scene was completed by 5:30 P.M. At that time Charles Danks, of the Reilly Gallagher Funeral Home in Greenwich, arrived and removed the victim's body. Police Officer Robert Lynch assisted Danks in bagging the body. Lieutenant James Gleason accompanied the body to the Greenwich Hospital morgue, where the autopsy would be done the following day. A police officer guarded Martha's body all night and the rest of the next morning. There in the morgue, Martha's body received better protection than at the crime scene, where she was basically ignored by the case detectives for five hours.

During those five hours, the Greenwich detectives should have been closely examining the immediate proximity for clues and learning what they could from the victim's body without touching or contaminating it.

Every homicide investigation should start at the body. Then it should move out from the body to encompass the surrounding crime scene. While the body of Martha Moxley grew colder and the night turned dark, the evidence that surrounded and was contained there was basically ignored. The body is the nucleus of the homicide investigation. The body will not lie. The body holds the facts that will lead to the suspect. It is your best witness. Unfortunately, this witness was ignored as the Greenwich police went after others.

By 5:30 P.M. on October 31, 1975, the best piece of evidence in the case was gone forever.

6

The Autopsy

*Chief Peter Robbins said he opposed an independent review
of the Moxley autopsy because, "I know where {the
information} is going—it's going into Fuhrman's book."*
—Greenwich Time, *November 7, 1997*

From the beginning, I knew that I would have to read the autopsy report, or at least learn its contents, in order to conduct a thorough investigation into the Moxley case. Without the autopsy information, I could not make any assumptions or hypotheses about how the murder occurred. It would be difficult, perhaps impossible, to determine who killed Martha Moxley and how it was done.

From newspaper accounts, the Sutton Associates files, and interviews with people who observed her body or were involved in the investigation, I had already heard a great deal about the method of death and the wounds inflicted on Martha. Many of the details were either vague, confusing, or contradictory. I had to find out for myself.

Reading the Sutton Associates files, I saw that Sutton, the Skakel attorneys, and the Academy Group had copies of the autopsy. Knowing that

Frank Garr had a copy of the Sutton files, I figured that he or Don Browne or Peter Robbins or whoever controlled the autopsy would allow me to read it. After all, what harm could I do if the defense attorneys for the suspect's family already had the information?

Days after the murder, the Greenwich police had told the press the cause of death, the weapon used, the estimated time of death, the position and location of the victim's body, and the condition of her clothes. They also stated that Martha was not under the influence of drugs or alcohol and had not been sexually molested. As the investigation progressed, even more details, particularly concerning the victim's wounds, were released. What other sensitive information could have been contained in the autopsy?

I found Dr. Elliot Gross, who performed the autopsy. Presently the medical examiner in Cape May County, New Jersey, Gross told me he could not remember any details of the case, did not have any records, and could not remember if he had any photos. "My policy," he said shortly before hanging up, "is not to discuss the case."

I asked Frank Garr if I could look at the autopsy. He said he would have to talk to Don Browne. When I asked Don Browne, he said he would have to talk to Frank Garr. So I went to see the Greenwich police chief, Peter Robbins. When I finally met with Robbins, I mentioned that Sutton and the Skakel attorneys had the autopsy. "I know,

Mark," he said wearily, confirming that they had it and the authorities knew. Then Robbins said he wouldn't let me read the autopsy.

Everyone said that they couldn't let me see the autopsy because it was an "open case." I was willing to agree to conditions and even suppress information if it could help catch a killer. I didn't think they were hiding the autopsy because it was an open case; too much information had already been made public. After all these years, I believe the only reason the Greenwich police might possibly have for not releasing the report was that they did not effectively use the information contained in the report. Or maybe they didn't even understand what was in it.

I asked Dorthy Moxley to request a copy of the autopsy, and she was told she couldn't have it. It is common procedure in most other states for the victim's family to be provided a copy of the autopsy, even in open cases, if they are planning an independent review of the document. In Connecticut, however, the autopsy report is controlled by the state's attorney.

During my conversations with Dorthy, she mentioned that she was a personal friend of Dr. Michael Baden, a renowned pathologist I knew from two previous cases in Los Angeles. In the first case, a victim's family hired Dr. Baden to review an autopsy report and help reclassify an accidental death as a homicide. The second case was *The People v. Simpson,* where Baden had been hired by the defendant. Even considering his work for Simpson, I had always thought highly of Baden's forensic skills and felt he was a scientist first, an expert witness second.

Dorthy and I discussed the possibility of having Dr. Baden represent the Moxley family in an effort to obtain the autopsy report and help me review it. Dorthy spoke with Baden, and he was eager to help in any way he could. When I spoke to him, I found Baden to be motivated and already familiar with the Moxley case. He was puzzled by the Connecticut authorities' refusal to release the autopsy report to the family after twenty-two years.

The Moxleys put their lawyer, Jack Zeldes, on the case, as they were also trying to get Martha's personal items, including her diary, returned to them. Zeldes determined that the autopsy report was officially controlled by the state's attorney office, and state law allowed them to withhold the autopsy report on any open case. The only way anyone could legally look at the autopsy report was with Don Browne's permission. How the Skakel lawyers had obtained the autopsy report is a mystery, but they had it. I told Zeldes, a personal friend of Manny Margolis, that if he knew someone who had the autopsy report, I would love to have it. I'm not sure if Zeldes made any overtures to the Skakel attorneys on my behalf.

Zeldes began negotiating between the Moxleys and Connecticut officials. The initial arrangement that Zeldes proposed was ludicrous: Don Browne

would allow Dr. Baden to review the autopsy
report, but he would have to sign a confidentiality
form that basically stated that Baden could not
speak with Mark Fuhrman about it.

When I was informed of this offer, I called
Zeldes and asked him what possible use this might
be to either me or the Moxley family. Zeldes
responded that Dr. Baden could provide the officials help with any "tips" he got from reading the
autopsy report. I told Zeldes that the only reason
Baden was involved at all was to talk to me. After
much frustrating discussion, Zeldes finally agreed
to push for a more useful arrangement.

Ultimately a deal was set up in which Baden
would be allowed to view the autopsy report and
photos in the presence of Henry Lee, Frank Garr,
and Don Browne. The police and prosecutors told
Baden that he could not be kept from discussing
the review with me.

However the autopsy was conducted, the
autopsy report was most probably the one piece of
evidence in this case that was still uncompromised.
Anatomical photos and lab reports are difficult to
change or ignore. For this fact alone, the autopsy
report is a very important document.

If used properly, the autopsy report can be a
significant tool in a homicide investigation. The
evidence acquired during this procedure is collected and analyzed only within scientific parame-
ters of fact. Knowledge and analysis of the autopsy
report are absolutely essential to understanding

how the evidence of the case does or does not match the physical evidence of the victim's body. In the Moxley case, I knew the autopsy report contained information that would answer several key questions.

One of the most important questions I had was the estimated time of death. The Greenwich police assumed that the attack occurred between 9:35 and 10:00 P.M. All they had to support such a narrow timeline were witness reports of dogs barking and Dorthy's hearing voices outside. There was no evidence that the attack occurred in that timespan, but the police never deviated from their assumptions, making it nearly impossible for them to solve the case, or even think about it clearly.

When contacting the state crime scene lab and medical examiner's office on October 31, 1975, the Greenwich police asked Dr. Elliot Gross, then chief medical examiner of the state of Connecticut, to respond to the Moxley scene. He said that he was hampered by a heavy caseload and unable to respond at the scene, and the mobile crime scene lab from Bethany was dispatched to the scene instead.

According to standard operating procedure, a qualified medical examiner or deputy coroner should have examined the body at the crime scene, preferably Dr. Gross himself. Had a qualified person been at the scene, he could have made many observations that would have resulted in a more accurate time of death. Dr. Baden, a medical examiner himself, agreed with me.

Two of the most important factors in determining time of death are rigor mortis and lividity. They can only be observed in the body during the crucial hours following death.

Rigor mortis is the contraction of the body muscles due to chemical changes occurring after death. This process begins within two to four hours and is complete eight to twelve hours after death. Once rigor mortis is complete, the body is "fixed" in the position assumed at death. The medical examiner should have established what stage of rigor mortis the victim was experiencing. Simply moving the victim would provide information establishing which portions of the body were limp or stiff.

Rigor mortis progresses from head to toe. When it leaves, the body slowly becomes limp again in the same order, from head to toe. It begins to disappear about eighteen to thirty-six hours after death. In the average body it is completely gone in forty-eight to sixty hours. Dr. Gross did not see the body of Martha Moxley until roughly thirty-six to thirty-nine hours after she died. By then effects of rigor mortis had almost entirely disappeared from the body, or at least were well on their way.

Postmortem lividity occurs when the heart ceases to pump and the blood pools toward the pull of gravity. It is important to establish not only time of death but also the position of the body at the time of death. Lividity begins about thirty minutes after death and becomes fixed in eight to ten hours.

It is identified by a purplish discoloration in the parts of the body closest to the ground. If lividity is not consistent with the body position—for example, there is lividity on the victim's back, but she is found facedown—then it can be concluded that the body has been moved from its original position at death.

Without having a qualified representative from the medical examiner's office at the scene of the homicide, these details could not have been documented properly, or even noted at all.

Therefore, an accurate determination of time of death was not possible. All Dr. Gross could determine was that Martha died sometime between 9:30 P.M. and 5:00 the following morning. He told this to the police and to the press.

On November 1, 1975, at approximately 9:00 A.M., Dr. Gross came to Greenwich. He was shown the Connecticut State Crime Lab videotape of the crime scene, and then taken to the Moxley property, where he was physically walked through the entire crime scene. He was also shown photos taken the day before and processed overnight. I don't understand what Gross might have been able to learn from the crime scene, since the body was no longer there. Perhaps the Greenwich police were hoping that he would solve the crime for them.

Most civilians, and some police agencies, are under the misconception that forensic pathologists are investigators. They watch programs like *Quincy*, and read Patricia Cornwell novels and think that the pathologist can take over a homicide investigation and solve it.

The role of the pathologist is to answer the following questions: What is the cause of death? How, by what means, and when did the victim die? The role of the detective is to prove who did it. The detective provides the pathologist with information about the scene, the victim, and the investigation. The pathologist provides the detective with information about the wounds and body condition of the victim. The pathologist and the detective are professional equals. They should work together with mutual respect for each other's expertise. The detective should ask the pathologist questions about his examination and conclusions, and the two should exchange theories on how the death occurred.

After viewing the crime scene, Dr. Gross performed an autopsy on Martha Moxley. The procedure began at 12:40 P.M. and concluded at 6:45 P.M. Several people attended the autopsy, including Gross's assistant, Dr. Alfred Tangney; a local pathologist named Dr. James Spencer; Dr. Coleman Kelly; youth officer Dan Hickman; and detectives Jim Lunney, Ted Brosko, Dan Pendergast, and Tom Sorenson.

Six hours is a very long autopsy, and five attending officers are a lot of spectators. Detectives Lunney and Brosko were there because they were assigned to the case. Detective Sorenson was the photographer/criminalist and took photos of the procedure. Officer Hickman was also at the autopsy, to make statements regarding his observations at the crime scene. After Hickman made his statements, he quickly left the room, as the sight of blood made him sick.

When I spoke to Detective Sorenson, he remembered taking photos at the autopsy, but when asked about the head wounds he stated that he didn't remember any details. "I might have blocked a lot of stuff out because I have a daughter who was the same age and that night my wife was having a Halloween party for her," Sorenson told me.

Although he did not attend the autopsy, Detective Steve Carroll was present at Greenwich police headquarters on January 7, 1976, when Dr. Gross showed the slides he had taken during the procedure. Also present were Jim Lunney and Jack Solomon.

Later that day, the police received the toxicology report from Dr. Abraham Stolman, chief of the state toxicology lab. Stolman determined that Martha was not under the influence of drugs or alcohol the night of her murder.

Once Dr. Gross presented his slide show, the detectives asked for their own set of photos. Gross refused, stating that the color slides were his personal property. The slides should be the property of the state of Connecticut, but Gross reportedly didn't give copies to the Greenwich police, who had only black-and-white photos of the autopsy.

In December 1997, I spoke to Dr. Baden about

his review of the autopsy. Frank Garr and state attorney Don Browne were present at the review. They did not allow Dr. Baden much time to examine the documents. Baden noted Garr's and Browne's visible discomfort whenever he started writing any notes. He was provided only black-and-white photos for reference, and when Baden asked about color photos of the autopsy, Browne and Garr acted as if they were surprised that color photos had not been included.

At this writing, Dr. Baden is still trying to locate the color photos of the autopsy, to examine more closely the condition of the wounds, abrasions, and lividity. The police say they are not able to find the photos.

Baden told me that the toxicology report confirmed that no alcohol or drugs were in Martha's system at the time of her death. The fact that she was not under the influence of any substance that might alter her judgment was an important factor in considering a possible motive for her murder.

I was very interested in Martha's stab wounds. The through-the-neck wound had been described by nearly every observer, but there was also talk of additional wounds. Dr. Baden told me that there was only one stab wound. It was in Martha's neck and hadn't punctured or severed any arteries or veins. The wound was perimortem; in other words, it was inflicted right around the time of death. That meant that the stab wound was most probably the last attack on the victim.

Dr. Baden noted that the stab wound was right to

left, with the victim's hair protruding from the wound on the left side of the neck. The stab wound had been repeatedly described to me as being left to right.

On April 29, 1991, Don Browne told *Hard Copy* that the victim was stabbed five times with the broken shaft of the golf club. I had not heard of these other four stab wounds, nor had any of the detectives I spoke to, nor the Moxleys. If Browne read the autopsy, why did he exaggerate the number of stab wounds?

According to Dr. Baden, the stab wound passed through the windpipe. He found evidence that there was blood in the lungs, indicating that Martha was still alive when the suspect stabbed her through the throat. Martha was still trying to breathe, and as she breathed she sucked blood into her lungs.

Baden's observations corroborated my hypothesis that Martha was lying with the left side of her face toward the ground, most probably on top of the eleven-inch portion of the shaft. She was in this position when she was stabbed. Dr. Baden agreed with me that an indentation on the side of Martha's head was most probably caused by her head lying on top of the eleven-inch piece of shaft in the pool of blood. The Greenwich detectives had thought that this indentation was the initial blow that had knocked Martha unconscious. I knew that if it had been a blow, there would have been bruising and at least lacerations, if not fractures, in that fragile part of the skull.

I had already spoken to two medical doctors
who confirmed that it would have taken some time
for Martha's wounds to expel that much blood from
her body as was described near the Japanese elm, so
I was very interested in Dr. Baden's opinion. He
also agreed that she lay there for a half hour or
longer, stating that any bleeding prior to the stab
wound would have been slow rather than rapid.

DET. STEVE CARROLL DESCRIBED AN
INDENTATION ON THE LEFT TEMPLE
LEADING FROM THE EYE TOWARDS
THE TOP OF THE EAR. THE FLESH
WAS DEPRESSED, AS WAS THE
BLOOD-SOAKED HAIR. THIS MOST
PROBABLY OCCURRED AS THE VICTIM'S
HEAD RESTED ON THE BROKEN
PORTION OF THE GOLF CLUB SHAFT. UPON
DEATH CIRCULATION CEASED AND
THE INDENTATION BECAME FIXED.

Mark Fuhrman

Despite the wounds to Martha's head, her heart
was still pumping, however slightly, for some time
in order for her to bleed significantly. Gravity alone
could not have accounted for the blood pool by the
Japanese elm, since Martha was laying facedown on
level ground.

There appears to be little doubt from the scientific evidence that she was beaten with the golf club
and left for dead by the suspect. The suspect returned
later to hide the body. Finding Martha still alive, he
stabbed her with the broken golf club shaft.

Dr. Baden stated that the head wounds were to

the back and sides of the victim's head, causing deep lacerations and fractures of the skull. He opined that the blunt-force wounds were definitely inflicted by contact with the golf club head, not just the shaft.

What surprised me was that Baden said the autopsy described only four wounds that could have resulted from the golf club head. The description of lacerations and fractures to the skull from these four wounds are the only injuries that can be directly connected to the murder weapon.

This conclusion supported my theory that the head of the club and a portion of the shaft broke off during the attack by the dwarf elm tree, not by the driveway. Had the head been broken off at the first blow, then the victim would only have one wound that could be matched to the golf club head. Instead, there were four.

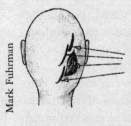

THE VICTIM HAD FOUR INJURIES TO THE RIGHT REAR OF THE HEAD, OF WHICH ONE HAD A VISIBLE SKULL FRACTURE. DR. DANEHOWER NOTED THE LACERATION TO THE SCALP ON OCTOBER 31ST, 1975, AND DR. BADEN CONFIRMED THAT OBSERVATION IN 1997. BOTH DOCTORS STATED THAT THESE TYPES OF WOUNDS TO THE HEAD WOULD "OOZE" BLOOD, NOT PUMP.

Mark Fuhrman

The fact that only a few specks of blood were present near the driveway where the club head and an eight-inch section of shaft were found would tend to indicate that the vicious attack on the victim was not committed there. If it had, there would have been more blood on the ground.

I asked Baden if there was any bruising to the victim in the neck or shoulder area that could have possibly been caused by the golf club. Dr. Baden noted one bruise on the left arm that could have been caused by the club, but no others.

Throughout the investigation, police and prosecutors spoke of twelve to fourteen blows to the victim's head. Where did they get that figure? Sometimes investigations intentionally leak false or incomplete information in hopes that it will provide some leverage with the suspect. However, I don't understand how overstating the number of blunt-force injuries, as well as stab wounds, could possibly help their case.

Another question I had concerned the stomach contents, which are an important factor in estimating time of death. Dorthy Moxley stated that she had given Martha a grilled cheese sandwich at approximately 6:00 P.M. Martha had ice cream at the Mouakad house around 7:00 to 7:30 P.M.

Under normal circumstances the stomach empties itself four to six hours after a meal. If the stomach contents showed that the food was almost completely digested but still remained in the stomach, we could state that she died four to six hours after her last meal.

Dr. Baden and I discussed at length the issue of the stomach contents and how this affected the estimated the time of death. The process of food

digestion is an approximation. Dr. Baden was of
the opinion that the stomach starts to empty itself
about two to three hours after the intake of food.

The autopsy report stated that Martha had three
ounces of digested, indistinguishable, semiliquid
food in her stomach. Based on the knowledge that
Martha ate a grilled cheese sandwich at 6:00 P.M. and
ice cream at the Moukads at 7:30, Dr. Baden confirmed my opinion that Martha's death could more
accurately be described as having most probably
occurred between 9:30 P.M. and 1:30 A.M.

Baden agreed that if a medical examiner had
responded to the scene and done a complete investigation of the victim regarding rigor mortis and lividity, coupled with the stomach contents, then a time
of death probably could have been established with
no more than a three-hour bracket.

Dr. Baden's observations and conclusions confirmed many of the theories I had but needed to corroborate through an expert's judgment. Baden is not
only a top-rate pathologist but also has good detective skills.

His review of the autopsy report answered many
of my questions, but it raised several more. Why did
the authorities try so hard to keep the autopsy away
from me? Why did they exaggerate the number of
blows and stab wounds? Why didn't they widen
their time frame for the attack and time of death?
Why didn't they scrutinize the autopsy for evidence
and information that could have helped them get a
clearer picture of how Martha Moxley died?

It is the job of the medical examiner to perform the autopsy and record his observations and theories, but it is the responsibility of the detective to make sense out of the process. A detective must arrange theory, scientific evidence, probability, and witness statements into a mosaic of the crime. He must have the right pieces in order for them to fit.

7

The Murder Weapon

The missing portion of the club has never turned up.
—Captain Tom Keegan

Three pieces of a golf club were found at the murder scene. The head of the club, with a couple drops of blood on it, was found on the north side of the driveway. An eight-inch piece of shaft was found by the club head. And an eleven-inch piece of the shaft was found in the pool of blood near the Japanese elm. That piece was covered in blood.

Police say the missing part of the golf club, approximately twenty inches of handle and shaft, was not at the crime scene. In the months ahead, they devoted extraordinary resources to finding that piece. They never did find it. Some immediate questions came to mind when I began investigating this case: Why did the police spend more time in the crucial early phases of the investigation looking for the murder weapon than the murder suspect? What did they think the missing piece would prove? Why were they so sure there was a missing piece? Why did the police assume it was a complete golf club to begin with?

The first and most important thing to do with a murder weapon is to link it to a suspect. The pieces of golf club found at the crime scene were linked to the Skakel house by the afternoon of November 1, 1975, at the latest.

According to the police report, on October 31 detectives Brosko and Lunney "had an occasion to be in the Rushton Skakel home" where they observed a Toney Penna golf club in a storage bin. At the time, Rushton Skakel was reportedly away on a hunting trip in Vermont, "and the investigators were unable to obtain permission to remove the golf club from his home."

This report was written on November 2, two days after the detectives' observation. In fact, the report actually reads "October 30, 1975," but that is a typo and indicates that Jim Lunney was writing the report retroactively in order to build a chain of events leading to probable cause that the murder weapon came from the Skakel house.

Lunney goes on to describe how on November 1, Dr. Elliot Gross had conducted the autopsy and stated that the weapon used to inflict Martha Moxley's fatal injuries was a golf club.

The next day, Lunney reported, "Since the golf club which was still at the Skakel home was similar to the one that caused the death of Martha Moxley, the investigators proceeded to the Skakel home in an attempt to obtain the golf club." Brosko and Lunney asked Rushton Skakel if they could take possession of the Toney Penna golf club that was still in his home. Skakel reportedly signed a consent-to-search premises without a search-warrant form (which is missing from the public police records).

The murder weapon was a Toney Penna six iron. Lunney and Brosko took a Toney Penna five iron from the Skakel house. The five iron was engraved with the name ANN SKAKEL just below the leatherette handle. Rushton Skakel told them that the Toney Penna clubs belonged to his wife, Ann, who died in 1973. He added that upon his wife's death, he gave the set to his daughter, Julie. The detectives interviewed Julie, who said that the last time she used the golf clubs was that past summer. She made a quick search of the house but was unable to find the rest of the set. Both Rushton and Julie said they would make a thorough search of the house in an attempt to find the golf clubs.

Toney Penna was a rare model of golf club. Subsequent investigation determined that the Skakels owned the only set in the neighborhood. The police didn't know that fact at the time, but they were obviously acting on the suspicion that the murder weapon came from the Skakel house. Once they found a matching club, they asked the family to produce the rest of the set. If the Skakels could produce a six iron from that set, then the club must have come from another set. But they couldn't.

Rushton Skakel had already been interviewed concerning the Toney Penna club by Detective Mike

Powell, father of current Greenwich patrolman Tim Powell. According to Powell's report, on November 1: "Mr. Skakel was questioned relative to the possibility of any golf clubs being left outside on his property and he related that with three teenaged sons that play the game, it was a good possibility that some clubs may have been left outside, further he was questioned relative to his owning any [Toney Penna] clubs and he related that he owned a set of [Toney Penna] woods, but no irons that he could recall."

Why would Rushton say he owned a set of woods, but no irons? That response becomes even more suspect when the detectives recovered a five iron from the house the next day.

Powell reported: "Mr. Skakel checked his clubs which are kept in a breakfast room on the first floor, northwest side of the home, and related that he was unsure if any were missing."

According to detectives who were in the Skakel house repeatedly during this time, the clubs kept in the breakfast room were a miscellaneous collection of clubs used by family members for walking sticks and to "whale golf balls" in the backyard. It would have been very difficult for Rushton to determine if any of those clubs were missing.

"He further advised that on or about Sept. 9, 1975, he had a company golf party at the house which was attended by many employees of his firm and that some [chip and put] was played on the lawn." Did Rushton Skakel, or the detectives for that matter, believe that a golf club left out nearly two months earlier would still be laying around a property that was looked after by a full-time gardener?

The next day, the Skakel boys told the same story. On November 2 at 7:00 P.M., Lunney and Brosko went back to the Skakel house and interviewed the family once again. "All the boys stated that on occasions after using the golf clubs some are left on the lawn and usually are retrieved the next day or so. It was noted by the investigators that the Skakel family own numerous sets of golf clubs which are stored at different locations in the house."

The possibility that the murder weapon was laying around on someone's lawn was a convenient story. It fit in with the initial suspicion that the suspect was a transient who wandered in from the turnpike. At the same time, the story focused attention away from the Skakels.

Greenwich police chief Steve Baran was offering this possibility as early as Sunday, November 2. According to an article in the next day's *Greenwich Time:* "'Kids are always leaving bicycles, tennis rackets, and golf clubs outdoors, after playing with them on the lawn,' he said, explaining that the murderer or murderers might simply have picked up the club."

When I was staying at the Homestead Inn, I took several walks and jogs around Belle Haven. In all my trips through that neighborhood, I never once saw a golf club, a golf ball, or even a golfer. Ken Littleton claimed in an interview with *A Current Affair* that Thomas and Michael killed chipmunks and squirrels with golf clubs. And Rushton

Sr. went for nightly walks armed with a golf club. "Walking with a golf club was a family trait," said one neighbor.

Baran also told *Greenwich Time:* "The fifteen Greenwich officers assigned to the case were attempting to trace the golf club back to its owner. . . ." He tried to downplay the possibility of linking the club to its owners: "The police chief pointed out that this in itself may not have any significance."

I would think that finding out where the murder weapon originated is very significant. Identifying the Toney Penna club didn't prove that one of the Skakels committed the murder, but it clearly pointed suspicion in the direction of the Skakel house, if anyone was brave enough to suspect them. It appears that the Greenwich police, and the community at large, were willing to accept any explanation as long as it directed suspicion away from a member of a wealthy and prominent family.

At the same time they were downplaying its importance, the police searched frantically for the missing piece of the murder weapon. The search began first thing the morning after Martha was found. On November 1 at 9:30 A.M. Captain Tom Keegan directed detectives Brosko and Lunney, Sergeant Hennessey, and youth officer Dan Hickman (why was a youth officer called in?) to respond to the crime scene and re-search the area. The local gas company provided personnel and the use of a metal detector to search the crime scene. Results negative.

The next day at 1:00 P.M. Sergeant Hennessey

and detectives Mike Powell and Ronald Timm went back to Belle Haven to continue the search. Armed with metal detectors and leaf blowers, the officers expanded the area of search to include all the adjacent and nearby properties, including the Skakels'. The investigators searched until it grew dark, but no luck.

When the officers returned from their search, Captain Keegan issued a Teletype containing information about the golf club. This Teletype was sent to other law-enforcement agencies. Five minutes before Keegan issued the Teletype, Chief Baran put out a press release revealing that the department "was seeking the grip & shaft portion of a stainless steel golf club, the approximate size is believed to be between sixteen inches and twenty-four inches in length. . . . This item is believed to have been used in the Moxley homicide and a concentrated search of the crime scene has failed to turn up the missing article."

I don't understand why the police were vague about the length of the golf club handle. Detectives had already obtained a complete club and determined the original length of the murder weapon by comparing it to the five iron from the Skakel set.

By 9:00 P.M. a citizen had already responded with the first possible clue. It turned out to be the broken piece of a ski pole. During the next few months, dozens of golf clubs, pieces of golf clubs, ski poles, metal shafts, and other objects were turned in to the Greenwich Police Department. None of them matched the murder weapon.

While the public and other law-enforcement agencies joined the search, the Greenwich police's own hunt for the missing handle continued.

On November 3, Captain Keegan called the Marine Division and requested a search of the Belle Haven waterfront. The shoreline was searched on foot, and a patrolman was dispatched in a skiff to check the shallow waters of Long Island Sound. The waterfront search was conducted at high tide, then again at half tide. The results were negative.

Police contacted the local garbage collector in charge of Belle Haven and told him to be on the lookout for a golf club shaft. Every morning after he picked up the Skakel trash, Greenwich detectives would wait around the corner and search his garbage. The gutters and storm drains of Belle Haven were searched. The Skakel family pool and a nearby pond were both drained and searched. The town Parks and Trees Department got in a cherry picker and searched all the trees, roofs, and gutters on the Moxley property.

Every outbuilding, fallout shelter, and hole in the ground near the crime scene was searched by the Greenwich police. They found nothing. On December 11, Detective Jim Lunney received permission from Rushton Skakel to search the Windham residence. Lunney drove up there that afternoon on overtime and searched the house. Results negative.

During late November and early December 1975, detectives Steve Carroll and Jim Lunney did some homework on Toney Penna golf clubs. They couldn't find anyone else in the neighborhood who owned them. They couldn't find any sporting goods store in the area that had sold them. They spoke to representatives of the company that manufactured the clubs and received information on sales of the particular model and size.

On December 3, Carroll and Lunney mailed the five iron taken from the Skakel house to the FBI crime lab for comparison with the pieces found at the crime scene. They did not get the results back until February 9, when the FBI finally completed its metallurgical testing of the two clubs and determined that they matched. The murder weapon did indeed come from the Skakel set.

The metallurgical tests would have been useful in court to nail down the fact that the murder weapon was a Skakel club. At this point in the investigation, they did not need those test results to determine that the murder weapon came from the Skakel house. Waiting for the results as confirmation of what they already knew only delayed and hindered the investigation.

The Greenwich police investigated every recent murder and assault committed with a golf club in the Northeast. What they didn't understand was that the golf club was a weapon of convenience. In the Bronx, murders are committed with steak knives, lengths of rebar, or bricks. In Belle Haven, murders are committed with golf clubs. A golf club was accessible, and the suspect must have felt comfortable with one, as probably did most males in Belle Haven.

If the weapon had been laying on the ground when the attacker picked it up, wouldn't it at least be possible that the club was broken already? This might have occurred to Sergeant Hennessey, who went over to the Moxley house to interview John Moxley on November 1 while searching for the missing piece on the Moxley property. Hennessey asked John if he owned any golf clubs, and John said yes. John then looked at all his golf clubs and determined that none were missing. Hennessey noted in his report: "John also stated that he mows the yard and could have run over a golf club that had been left in the yard." John Moxley had enough sense to know that the golf club could already have been broken. Did the Greenwich police know something that he didn't?

The search continued, and police officials often acted as if the missing golf club handle were the key to the case. Many casual observers of the investigation seemed to think the same thing—if only that handle had turned up, it might have had the killer's fingerprints. If the police had found it, they would have solved the case.

In fact, the missing handle was not necessary to solve this case. And the search was more than just a waste of time. A gross misallocation of resources, the search ultimately served as a convenient excuse for why the killer hadn't been brought to justice. To me, the search was so frantic and so fruitless that it almost seems as if it were conducted merely so the police could say that they covered all the bases.

On October 11, 1997, I spoke with youth officer Millard Jones. At the time, I was attempting to reconstruct the crime scene and wanted to speak with everyone who had seen Martha's body beneath the tree. My questions to Jones initially focused on the position of her body and whether anyone had moved or touched her. His answers quickly turned the interview, and my investigation, in an entirely different direction. During Jones's description of his observations at the scene, he said the following:

MJ: Her pants were kind of down and the golf club was through her head from one side to the other.

MF: The golf club was still there?

MJ: The shaft was there. Part of the shaft, not the whole thing. Part of the shaft was there. That was always a bone of contention, that they never found the set of clubs that this club matched. I don't know what the exact police report says, I don't even remember what I wrote at that point, to be honest with you, it's been a lot of years ago.

MF: So when you saw the body under the tree, she had a shaft sticking—

MJ: The shaft was sticking through her head and the hair from the one side of the head was through the hole with the shaft and sticking out the other.

MF: Was there a handle on this shaft?

MJ: I'm not a golfer, I don't know much about golf, but it was, I guess it was like a leatherette or whatever you call it, the holder or the handle whatever you call it. And whatever side of the club it was, the end of the club was missing. And the shaft was just stuck through her head.

MF: And it was just sticking up there?

MJ: She was laying down and it was sticking right up.

I was shocked to hear this from Jones, and initially viewed it with skepticism. But he wasn't the first person ever to describe the golf club handle and shaft left embedded in the victim's body. Michael Skakel had made a similar statement during an interview at Elan School, a residential treatment facility he attended for several years. Jones was the first person at the crime scene who had said anything about it.

I needed to corroborate this information. I wanted the corroboration to be independent, both in source and interviewer, so I called Steve Weeks and told him what Jones had said. Then I asked him to call Jones's partner, Dan Hickman.

During Steve's interview, Hickman corroborated Jones's statement.

SW: When you saw the body, what position was it in?

DH: She was laying down, her face was down.

SW: Was any part of the weapon there?

DH: When you say weapon, I don't know, we don't know, what was the weapon?

SW: The golf club, because there were pieces scattered on the lawn and—

DH: The only piece that was there that I saw was just the shaft was right through her head. All the way through her head. That's the only part I saw.

SW: And it was still there when you got there?

DH: Yeah, that was embedded in her head.

This information was explosive. It meant that the murder weapon that police had been trying to find for twenty-two years had actually been at the crime scene, in the victim's body. What happened to it? Who else knew it was there? I had to make sure this information was absolutely solid.

I asked several people about Hickman and Jones, and everybody said they were stand-up guys. Jones was a blue-collar cop. His wife confirmed that he described the shaft sticking out of Martha's head when he came home from work that night in 1975. Hickman is now an ordained minister. "Danny's probably one of the most forthright, upright guys I've known in my life," said a retired patrolman, and several other people echoed those sentiments.

Both officers described the club as being in her head. I knew there was a stab wound through Martha's neck, but the angle and point of entry could make it appear that the handle was embedded in her head.

Jones and Hickman said they had never been formally interviewed by the detectives investigating the case. It didn't make any sense for them to lie about something like this. Still, I needed additional corroboration.

I called Jean Walker again, and she said she didn't see anything sticking out of Martha's head.

I called Dr. Richard Danehower, who saw the body next after Jones and Hickman. He said that on the ground next to Martha's body he had seen a shiny metal object, which looked like a golf club handle.

The next person to see the body was Captain Tom Keegan. He wouldn't talk. After Keegan came Carroll and Lunney. I went to Steve Carroll's house with tape recordings of the interviews with Hickman and Jones. When I told Carroll what they had said, he was incredulous.

During my work on this book, I got to know Steve Carroll fairly well. I am dead certain that his reaction to my information was genuine. He didn't see the golf club handle in Martha's head or at the crime scene. "If the shaft was there it would have had Ann Skakel's name on it," Steve said. "We wouldn't have been chasing all over God's little acre to find out where it came from."

Somehow the golf club handle disappeared from the crime scene. Maybe it was lost. Maybe it was taken by one of the many civilian bystanders, or even a corrupt police officer. Either way, the club handle was there, and then it wasn't.

Someone knew that the golf club handle was missing from the crime scene. And whoever did had been lying to other police officers, lying to other law-enforcement agencies, lying to the press, lying to the public, and most significantly, lying to the Moxley family about crucial evidence in the case. I couldn't sit on this information. If I did, I would be just like the person who had been covering it up for twenty-two years.

I decided to go public, but first I had to tell the Moxleys. I called John Moxley and arranged to meet him near his office in lower Manhattan. When I told John, his face froze in anger and I could see his hand shake. For twenty-two years, the police have been telling him and his family that one of the reasons they can't prosecute Martha's killer was that the missing piece of the murder weapon had never been found.

"I have put all my faith in the police for so long," Dorthy said after she found out, "and now I realize more and more they have let me down."

Joe Johnson ran the story in the October 23, 1997, *Greenwich Time*. He had interviewed Jones and Hickman himself, further corroborating what they had told Steve and me.

"What really blew my mind," Hickman told the reporter, "I remember seeing a shiny object impaled through the skull and it came out the other side. It obviously was the shaft of the golf club."

"You could see the leatherette or vinyl grip [of the golf club shaft]," Jones said, "and my wife swears that's what I told her when I came home that night."

Tom Keegan, who was running for reelection at the time, told Johnson, "That is not correct. The missing piece was the club handle on which the grips are found, and this section of the club was not present at the scene or in the body."

Once the story broke, Frank Garr said, "I didn't personally see the need to reinterview Millard Jones or Danny Hickman" during his reinvestigation of the case. He went on to state, "Obviously, they are not remembering things correctly."

To this day, Jones and Hickman stand by their observations. Hickman said that he didn't come forward with the information because he "blacked out" the details of his involvement at the crime scene. Those details came flooding back, he said, when Steve interviewed him. Jones said, "I never talked to anyone about it because no one asked me." Today both Hickman and

Jones have retained attorneys and refuse to be interviewed.

Before I started working on this book, I would
have been surprised that two experienced police officers didn't come forward with this kind of information. After spending several months investigating
the Moxley case, I am no longer surprised by these
lapses in communication.

Still, the question remained——what happened to
the golf club handle? When was it taken out of the
victim's head? Where did it go?

Detective Dan Pendergast attended the autopsy.
He told me that nothing was removed from Martha's
head there in the morgue. Mike Powell, a detective
who handled most of the evidence, told me that he
never booked a golf club handle. Tom Sorenson, the
Greenwich criminalist and photographer, said that
the handle was never found, and neither Hickman
nor Jones ever said anything to him about it.

Jones was the first officer to see Martha and probably the first person to move her. Jean Walker touched
Martha's back to see if she was cold, but that probably
did not affect her position. Martha's hair was long,
past her shoulders, and clotted with blood. Her hair
could have been right over the shaft, covering it from
view. Jones moved her body—as he says in his
report—to check for her vital signs. She was facedown, so he had to turn her over to check her carotid
artery on the side of her throat. He might even have
felt the end of the shaft in her neck. Once he rolled her
over, he certainly could see it. When Jones let her go,

Martha's bloody hair might have covered the shaft. Could Jones, Hickman, or Danehower have removed the golf club handle from her neck, either intentionally or inadvertently, and left it lying by the body? Of course, that's possible. When Steve Carroll and the others observed the body, they did not see the handle. Whether it was still in Martha's neck and obscured by her bloody hair, or lying on the ground, after being dislodged or removed, the handle would still have to be lost at some point.

That is the innocent explanation. The not-so-innocent explanation is that a citizen or police officer took the golf club handle from the scene and either disposed of it or gave it back to the Skakels and they disposed of it. I didn't want that to be the case, but I had to know the truth.

I called Tom Keegan again. I told him that Jones's and Hickman's statements left him exposed, and I gave him the opportunity to tell his side of the story. He refused. "Do what you got to do, Mark."

I called Jim Lunney again. Although he had refused to speak with me earlier, I thought that the recent revelations might make him want to talk. I was wrong. As soon as I identified myself, Lunney said, "I'd rather you lose my phone number."

"Well, unfortunately, Hickman and Jones kind of changed the game here," I told him.

"Wait a second," Lunney said. "I just asked you please lose my phone number."

"Well, I won't do that, Jim, this is about a murder investigation."

"Well, if you won't do that, then I'm sorry, I won't talk to you."

Lunney hung up.

More than one person I spoke to wondered if there had been a police conspiracy in the Moxley case. Having been on the receiving end of some pretty ludicrous conspiracy theories, I'm the last person to assume that such is the case.

I don't know whether there was a conspiracy to destroy evidence or just cover up police mistakes. A conspiracy occurs when people will not admit that they know something and take steps to alter the truth. On those grounds, I do believe there was a conspiracy to cover up the fact that the police found and then lost an important piece of the murder weapon.

The irony of all this is that the police didn't need the missing piece of the golf club to make their case. It happens all the time in homicides. The weapon is never recovered, but enough physical or eyewitness evidence remains that the suspect can be arrested and prosecuted. A golf club, or any object used to inflict deadly blunt-force trauma, is not an essential piece of evidence. Sure, it would be nice to have the complete murder weapon, but its loss is something that can be overcome.

8

"The Evidence Is Askew"

The evidence that they do have is so askew that they would never be able to do anything about it.
—*Steve Carroll*

The murder weapon wasn't the only piece of evidence the Greenwich police mishandled. From the first few minutes of their investigation, they lost, ignored, and bungled important evidence that could have been used to convict the killer.

In 1975 the Greenwich police had no homicide manual and no manual for detective procedures. There was no detective school established at Greenwich, nor any type of formal training for investigators. It was basically on-the-job training in a town where the last homicide investigation was conducted in 1949. The uniformed officers had even less training in the area of crime scene protection and there was very little communication between them and the detective division.

While not a substitute for real-life experience, proper training and management can at least give police officers the tools they need to perform effectively. Police, like firemen, paramedics, and other emergency personnel, should be trained and ready for any potential challenge they might face on the job. They should know what to do, and their management should be able to direct them if they panic or forget their training.

From top to bottom, the Greenwich police were not prepared to investigate a homicide. Not only did they fail to collect evidence properly or thoroughly, but they also misread what little evidence they did have.

The police assumed the murder to have occurred between 9:30 and 10:00 P.M. This determination was made because Dorthy Moxley heard voices outside her window and several neighborhood dogs were barking wildly around that time. The Ixes' dog came to the edge of their property closest to the Moxley house and started barking and howling; the Bjorks' dog did the same. The police never went out on similar evenings to see if dogs were normally barking loudly at night. I would bet that anytime kids walked through someone's backyard, dogs would start barking. They also believed the murder occurred before ten o'clock because Martha was a good girl who wouldn't stay out that late. Martha was a good girl, but she had also stayed out very late the week before.

The detectives should have determined time of death using information from the autopsy, combined with their knowledge of the evidence and the witness statements. And they should have kept their estimated time of death wide rather than narrow. There was no reason to determine the time of death any closer than 9:40–1:00 A.M. Once the time frame is opened up, Michael Skakel becomes a possible suspect, since he reportedly returned from the Terriens' at 11:20 P.M.

Does other evidence from the crime scene point toward the younger Skakel? It's tough to say, since the police don't seem to have much evidence of any value.

In 1996 Don Browne said trace evidence had been sent away for DNA analysis and the results were expected in early 1997. He said that he would decide whether or not to call a grand jury based on the results of those test results. Those test results were never announced and, of course, no grand jury was ever called.

In August 1997, Frank Garr told the press that an important piece of evidence was in the process of being tested. When results of that testing returned sometime in 1998, Garr said, they might be able to proceed with a prosecution. Garr personally transported the evidence to the Armed Forces Institute of Pathology in Washington, which had developed a new kind of DNA testing in which minute amounts of genetic material can be identified years after the subject's death. This technique has been used to identify remains of soldiers killed or missing in action as far back as World War II.

Henry Lee had already told *Greenwich Time* three years earlier that his office had done everything it

could with the evidence in the Moxley case. Several
times during the reinvestigation, Lee said that a male
Caucasian head hair had been found at the murder
scene. He said that hair was compared to samples
taken from suspects, but no match was made. He also
said that the hair was "so minute" that there was not
much left to test, and that DNA tests could not be
used. Elaine Pagliaro, Lee's assistant at the state laboratory, confirmed to the press in 1996 that DNA
tests were not performed on the Moxley evidence.
Apparently, Lee conducted only blood-type and comparison tests on the hair.

In 1997, Lee said that the Defense Department
tests would be performed on minute amounts of evidence found on Martha's clothing. If that evidence
consisted of semen or saliva, then the Skakel boys'
revised statements to Sutton Associates provided an
explanation for their DNA being present. If that evidence consisted of the single human hair found on
Martha's body and thought to belong to the suspect—then the tests were a waste of time and money.
As a piece of evidence, the hair is useless.

More than a dozen people closely viewed
Martha's body at the crime scene. Most of them were
male Caucasians. There is a very good chance that the
hair came from someone at the scene.

The police took hair samples only from Thomas
Skakel, Ken Littleton, Ed Hammond, and a couple
other suspects we know were not involved. They
never took hair samples from Michael Skakel.

Let's suppose they had taken a hair sample from

Michael and it turned out to match the hair found on Martha's body. What would that prove? Michael was with Martha the night she died. They sat together in the front seat of the Skakel car. It would not be at all surprising or suspicious if one of Michael's hairs was found on Martha.

The same for Thomas. He was sitting next to her in the car, then fooling around with her in the driveway, and finally engaging in a sexual encounter with her. It would be surprising if one of Thomas's hairs were *not* found on Martha, and its presence would have no evidentiary value whatsoever.

The male Caucasian head hair was not the only hair found on Martha. A male negroid hair was found in the sheets that Charles Danks wrapped around Martha's body. That evidence was quickly eliminated, because the police decided it must have come from Dan Hickman, the only black officer close to Martha's body at the crime scene. How did they know this hair was Hickman's? I don't understand why they would immediately eliminate this possible piece of evidence. At this point, the police supposedly thought the killer must have been somebody from outside the neighborhood. Here was the one piece of evidence that might have supported the Turnpike Transient Theory, and the police dismissed it.

A stained pair of Wrangler jeans and a single Tretorn sneaker were found during a search of the Skakel garbage. Rushton Skakel eventually identified the jeans as belonging to Michael. The stains on the jeans turned out not to be blood, but a long blond hair was found on them. If this hair proved to be Martha's, it had no evidentiary value. She was with Michael that night and previously. And since the jeans were collected from the back of a garbage truck, there is nothing to prove that the hair had actually come from those jeans, or even from the Skakel house.

The Tretorn sneaker contained dyed red wool fiber, and they seemed extra clean on the soles. A red mat at the back of the Skakel house was said to have been used by the family to tee off golf balls. Fibers from that mat matched fibers found on the sneakers and on the Toney Penna five iron surrendered by the Skakels. Apparently no matching fibers were found on the murder weapon, but the police had already traced it to the Skakel house, so what would matching fibers prove?

Aside from evidence collected during the search of the Hammond residence, evidence lists are redacted from the police report. However, in most of those evidence lists only the item description is redacted. The item numbers remain, showing that few individual pieces of evidence were actually collected.

"Sometimes you're able to recover a lot of physical evidence," Frank Garr said. "Other times you are not. Unfortunately, in this case, there was not much physical evidence at the crime scene."

How does Frank know that there was not much evidence at the crime scene? He was the dispatcher that night. What Frank should have said was that there wasn't much physical evidence *recovered* from the crime scene. A great deal more evidence may have been at the scene, but in their haste and confusion, the Greenwich police and the state crime lab missed it.

Henry Lee said that all of the blood recovered from the crime scene came from Martha. That is very possible, since there appears to have been no struggle, the attack came as a surprise, and Martha knew her assailant. The police could have recorded and analyzed blood spatter on the ground and trees of the crime scene, but they did not. By the next morning, with the wind blowing the leaves all over the Moxley property and police tramping around with metal detectors, that important blood evidence was lost forever.

More blood evidence could possibly have been recovered from the Skakel house, but the police never conducted a formal search.

"To the best of my knowledge," Steve Carroll said, "we never thought there was any reason to get a search warrant because we had already been through the house. Up one side, down the other."

Even though they did get to look through the house, the Greenwich detectives' searches were neither official nor thorough. They should have gotten a search warrant on that first day and searched the entire house, grounds, and vehicles immediately.

Despite the fact that they had permission, the Greenwich police still should have obtained a warrant. You get a search warrant to protect yourself and any evidence you might find. A consent-to-search form can be revoked at any time, and any searches done under that type of permission are vulnerable to attack by defense attorneys. If the Greenwich police had gotten a search warrant and done a thorough search that day, they could have uncovered important evidence. If they found nothing, then they would have at least been able to leave the Skakels alone and look elsewhere.

Had they obtained a search warrant for the house and vehicles the first day, not only might they have collected some valuable physical evidence but they also would have established their authority and gotten a good indication of how cooperative the Skakel family really were. If the Skakels truly didn't have anything to hide, then they wouldn't have minded a full search of the house. Although they clearly thought it was easier just to look through the house with Rushton's permission, not obtaining a search warrant that first day made the entire investigation more difficult.

Six months into the investigation, after consultation with Gerald Hale from Detroit homicide, the Greenwich police requested a search warrant of the Skakel house. They were looking for the missing part of the golf club and the clothing Thomas wore on the night of the murder. The warrant request was denied by Don Browne. In several interviews as early as 1983, Browne could not remember the circumstances that caused him to refuse the search warrant but said perhaps too much time had elapsed between the murder and the search-warrant application. The Greenwich police did unnecessarily delay asking for a warrant, but I'd like to know how long Browne thinks forensic evidence would last in the house.

According to Steve Carroll, the Greenwich police received the Skakel family phone records through an employee who worked for the phone company. Since these records were illegally obtained, the police could not use them as evidence. They never booked the records as evidence and apparently returned or destroyed them after about a week, without even looking at them closely. What they should have done was obtain the records legally, through a search warrant. Not only the Skakel phone records but also the Terrien residence and Great Lakes Carbon corporate office records should have been requested.

It would have been interesting to see if any phone calls had been made to Ethel or Ted Kennedy, or Stephen Smith, the Kennedy family fixer. It would have been interesting to see at what time phone calls were first made to wherever Rushton Skakel was vacationing. If the phone calls occurred before 12:30 P.M., then someone in the house knew something had happened before Martha's body was discovered. It would have been interesting to know what time the offices of Great Lakes Carbon were first contacted, and who was called. It would have been interesting to know when family legal adviser Tom Sheridan got involved. The phone records could have answered these and other important questions. Since phone records are only recorded for a few years, those records are no longer available and a useful source of evidence is lost forever.

The paperwork on the case is at best sloppy and at worst intentionally misleading. In at least two written police reports, Greenwich officers state that a suspect was read his rights when in fact he wasn't. Some consent-to-search forms are included in the police record, but others are not. Are these forms lost or were they never obtained in the first place?

If Millard Jones's full October 31, 1975, report of his and Dan Hickman's first observations of Martha's body did not include the description of the golf club handle in her head, then Jones did not fill out a complete and accurate report. That's not such a big deal. If he did mention the handle, and it was redacted from the public report, or even suppressed from the internal police documents, then someone is guilty of tampering with evidence and falsifying statements on a police report.

In my opinion, Ted Brosko's report dated November 2, 1975, is a clear attempt at creating retroactive probable cause. In that report, Brosko described his actions and observations from October 31 to November 2, developing probable cause to believe the murder weapon came from the Skakel house and building a case history of how the other Toney Penna club was discovered and obtained.

Several other reports were obviously written days, even weeks, after the events described actually occurred. I noted these discrepancies in the redacted police report and can only assume that some of the redactions include similar discrepancies, whether they are unintentional inaccuracies or willful misstatements.

A videotape was taken by the Connecticut State Crime Lab and viewed by Greenwich detectives on December 17, 1975. Peter Robbins told me that the tape does not exist. I do know that the tape was not properly preserved, it had not been rerecorded, and had not been kept in a temperature-controlled room. As a result, the tape could have deteriorated beyond recognition.

Photos of the crime scene have been seen by outside police departments, consultants, psychics, and others. According to several of these sources, the photos include several shots of Martha's body at the scene. Tom Sorenson, the Greenwich criminalist and photographer, told me that he never took any pictures of Martha's body underneath the tree. When he walked toward the tree, someone told him not to photograph the body. He does not remember who told him not to photograph the most important piece of evidence in the case. Instead, he photographed the rest of the crime scene. Tom Keegan was known to be a photography buff. He personally took pictures of the mourners at Martha's funeral and often directed the photographing of crime scenes. There is no indication that Keegan took photos at the Moxley scene on October 31, 1975. Were pictures ever taken of Martha's body beneath the pine tree? Several detectives have told me they saw such pictures, but nobody with whom I spoke admitted to taking them.

As far as I can determine, here is the only physical evidence the Greenwich police collected that has any viable connection to the crime:

1. Three pieces of the broken Toney Penna six iron.

2. The matching five iron surrendered by the Skakels.

3. The clothes Martha was wearing the night she was killed.

4. Martha's personal effects surrendered by her family.

5. Crime scene photos (whether they include Martha's body under the tree or not).

6. A single male Caucasian head hair.

This isn't much. The evidence room is filled with other items, but those no doubt include all the pieces of scrap metal turned into police after they issued the press release and Teletype seeking the missing handle and shaft of the golf club, along with other pieces of evidence the Greenwich police must know have no connection to the crime. They also still control several of Martha's personal effects, including her diary, despite Dorthy's repeated requests that these items be returned.

Evidence collected by the Greenwich police was sent to the state police lab in Bethany, the toxicology lab in Hartford, the FBI lab in Washington, the reinvestigation office in Bridgeport, Henry Lee's forensic crime lab in Meriden, and the Department of Defense in Washington. Most of the evidence has traveled to all of those locations at one time or another. Do the police even know where all their evidence is? Does the state's attorney office refuse to prosecute because they are afraid of being embarrassed in court?

I think the Moxley investigators know just how "askew" their evidence is. That's why they continue to hope for a confession. Numerous statements to the press by Donald Browne, Jack Solomon, Kenneth Moughty, Tom Keegan, Frank Garr, Peter Robbins, and others associated with the case seem to imply that a confession is the only way it will ever be solved. Given the state of their evidence, they could be right.

PART IV

Profiling the Participants

9

The Skakel Family

*If you walked into one Skakel house, you walked into
all of them: servants running around, no meals on
the table, crazy, undisciplined.*
—Skakel family friend

When suspicion focused on the Skakel family,
their neighbors, town officials, and the
press all said publicly that the prominent
Greenwich family could not have been involved in
the murder of Martha Moxley. In secret, according
to one local, "no one was surprised."

While the family had many friends and sup-
porters—and still does to this day—everybody who
lived in Greenwich had heard the stories of the
Skakels' reckless behavior. The Skakels were more
than just local troublemakers. The family had been
living in Greenwich for nearly fifty years. At the
time of Martha's murder, they were among the richest and most powerful families in town.

The Skakel money came from Great Lakes
Carbon, a processor of industrial coke and other min-
erals, which was for a long time one of the largest privately held companies in the world. Family patriarch

George Skakel started out as a railroad clerk in Chicago, making eight dollars a week. In 1919 he established Great Lakes Carbon, along with two partners. Soon the company was all his, and making a great deal of money.

George and his wife Ann Brannack Skakel had seven children, Georgeann, James, George Jr., Rushton, Patricia, Ethel, and Ann. The family first moved to Greenwich in the depths of the depression. When everyone else was going through hard times, the Skakels were very wealthy. George Skakel bought a furnished mansion on Lake Avenue from the widow of the Simmons mattress heir. He paid $100,000 cash.

It was not easy for the Catholic family to assimilate into staid, WASPy Greenwich. The Skakels did not make it any easier with their reckless, drunken, and sometimes violent behavior. Though George Skakel's philosophy was "You can't quote silence," it often wasn't easy keeping his family's misadventures secret. According to Jerry Oppenheimer's book *The Other Mrs. Kennedy,* here are just a few of the incidents that George Skakel and his family were unable to cover up:

- The Skakels were such reckless drivers that the Greenwich police routinely stationed a motorcycle cop at the end of their driveway.

- One of the Skakel boys' favorite games was to shoot the arms off sculptures on the family estate.

- They would sit in the upper windows of the Lake Avenue estate and shoot at their sisters' arriving dates with air rifles.

- While working as roughnecks on the 1,100-acre Skakel ranch in Moab, Utah, George Jr. shot his brother Jim in the stomach with a .45 automatic. Fortunately, the gunshot wound was not serious.

- Greg Reilly, a Skakel friend, was shot at the Lake Avenue estate when Jim Skakel and his friends were shooting squirrels on the property. Instead of taking Reilly to nearby Greenwich Hospital, they drove him to Port Chester, where the incident would not attract the attention of local authorities.

- Early in 1962, Pat Corroon Skakel caught her husband George with another woman in their guest house. She burned the guest house to the ground. Although the house was filled with priceless family heirlooms, they didn't file an insurance claim. George Skakel told his brother-in-law George Terrien, "I don't need to add insurance fraud to arson and adultery."

- On Thanksgiving Day 1966 Kick Skakel, the eldest daughter of Pat Corroon Skakel, was driving around the neighborhood in her brand-new Mustang convertible with the top down and several young children sitting on the trunk lid. When the car hit a speed bump, six-year-old Hope O'Brien flew off the back of the car, landing on her head. She died a week later. Greenwich police chief Stephen Baran blamed speed bumps for her death. The Skakels' insurance company eventually settled with the O'Briens for $25,000.

In 1955 George and Ann Skakel died in a plane crash in Oklahoma. Eleven years later, George Skakel Jr. was killed, along with four other passengers, when their single-engine Cessna, loaded with booze and guns, crashed into Crooked Creek Canyon in Idaho.

After his brother's death, Rushton Skakel was put in charge of the family company. Jim Skakel remembered how Rushton decided the future of the company "while my brother George's body was still warm." Rushton appointed his cousin Joe Solari president of Great Lakes Carbon. The Solari family had been fighting for control of the company with the Skakels. Rushton's brothers and sisters were furious.

Although Rushton officially served as chairman of the board, he did not have many responsibilities. One source told me, "Rushton was basically paid to stay out of the office." An admitted alcoholic, "Rushton lived in the bottle," according to one Greenwich resident. His inability to run Great Lakes was the beginning of the end of the Skakel business dynasty, which took only one generation to build and another generation to dismantle.

While the business fortunes of the Skakel family rose and fell, one thing remained constant— their wild behavior. In conversations about Rushton Skakel's family with their friends, neighbors, and schoolmates, I kept hearing the same comments: "The boys were wild" and "There was no structure."

Dorthy Moxley said of her Skakel neighbors: "They didn't seem to act like everybody else in that neighborhood. They just didn't do things like other people. Our kids got up in the morning and went to school and came home at night when they were supposed to and I was there. My husband went to work and came home at the end of the day. They had a housekeeper and no mother and Rush was always off somewhere. Every once in a while, I'd see one of the children straggling home, but that was about it."

Some Belle Haven parents would not allow their children to hang out with the Skakel kids. All the boys were rowdy, but Thomas and Michael were by far the worst. "Michael was like a junior Tommy in a lot of respects," said a boyhood friend. "He would definitely follow his brother's lead."

Despite their social prominence, the Skakels usually found their friends among family members rather than outsiders. Rushton's sons were very close with Jim Terrien, son of Georgeann Skakel Terrien. Georgeann had first married John Dowdle, an alcoholic who died in 1957 of what was said to be a heart attack. Shortly after Dowdle's death, Georgeann married George Terrien, a close friend and former roommate of Bobby Kennedy. One of Georgeann's sons from her first marriage was Jim Terrien, born in 1957, who preferred to go by the name Jimmy Dowdle.

Jim Terrien was "like a brother . . . a best friend . . . member of the family," according to one source, and that observation was echoed by many others. A childhood friend says, "Tommy and Michael were wild as kids, along with Jimmy Terrien. Absolutely cut from the same cloth. The kids who would gang up on a nerdy kid."

In 1991 Jim Terrien's older brother John Dowdle was arrested for assault, allegedly breaking into the Terrien home, tying up his stepfather, George Terrien, and beating him severely. Dowdle was released on bail and the charges were eventually dropped. A year later, George Terrien, also an alcoholic, died waiting for a liver transplant.

A Greenwich man told me that one day he was pruning apple trees on the Terrien estate, Sursum Corda. Suddenly he heard gunfire. Shotgun pellets whizzed past his head. He looked back and saw the Terrien boys shooting at him from the balcony of their house. He went to the house and screamed at them, but they pretended they didn't know he was in the tree. Once he got back up in the tree, they shot again at him. "They did whatever they wanted," the man said.

"If the Skakels ever did something really bad," one Greenwich resident said, "they would have the

Cardinal in and they would feel absolved." The Skakels were "front row Catholics," who took up the first pews in church. Their local priests and other prominent Catholic clergy were close friends and advisors.

When Ethel Skakel married Bobby Kennedy at St. Mary's in Greenwich in 1950, the Skakels were linked to another wealthy, large, and well-connected Catholic family. Although not as famous as their Kennedy cousins, the Skakel family was richer and almost as powerful in their time. Despite their being related by marriage, the Skakels and the Kennedys were initially not very close. In previous generations, the families seemed actively to dislike each other. The Kennedys were liberal Democrats, the Skakels were conservative Republicans. The Kennedys pursued fame and political position; the Skakels quietly built a family empire.

It didn't hurt to be related to one of the most famous and powerful families in America. Dorthy Moxley said that as soon as she moved into Belle Haven, a neighbor told her, "'That's where the Skakels live, they're related to the Kennedys.'"

During the years, both embattled families have put aside their social and political animosity and appear to be getting along. Several of the younger Skakels associate with their Kennedy cousins, socially, professionally, and even politically. Both Thomas and Michael Skakel have worked on Kennedy campaigns.

However much they might take advantage of

the relationship, the Skakels did not need the Kennedys. Someone close to Thomas described his attitude toward the Kennedys this way: "He felt that they were riding his coattails, rather than the other way around."

The Skakels took an important place in the hierarchy of what several people have called "the Irish Catholic Mafia," a close-knit group of large, wealthy Catholic families. One of their closest friends and associates from that group is Tom Sheridan, an attorney who handled Skakel family legal matters concerning the Moxley murder and formally represented Michael and Julie Skakel in the matter.

Sheridan was also one of the founding fathers of the Windham ski resort in the Catskills region of New York. After Sheridan helped establish the resort, the Skakels bought the house most accessible to the ski mountain. The Skakels felt very comfortable in Windham, a community of mostly Catholic families with close business, social, and family ties. It didn't take long for the Skakel family to bring their unique brand of hell-raising up to Windham. One local said, "Friday nights when the lights went on in the Skakel house, the cops at Windham knew they were in for trouble."

The Skakels, Terriens, and Sheridans also helped establish the Whitby School. A small private school that combined Catholic religious instruction with Montessori classroom technique, Whitby's initial classrooms were the former stables of Sursum Corda, the Terrien estate in the "backcountry" of Greenwich. As Whitby grew, it moved off the Terrien property to its present location on Lake Avenue, but the founding families retained their clout at the school.

The Skakels lived in a different zone of security from most of us. They knew they could pretty much do what they wanted and not have to worry about the consequences. Sheltered by money, power, and prominence, the Skakels lived a privileged existence. And they frequently abused that privilege.

As comfortable as they felt in Windham and Whitby, the Skakels enjoyed the same sense of security at home in Belle Haven, particularly when it came to the Greenwich police. Instead of being public servants, working for all the citizens equally, the Greenwich police, then and still today, were more like servants of the rich and powerful. This was achieved not through direct graft—at least none that I could uncover—but rather through a more subtle and insidious influence.

The Greenwich police worked for the Skakel family, literally. During their off-duty hours, they performed various side jobs—driving the Skakel children to school, parking cars during Skakel parties, running errands, and fixing problems for them. These side jobs were important to the Greenwich officers, who didn't make much money. In 1975, a Greenwich detective's salary was $14,800.

Not only did the rank and file work for the Skakels, but their bosses were frequent visitors to the Skakel houses, off duty and on. Police captain Hilbert Heberling was a frequent guest at the Skakel and Terrien houses for dinner and was present at a dinner when Pat Skakel choked to death on a piece of kabob meat.

At Rushton's house in Belle Haven, the police were constant visitors, even before Martha's murder. Belle Haven security guards, who were often off-duty Greenwich cops, and town patrolmen were often stopping in at Otter Rock Drive for a cup of coffee and a sandwich prepared by the Skakel help.

After the murder, this casual relationship between the Greenwich police and the Skakel family continued. Steve Carroll described Rushton Skakel as "a Jack Ruby kind of guy. A real police buff."

In return for hospitality and side jobs, Rushton was able to keep his boys out of trouble. "Anything that the kids did, and they did a lot, especially Michael, they would always squelch it," a Greenwich officer said.

Is that what happened in the Moxley murder?

On October 31, 1975, the Skakel household was even more crowded and chaotic than usual. Amelia Rodriguez, the Skakel family maid, arrived at the house on Otter Rock Drive at approximately 9:30 A.M. and left around 2:00 or 2:30 P.M. She said that there were many people and much activity in the house during her shift there, including at least one attorney.

According to several witnesses in the house, the phone was ringing constantly. For a while, Julie or the housekeeper answered. Then next-door neighbor Mildred Ix came home early from a trip with her husband and tried to take charge of the children. Mildred Ix had been Ann Skakel's best friend. When Ann died of cancer in 1973, Mildred became very close to Rushton and often acted as surrogate mother for the Skakel children. That afternoon, Mildred tried to manage the Skakel household while they waited for a lawyer to arrive.

The lawyer was Jim McKenzie, a junior associate counsel at Great Lakes Carbon. McKenzie told me he doesn't remember why he was called to the Skakel house or who called him. He thinks he was asked because Joe Donovan and Tom Hayes, the senior attorneys for Great Lakes Carbon, were out of the office.

When McKenzie arrived at the Skakel house at 5:15 P.M., the place was a madhouse. "The kids were sort of high-strung . . . and they aren't really disciplined anyway," McKenzie said. The first thing McKenzie did was get rid of the reporters and neighbors who were hanging out in the front yard. Then he told the Skakel kids to go to their rooms.

"Cissy Ix . . . was being really nice about it and trying in effect to act as the mother but that was sort of impossible," McKenzie said. "And so you had this chaotic scene and so I just was there to wait because the father was going to fly down that night and was coming back from this trip he was on."

According to McKenzie, eighteen-year-old Julie Skakel was like a mother figure in the household. "She had a little sense and was a little more calm about the whole situation, trying to act as a mother and yet a teenager at the same time. Trying to be a calming influence, but clearly the sister couldn't calm some of this crowd down."

Were the Kennedys involved that afternoon? George Terrien told Jerry Oppenheimer that his wife Georgeann had called Ethel Kennedy when she heard that Martha's body had been found. "My wife told Ethie that the Moxley girl was hanging out with Tommy the night of the murder," George said. "Ethel was a nervous wreck. Georgeann told me later that Ethel said she was going to call Ted right away. She also called her other advisors. She said, 'We can't let this touch the Kennedys.'"

Noelle Fell, secretary for Ethel Kennedy, said that on October 31, 1975, "Something happened and Mrs. Kennedy was very upset, very agitated. Senator Kennedy, looking very serious, had been at the house, meeting with her in private, and there were all these hush-hush telephone conversations."

Later in the day, Fell said that Ethel called a friend and said, "I've got to get out of here." Ethel looked distressed when she left wearing a witch mask, dressed in black and carrying a broom.

The Greenwich police never interviewed Ethel Kennedy or Ted Kennedy. They never looked at Skakel phone records to see if there were any calls to Ted Kennedy or Ethel Kennedy or Stephen Smith or any one of a dozen Kennedy associates.

When I asked Jim McKenzie if Ethel or Ted

Kennedy ever called the Skakel house that afternoon, he said no and appeared to feel comfortable
with both my question and his answer. But when I
asked if anybody associated with the Kennedy family called, he appeared very uncomfortable. Here is
the line of questioning verbatim:

MF: Did Ethel or Ted Kennedy ever call?

JM: No.

MF: Did anybody associated with the Kennedy
    family or business or political group ever
    call?

JM: Never from the Kennedy family. That ever
    talked to me. And because I don't know
    that I would have been the one they would
    have called. Because after twenty-four
    hours I was sort of out of it.

His answer to the first question was crisp and certain.
His answer to the second question was vague and
stumbling. He said no one from the family, not anyone from the business or political group. And he
qualified it by saying that no one ever talked to him.
Did somebody from the Kennedy business or political groups talk to McKenzie? Did someone from the
Kennedy family talk to Mildred Ix or Julie Skakel?

Remember that Jim McKenzie is a lawyer.
Throughout the interview, he was very careful about

what he said. I don't think his word choice on those questions was unintentional.

While Jim McKenzie tried to minimize his use of the phone in the Skakel home, a family friend recalled: "There was someone older than Tommy who was on the phone, but I don't know who it was. It wasn't Ken Littleton."

When Rushton got home, McKenzie briefed him on the situation, although he doesn't remember what he told Mr. Skakel. Then he was driven home by Franz Wittine, the Skakel gardener. McKenzie said after that time, Rushton only spoke to him "in terms of thanks very much for coming up, and you know, we really appreciate it, and in the clutch, and a couple of nice things like that." In 1975, Jim McKenzie was a junior associate counsel at Great Lakes Carbon. Now he is vice president and chief counsel.

Rushton left to go on a hunting trip the afternoon of October 30. He came back on the Great Lakes Carbon corporate jet the next day, landing at Westchester Airport, where he was picked up by Franz Wittine and returned to Otter Rock Drive at 8:00 P.M. Why did he come back so quickly?

Police were either in the house or, at least, still in the neighborhood when he returned home, but none of them seemed to know that Rushton came back that night. Rushton didn't talk to the police until November 1, but many were under the impression, even to this day, that he did not return from his trip until November 2. Police sources were unclear whether he was on a business or hunting trip or whether he had been in California, Canada, or Vermont. They never did establish where Rushton had been and when he returned.

The trip Rushton took on October 30 was pleasure, not business. I know this because I have spoken to the woman who was his companion on that trip.

Eleanor Stude originally met Rushton Skakel at Harbor Springs, a Michigan resort. She told me that they had a dating relationship. In the fall of 1975, Rushton asked her to go to California with him. She agreed on the condition that he got someone to look after his own children. So Rushton hired Ken Littleton, and they went away. While they were in California, something happened and Rushton had to leave early. Sometime later, Rushton called Eleanor and said that he had terrible news: There had been a murder. Rushton told her that when the murder was committed, the children had all been drinking. Eleanor said that she found it odd that nobody ever asked her any questions about her trip with Rushton or his comments afterwards.

In February 1996, Eleanor Stude saw the television show *Unsolved Mysteries* on Martha's murder. She called the tip line and gave an operator the information above. The operator misunderstood or mistyped the tip sheet and Eleanor was described as a girlfriend of Michael's, not of Rushton's. The tip was passed on to the Moxley investigators, but no one had ever spoken to Eleanor until I did. I asked several people involved in the case if they recognized her name, and no one did.

When Eleanor Stude called *Unsolved Mysteries,* she said that she had been in California with Rushton. On two separate interviews in 1997, Steve Weeks and I both confirmed that Eleanor went on a trip with Rushton in late October 1975, but she claimed not to remember where they went. Jim McKenzie told me that Rushton had been in Canada. Why the discrepancy? Maybe Rushton was just trying to protect his children from knowing what he was up to. Or perhaps there is a more suspicious explanation. If Rushton had been in California, his trip would have taken at least five hours. In order to return to Greenwich by 8:00 P.M. Rushton would have had to know that Martha was dead shortly after—or even before—her body was found.

The Greenwich police believed that the Skakel family left for Windham on Saturday, November 1. According to the police report, Detective Mike Powell spoke to Rushton in person that afternoon. When asked about this interview, Powell said that he did not remember it. Powell's memory aside, why would the police assume that Rushton was away that day when they had written reports saying that he had been interviewed by a detective?

The Greenwich police thought that the family had gone on a ski trip because the Revcon camper was not in the driveway. They did not know that two Skakel cousins drove the camper away the day after the murder. George Skakel flew into Westchester airport on a commercial flight from Boston, arriving at 2:00 P.M., October 31. Rush Jr. picked up his cousin at that time and drove him to Belle Haven. At 4:00 P.M., George Skakel and John Pinto, another Skakel cousin, took the Revcon camper to Washington, DC, for a Georgetown reunion weekend.

At 4:30 Rush Jr. left for Dartmouth.

At 5:15 Jim McKenzie arrived.

Shortly thereafter, Thomas returned from the field hockey game in Rye.

Detectives Jim Lunney and Ted Brosko were in the Skakel house from 3:00 P.M. until at least 5:40, when Thomas was taken to police headquarters for his statement.

Why didn't the detectives notice all this activity? Why didn't they find out who Jim McKenzie was? Did they even notice him? Why did they let George Skakel and John Pinto take the Revcon? Why did they let Rush Jr. leave? Why didn't they take Michael to headquarters for a statement?

While they were in the Skakel house, detectives Lunney and Brosko reportedly saw a golf club that was the same model as the pieces found at the crime scene. Why didn't they seize it as evidence? Why didn't they get a warrant and search the entire house? Why—once the golf club was determined to come from the Skakel house—wasn't 71 Otter Rock Drive made part of the crime scene?

Initially, at least, the Greenwich police seemed

to think that while the Skakel boys might be feisty, even troublemakers, they would never kill anybody. Thomas was reportedly a suspect from the beginning, but he was not treated like one.

When Thomas was brought into the Greenwich police headquarters for questioning on October 31, Detective Ted Brosko remarked on his presence to other detectives by saying, "Tommy Skakel, good ballplayer." Then he greeted the boy with, "Hey, Tommy."

From the evening of October 31, the police knew that Thomas was the last person seen with Martha the night she died and that the golf club came from the Skakel house. But Rushton was cooperating with the police, allowing them to look around and inviting them to use the house as an informal neighborhood headquarters while they pursued other suspects. "Rushton Skakel would go out of his way to be hospitable," Steve Carroll said. Over coffee with the detectives, Rushton often said, "I hope you catch this guy."

Detectives Carroll and Lunney conducted several casual searches of the Skakel residence. "It was open house, he'd never even go with us," Carroll recalled.

During the first couple months of the investigation, as the police looked for other suspects and found none, suspicion kept coming back to Tommy. On December 11, when Helen Ix and Geoffrey Byrne reported that he was engaged in horseplay with Martha and made repeated advances to her, that suspicion hardened into a belief that Thomas could be the killer.

They finally had a motive—Thomas wanted to have sex with Martha and she refused him. As she headed home, Thomas pursued her. Picking up a golf club from the back of the house, he tried to hook her with it. He hit Martha harder than he had planned, and she fell down. Once she was down, he began a maniacal attack.

Unfortunately for the detectives' theory, Thomas had passed a polygraph on November 9. If he was the killer, how could he have passed the examination? During interrogations, Thomas seemed to draw a blank when asked about attacking or injuring Martha. Perhaps, Greenwich detectives conjectured, he didn't remember killing her. In order to support that theory, the detectives needed proof that Thomas was subject to violent fits and blackouts.

On January 16, 1976, Detective Jim Lunney went to the Skakel house, where he received written permission from Rushton to obtain Thomas's school and medical records. Armed with the permission letter, Steve Carroll went to see Dr. Walter Camp, the Skakel family pediatrician. Camp told detectives about Thomas's epilepsy of the stomach and gave them a large file regarding the boy's health and discipline problems. The files reported that Thomas was often uncontrollable and had to be physically restrained.

Then Carroll went to see Dr. Anderson, a neurologist who had operated on Tommy when he had a linear fracture of the skull from jumping out of a moving car. Anderson would not cooperate and gave the detectives nothing.

Steve Carroll arrived at the Whitby School and was told to wait—Headmaster Paul Czaja was attending a meeting outside the school. When Czaja finally returned, Steve introduced himself and showed his badge. He asked to look at the Skakel boys' records, saying that he had a letter from Rushton giving him permission. Czaja just said, "Get out!"

As Steve started to leave he asked, "Does Tommy throw temper tantrums? His dad said he has problems."

Czaja repeated, "Get out!"

"Did Tommy or Michael break any statues?"

Czaja screamed louder, "Get out!"

"Did he ever attack any of the other kids?"

"Get out!"

Carroll left Whitby, having no idea what kind of trouble he had caused. Paul Czaja called Mildred Ix, who got in touch with Rushton. Soon Chris Roosevelt, a former Justice Department attorney who was a board member and counsel for the school, was also contacted.

The next day, Roosevelt called detectives Carroll and Lunney at the police station. He told them that he would personally contact Rushton and Thomas to obtain their permission to release the requested records. According to the police report: "During this conversation Mr. Roosevelt became highly agitated by the investigators' request and interpreted the request to be something akin to an actual arrest, and his attitude was such that the youth had already been arrested.

"He further related that if this in fact happened, Thomas would be defended by a battery of lawyers who would claim that Thomas was temporarily insane. Mr. Roosevelt was very strong in that attitude."

At 1:20 P.M. the next day, Rushton Skakel appeared at the complaint desk at Greenwich police headquarters. He turned over a letter addressed to Chief Baran and requested that the letter be delivered immediately. In that letter, Rushton withdrew his authorization to release medical and school records.

Twelve minutes later, the Greenwich police ambulance got a call to respond to the Ix residence, Walsh Lane, Belle Haven. A person was in need of medical attention. The injured person turned out to be Rushton Skakel, who complained of chest pains. When the emergency officers responded, Rushton said that he had just received some bad news.

Rushton was taken to the hospital and admitted for tests and observation. When detectives Carroll and Lunney heard about the call, they first went to the Ix residence and interviewed Mildred. She stated that shortly before the attack Rushton arrived at her house in the company of Joe Donovan, a corporate attorney for Great Lakes Carbon. Mildred seated them in the study and went to get some "refreshments." When she came back, Rushton was holding his chest and complaining of pains.

Rushton told Mildred that he had received some bad news during a telephone conversation, but he didn't tell her to whom he had spoken or what the bad news was. Mildred said that she knew Rushton had met earlier that day with Paul Czaja and Chris Roosevelt and that he was upset after that meeting.

Years later, Roosevelt told Len Levitt, "I gave Mr. Skakel one piece of advice: to get competent legal advice on this. I told him to put his emotions in the background, and to best represent the child's interest."

Carroll and Lunney continued to Greenwich Hospital, where they were met by Father Mark Connolly, a Skakel family advisor and television priest. Father Connolly said that Rushton had been sedated and could only submit to a brief interview. When Carroll and Lunney spoke with Rushton, he told them he had hired Manny Margolis, a criminal attorney, for his son's protection and that he had rescinded his permission for background records.

Years later, Rushton Jr. told Sutton Associates that during this period his father had been on a massive drinking binge, so it is highly probable that the attack was an alcohol- and/or stress-related seizure. After a series of tests, Rushton Sr. was finally released from the Greenwich Hospital on February 9, 1976. He spent the next two weeks being treated for alcoholism in High Watch Sanitarium, according to his son.

Rushton Skakel was an admitted alcoholic who told Jerry Oppenheimer that he and his siblings began drinking "as little tots." Rushton's drinking is only pertinent in this light: Was his drinking binge precipitated by the realization that his family was involved in the Moxley murder and that the police were not going to let this go away? Is that why his cooperation swiftly ended?

His personal and medical problems aside, what could have caused Rushton Skakel to rescind cooperation? Carroll's question of Czaja concerning Thomas and Michael possibly vandalizing school property was the first time that Michael was ever mentioned by the police as a possible suspect. Until then, he had been ignored by police because of his alibi with his brothers and Jim Terrien. As soon as Steve Carroll mentioned Michael Skakel, the case seized up like an engine with no oil.

Manny Margolis shut down any cooperation between the Skakels and the police. When the police continued to request medical and psychological information on Thomas, the Skakels had him tested privately, then refused to turn the results over to the police.

As the investigation continued and suspicion, rumors, and gossip focused on the Skakels, the family dynasty quickly fell to pieces. In 1983 Great Lakes Carbon was put up for sale. Two years later, Horseheads Industries gobbled up the company in a leveraged buyout. Because the Skakels were so eager to sell, the price of $150 million was a bargain.

"The word was that the Skakels weren't bright enough and weren't smart enough and all they knew was how to fight among themselves, so why not go for the jugular vein," Georgeann Terrien said. "We got nailed."

Living under a cloud of suspicion, Thomas Skakel attended several different schools, held several different jobs, and traveled around the world, until he eventually married and settled down in Stockbridge, Massachusetts. Michael kept a much lower profile, living for the most part in residential rehabilitation facilities before moving to the Boston area, where he finally graduated from college in his thirties, got married, and began working for his cousin, Michael Kennedy, who died in a skiing accident in Aspen on New Year's Eve 1997.

Rushton sold the house on Otter Rock Drive in 1993 for $3 million. He moved to an exclusive condominium development in Hobe Sound, Florida. In 1997 he was seventy-four years old and reportedly suffering from serious health problems.

Shortly after Martha's murder, Michael Skakel was suspected of vandalizing a kitchen in a local private school. Juvenile officer Millard Jones went down to the Skakel house to speak with Rushton about the incident. When he arrived, Rushton thought that Jones was there about the Moxley homicide. In Jones's words, "The old man went wild."

When Jones told him that he was there regarding a separate vandalism incident, Rushton finally calmed down. He said to Jones, "Just tell me what it is and I'll buy them a new goddamn kitchen."

The vandalism case, like so many other Skakel offenses, was taken care of quietly. But the murder of Martha Moxley would not go away because her family wouldn't let it.

10

The Moxley Family

*Martha wasn't the only victim. The family is also
a victim because her murder changed our lives.*
—Dorthy Moxley

The Moxleys moved from Piedmont, California, to Greenwich, Connecticut, in the summer of 1974. "We came from California and people in this area think anybody who came from California had to be like granola, all nuts and flakes," Dorthy said. In fact, the Moxleys were not Californians, they were midwesterners. David came from Kansas and Dorthy came from Michigan. They were honest, down-to-earth, hardworking people who believed in getting along with others and doing the right thing.

That first year in Greenwich, Martha went to Western Junior High. John went to Greenwich High School, where he made the varsity football team. Both Martha and John made friends easily.

"Growing up in northern California, then moving to Belle Haven was a change," John said. "Blue jeans, Converse, and T-shirts versus wide-wale corduroys and Izod shirts."

Getting along in Greenwich isn't easy—I know, because I experienced its snobbery and pretension firsthand—but the Moxleys didn't have any trouble. "It just didn't take any time at all" for the Moxleys to make friends, Dorthy said. "I feel so comfortable in the East. I never felt really that comfortable living in California. I was always a half step off."

The Moxleys received a warm welcome to Belle Haven. Mildred Ix, who lived across the street, came over and introduced herself, saying she wanted to have a cocktail party so they could meet all the neighbors. At the Ixes' party the Moxleys met Rushton Skakel. Neighbors invited the Moxleys to other parties. Quickly, the Moxleys knew everybody in the close-knit community of Belle Haven and had made several friends.

"Moving to Greenwich was one of the easiest things we had ever done," Dorthy said. "And if Martha had not died, we would be living there today and just be very happy."

The Moxleys had always been very social. "Nothing would please my mother more than to hang out at the backyard fence, have a cup of coffee with the neighbors," John said. "She was always on the phone talking to somebody."

David and Dorthy were always the last to leave a party. Dorthy would get a vacuum cleaner and help the hostess clean up or help with the dishes. "It's the whole midwestern value system," John explained.

As partner in charge of the New York office of Touche Ross, David Moxley traveled a great deal. When David was coming home late, Dorthy would often feed the kids a large snack, then wait for their father. "When their dad came home, we'd all eat together," Dorthy remembered, "because for me that was important."

David was usually up and out of the house before anyone else was awake. And many nights he would come home after everyone had gone to bed. One Saturday afternoon, John Moxley encountered his father in the kitchen. "Hey, who are you?" John asked. "You look a little bit like I remember my father, but you look different." David didn't like hearing that.

"David was a workaholic," Dorthy said. "He enjoyed being at the office." And the rest of the family followed his example. John was busy with school and sports. Martha was very active at school and had many hobbies, including art and music.

"David was very smart, and everything worked like it was supposed to. When things got broken, he got them fixed. And that was the way we lived," Dorthy said.

Things ran smoothly in the Moxley household. There was order; the rules were clear. The children were expected to do certain things, and they did them. John and Martha both helped with chores around the house, like mowing the lawn.

"I was sort of compulsively clean," Dorthy said. "I was picky." While the Moxleys had a cleaning lady, Dorthy still did much of the housework, and the kids were expected to keep their rooms neat.

They were an open family. "We were not sneaky people," Dorthy said. Martha told her mother all about her school and friends. When Martha died and Dorthy read her diary, she realized that Martha had kept one thing secret—her relationship with the Skakel boys.

Although they weren't close social friends, Rushton had sponsored the Moxleys for membership in the Belle Haven Club in spring 1975 and helped David Moxley join the prestigious University Club in New York. Martha spent a good part of the summer of 1975 swimming and playing tennis at the Belle Haven Club.

Dorthy doesn't know where Martha started hanging around with the Skakel boys. She suspects it might have been at that party at the Fuchses' the week before her murder, when Martha stayed out until three in the morning.

Martha's friend Christy Kalan remembered Thomas letting Martha drive the Skakel car up and down Walsh Lane. "We were all dying to drive," Christy recalled. "Tommy would try to kiss her or put his hand on her knee. You know, a quasi-pass. But nothing ever happened." Martha noted in her diary that Thomas was trying to get to "first base" and "second base." At the same time, Michael was also interested in Martha, and some sources have referred to her as Michael's girlfriend, or ex-girlfriend. According to Frank Garr, Martha's diary noted that while she liked Thomas, she had to be careful of Michael. As far as Dorthy knew, Martha was still going out with Peter Ziluca when she was killed.

The Skakel boys didn't hang out much with the neighborhood kids. They stayed closer to their own family. "They just didn't associate with the people around," Dorthy remembered. "You would have thought that I would have been aware of them, but I wasn't."

John Moxley didn't hang around with the Skakels. "I didn't know them from Adam," he said, since they attended private schools and John went to Greenwich High.

The morning after Martha's body was found, Rushton and Thomas came over to the Moxley house with a ham. Lowell Robertson, who stayed with the Moxleys for about ten days following the murder, accepted the gift.

The next time Rushton visited the Moxley house was on Sunday, March 28, 1976, when he told the Moxleys that Thomas had undergone tests proving he did not kill Martha. When the Moxleys tried to get the Skakel attorneys to turn the test results over to the police, they were stonewalled.

The Moxley family repeatedly found themselves in situations where their efforts to help solve the case were turned against them. Dorthy surrendered her daughter's diary and other personal effects to the Greenwich police early in the investigation. In 1980, she requested that those items be returned.

They refused. In 1997 she requested again, and Frank Garr refused her again.

The Moxleys were often treated like suspects rather than victims. Early on, detectives took Dorthy aside and asked if she had a boyfriend or a drinking problem. She told them that she didn't have a boyfriend, but she did drink, although she didn't think it was a problem. She said the police never explained why they were asking these types of questions.

On December 2, 1975, John was taken to Bethany for a polygraph test. The whole experience was a "horror" to the seventeen-year-old boy. "It never even dawned on me what was happening," he said twenty-two years later. They didn't tell him he was being taken in for a polygraph until he was already in the car. Of course, John passed the poly. The police showed him the charts and told him why they believed he was telling the truth.

"I was so pissed, I was so hurt that my mom and dad could even agree to have it done," John said. "I remember sitting there with my father afterwards and saying, how could you let them do this?"

On December 17, 1975, the Greenwich police took Dorthy to the state crime lab in Bethany for a polygraph test. "I was willing to do anything they asked, I didn't question anything," Dorthy said. "If they told me it would have helped, I would have jumped out of a second-story window."

After preliminary tests, the polygraph examiner stated that Mrs. Moxley was too nervous and upset to get a conclusive reading. "I was such a wreck," Dorthy said, that they stopped the test and let her go home. Although the police talked about rescheduling a test, they never did.

"I don't mean to defend them," Dorthy said years later, "but I just don't think they knew what they were doing."

David Moxley had the same suspicion almost from the beginning. He wanted to trust the Greenwich police, but their disorganization and inexperience quickly became apparent to the management consultant.

When David Moxley returned home the day Martha's body was found, a colleague at Touche Ross called him to express sympathy. He asked David if the investigation was under way. David looked out his window and said, "They've got this thing covered, I can hardly see the front lawn for all the police officers." His colleague replied, "You're not going to like what I'm going to say, but they're never going to solve this by themselves."

In the beginning, David Moxley gave the Greenwich police the benefit of the doubt. As the weeks passed and no progress seemed to be made, he began wondering if his daughter's murder was being investigated properly. When he asked the police questions, they didn't give him straight answers. Coming to the conclusion that they were not capable of solving the crime, David felt that they ought to bring in outside experts. He tried to get the Greenwich police to meet with homicide

Martha Moxley, Summer 1975.

Martha, nine years old.

Martha, age ten, and her mother, Dorthy.

John, Dorthy, Martha, and David Moxley at Lake Tahoe, *top.*

Martha and her friends, Kerry Schwab and Karen Derr, *center.*

John and Martha Moxley, months before her murder, *bottom.*

Moxley house and driveway, where Martha was first attacked, *above.* (Ed Hausner/*New York Times* Pictures)

Old Moxley driveway with Japanese Elm on right, *above.* (Mark Fuhrman)

The former Skakel residence at 71 Otter Rock Drive, *right.* (Mark Fuhrman)

Master bedroom and terrace of the Skakel house, as seen from the Moxley front yard. (Mark Fuhrman)

Security guard booth at the entrance of the exclusive Belle Haven neighborhood. (Helen Neafsey)

The Belle Haven Club, where the Skakel family dined the night Martha was killed. (Mark Fuhrman)

Martha's classmates console each other after her funeral, *above.* (*New York Times* Pictures)

Greenwich police detectives, at a retirement party, 1978. Standing (*l-r*): Joe Smolewski, Tom Sorenson, Don Verboven, Mike Powell, Dan Pendergast, Jim Lunney, Ted Brosko, Tom Keegan, Vincent Ambrose. Seated (*l-r*): Audrey Adinas, Bob Dell, Bill DePra, Steve Carroll, Frank Garr, Joe McGlynn, *below.* (Courtesy of Steve Carroll)

Michael Skakel on the grounds of St. Martin's rehab, around 1987, *right.*

Mark Fuhrman with Joe Johnson, *Greenwich Time* police reporter, *below.* (Helen Neafsey/*Greenwich Time*)

Martha Moxley's grave site at Putnam Hills Cemetery.
(Helen Neafsey)

investigators from Detroit so they could offer advice and assistance but, according to the Moxleys, the Greenwich police didn't want help from outside.

Meanwhile their investigation wasted valuable time. "It was just like a half-gallon of ice cream on the kitchen counter that was just melting and melting and melting with every passing day," said someone close to the case.

Days after the Skakels shut down cooperation, the Greenwich police finally agreed to meet with the investigators from Detroit homicide. While the Detroit officers were helpful, they couldn't do the investigation for them, nor could they repair the mistakes Greenwich had already made.

"Whoever killed Martha Moxley should not have been able to get away with it," Detroit commander Gerald Hale told Len Levitt in 1982. Hale felt strongly that the Skakel house should have been formally searched. However, "When it came to the Skakels, the Greenwich police were treading lightly."

While David Moxley was deeply involved in overseeing the investigation, he wouldn't talk about it with his family. John said his father never once talked to him about Martha's murder in any depth. John didn't feel comfortable talking about his sister's death. He didn't know much about the investigation. "My way of dealing with it was not to deal with it," John said. His sister's death was "like a black closet that you never went in."

Lowell Robertson was a longtime friend and business associate of David's. He first met David Moxley in 1958, when they were young executives moving up the corporate ladder in Touche Ross. "I never saw him shed a tear," Robertson said. "He never expressed any opinions about possible suspects."

The only time David ever said anything about Martha's death to his good friend was the night of the funeral. The two were eating dinner when David asked, "How did you know it was Martha?"

"I knew," Robertson replied.

"How did she look?"

"She looked fine." Robertson didn't want to tell David how she really looked.

"Why wouldn't they let me see her at the funeral?"

"I don't know."

For the next several years, Robertson worked, traveled, and socialized with David. That was the last thing David ever said about his daughter's murder.

"My father and I were more quiet about things and more inclined to keep things inside," John said. "My mom is the kind of person to invite ten people over and talk about it. In hindsight, she was the smart one."

Dorthy tried simply to cope. She got up every morning to drive David to the train station, an arrangement that her husband suggested in order to give her a reason to get up and moving. Going out in public was difficult initially. "I remember it was so hard to go out the first time after the funeral," Dorthy said. "I went to the grocery store and everybody was looking at me."

Her friends were a great solace. They kept her busy and involved, always inviting her out to lunch and social gatherings. Jean Wold and Mildred Ix were among her most intimate friends at the time. "I saw Cissy every day and we talked about it all the time," Dorthy remembered. During these conversations, Dorthy said that Mildred told her, "I just can't believe it was Tommy, but I would give you Michael any day."

While she found comfort in talking with her friends about Martha, she protected herself by avoiding the details of her murder. Dorthy never even found out where Martha's body was discovered. She didn't want to know, or else she would never be able to go out in her yard without being reminded.

After Martha's death, the house was much too large for them and held too many memories, but the Moxleys remained in Belle Haven for a year. "We thought maybe it would help the investigation if we stayed," Dorthy said. "And I was just getting fruitier and fruitier." The memories of Martha were too much, and they had to move out.

They lived in a condominium in Greenwich for a few months, but David was never home and John was away at Choate. "I was falling apart, I just couldn't stand it," Dorthy said. When John got out of school, they moved to New York City.

"My father's idea was just to get out of town," John said. Martha's case wasn't going anywhere and they weren't doing much good by staying around. Both parents enjoyed living in New York. David buried himself in his work, while Dorthy made friends in Manhattan.

From New York, David still kept a close eye on the investigation. Sometimes he would give Dorthy updates on the case, but he still wouldn't talk about Martha. "If David were to walk in the door and I said, 'Come on in and sit down, I want to talk to you about Martha,' he just wouldn't do it," Dorthy said. "I think he felt he was protecting me by not talking about it."

Although he had always worked long, hard hours, David worked even longer and even harder after Martha's death. He was not one to sit around the house. As Dorthy puts it, "David was not a domestic sort of person. He really didn't have any idea where the kitchen was."

David Moxley was an ambitious and talented man. He was quarterback and captain of his high school football team and swam for the University of Kansas. On business trips he always brought a fishing rod and found time to fly-fish. A powerful intellect and voracious reader, he edited a couple of books, including one volume of brief essays written by one hundred prominent people about the federal deficit. David circulated the book to all members of Congress and the heads of major corporations in 1976.

David served on several nonprofit boards, including the Metropolitan Opera and New York Public Library. He was also head trustee for Manhattanville College, a Catholic girls' college that Ethel and Joan Kennedy attended.

David was elected to managing partner of Touche Ross, but his work no longer offered him solace. "The office politics was just awful," Dorthy remembered. "People were stabbing him in the back." At the end of his term, David was made managing partner of the international branch of the firm.

After David retired from Touche Ross in 1986, he and Dorthy moved to a waterfront condominium in Annapolis, Maryland, and bought a boat. While David enjoyed sailing, he wasn't happy with retirement. So he started working for Bob Dole's 1988 presidential campaign. The native Kansan quickly moved up in the campaign organization. By the time Dole withdrew from the race, David was in charge of the campaign's budget and finance.

When the campaign was over, David got a job in New York, serving as business manager for two law firms that had recently merged. They moved back to New York, while keeping the condo in Annapolis and an apartment in Washington. David was busy and loved his new job. "Everything was really going very well," Dorthy said.

The Moxleys planned to have Thanksgiving dinner at the house of John's future parents-in-law. The weekend before Thanksgiving, Dorthy and David were in Washington. On Sunday morning,

Dorthy took David to Union Station so he could take a train and be back at work in New York Monday morning. He didn't call Dorthy for the next couple days, which Dorthy found odd because he usually called. She assumed he was just busy and enjoying work.

Dorthy still hadn't heard from David when she drove up to New York that Wednesday. She arrived in the city in the afternoon and went straight to the apartment. When she opened the door, she could see David's foot sticking out from the bed. She said, "David, you're home." Then she walked in and saw him. "My god," she said, "you look terrible."

Then, she realized her husband was dead. "He looked very peaceful," she said years later. "We don't know exactly what day he died, but he died exactly how he wanted. He was happy, everything was going very well, he was doing what he wanted to do."

David was buried next to Martha in Putnam Hills cemetery. Dorthy settled back in New York and John moved in with her until his marriage. After the wedding, Dorthy moved back to Annapolis. There she realized that if she didn't do something to keep Martha's memory alive, her case might be forgotten and never get resolved.

"David was the one who was in charge of Martha's case, in charge of working with the police and everything," Dorthy said. "And I was the dutiful wife who would sit back and do everything I was told to do. I never stood up and screamed, 'Why aren't you doing something?' Maybe I should have done that a couple times, I'm sure I did feel like that."

Dorthy expected to find a full record of the investigation in David's personal files. Instead, there was only one memo about Ken Littleton calling him and asking for money.

John Moxley was worried that his mother would become a recluse. David Moxley's work at Touche Ross, his standing on the nonprofit boards, and political work had been the basis for the Moxleys' social life. Instead of becoming a recluse, Dorthy came out of her shell. "I'm a stronger person now," Dorthy said. "You just pull up your socks and go on." John Moxley says of his mother, "She's always been incredibly resilient. She will bend, but she won't break."

Martha's death was more traumatic to Dorthy than losing her husband. "As much as I loved him," she said of David, "his death has not shaken me the way Martha's did. I say that because my husband had a life, and Martha didn't."

Now Dorthy had the responsibility to look after Martha's case, but she would have to handle it differently than her husband. "It was like someone walking in the door and saying here's a polar bear for you to raise," Dorthy said of the responsibility. "Now what do I do with a polar bear?"

Dorthy wasn't a manager or an investigator. She was Martha's mother. So she did what she could do—she talked about Martha, not only to her friends but also to representatives of the media. She felt that by keeping Martha's memory alive, public attention and pressure might help bring the case to some kind of resolution. And she talked to John about how they should handle the case themselves.

"It became clear to us that neither one of us really knew what was going on," John said. "And with my father gone, we didn't want it to die on the vine."

In 1990, Dorthy and John Moxley, together with Touche Ross consultant John McCreight, came up with an ambitious "Ten-Week Plan" to reinvigorate Martha's case. They offered to hire experienced investigators to review the evidence. They offered to pay for the computer hardware and personnel to allow the Greenwich police to automate the investigation. At his own expense, McCreight had all the information from the redacted police reports typed into a computer, to show the police how advanced technology can be used as an investigative tool.

The police rejected all the Moxleys' offers. "It went over like a lead balloon," John Moxley said later. "They were very territorial."

After the ten-week plan was rejected, the Moxleys got a lucky break. William Kennedy Smith was accused of rape. If not for the publicity surrounding the Palm Beach rape trial, the Connecticut authorities might never have reopened the case.

At the August 9, 1991, press conference announcing the reinvestigation, the Moxleys raised the existing $20,000 state reward to $50,000. They also pledged to finance the toll-free tip line. And they granted countless interviews to the media over the next few years.

After four years of reinvestigation, no real progress had been made, but the Moxleys were still grateful for the efforts. As a gesture of gratitude and friendship to everyone who had worked on the case, Dorthy and John Moxley hosted a dinner at the Belle Haven Club on November 3, 1995. They invited thirty-nine law-enforcement officials, lawyers, and journalists who helped keep the investigation going. The guest list included Steve Carroll, Jim Lunney, Jack Solomon, Frank Garr, Donald Browne, Ken Moughty, Henry Lee, and family friends.

"It's hard for us to express everything we feel," John Moxley said in an informal speech. "Thank you for caring."

"You are such wonderful people to be out there working for justice," Dorthy told the crowd.

In June 1996, the Moxleys doubled the reward to $100,000. The reward expired a year later and was converted into a scholarship fund in Martha's name. Still, the Moxleys haven't given up.

"The fact that things keep happening, books keep getting written should prove that when you get something the magnitude of this, you just can't put it in the closet and shut the door and say it didn't happen," Dorthy said. "If Martha were missing, or I thought it would bring her back, I would do anything, I'd be out there scratching and kicking and screaming and hollering."

By nature Dorthy is quietly persistent. Without

ever saying that she suspects her former neighbors of Martha's murder, Dorthy continues publicly to ask the Skakels at least to cooperate with the police.

"All I know is that Martha was at the Skakels', the golf club that killed her was at the Skakels', and somehow Martha and the golf club came together," Dorthy said. "All I'd like to see is some cooperation from the Skakels to clear this up. They claimed they didn't do it. If they didn't do it, why won't they help me?"

Someone out there lives with what he has done and doesn't appear to be bothered by it. Meanwhile, the victim's family has to cope with their loss. Both John and Dorthy say that with the passage of time, "It doesn't get better, it gets worse."

"I get married and wonder what it would be like if she had married," John said. "I have kids, I wonder what her kids would be like."

"I know I will only have half a family, only half the grandchildren," Dorthy said, fighting the tears. "I was never able to put a wedding dress on my daughter."

11

The Victim: Martha Moxley

*When Martha enters a room it's like the sun
coming up in the morning.*
—*Martha Moxley's seventh-grade teacher*

Detectives often profile a suspect. It is fairly easy
to piece together a picture of the suspect from
the evidence: what he does at the crime scene;
what he leaves or doesn't leave there; the method he
uses to kill; his possible motive. The elements that
eventually make up a suspect profile are all provided
by the suspect himself.

The victim is more difficult to profile, since the
victim did not create or control the situation. A detective should always be careful not to add to the stigma
of a victim. The one group of people who commonly
profile victims are defense lawyers in rape cases, trying
to establish that the victim "asked for it." The case of
Martha Moxley is exactly the opposite. Not only do all
witnesses and documents report that she was a good
girl, but that is probably the very reason she was vic-
timized.

At first glance, Martha seems an unlikely victim.

She was popular, vivacious, and self-confident. She felt secure in any situation. Everyone liked her and she succeeded in nearly every endeavor.

"Martha was just a very easy child from the beginning," Dorthy said. "She did all the things she was supposed to do."

Her constant companion and playmate was a cat named Tiger. When they moved to Greenwich, Tiger was joined by another called Junior.

Wherever she was—California or Greenwich—Martha always had a lot of friends, but she was also content to spend time by herself. With her cats nearby, she would sit at her desk and draw pictures or write in her diary.

Martha was very creative. She played violin and piano, and excelled in drawing and painting. One whole room in the Walsh Lane house was turned over to her art projects, including a collage made of magazine clippings that took up the entire wall. A bright girl who did well in school, Martha did her assignments as soon as she got home.

Years later John Moxley remembered with sadness what probably bugged him while Martha was alive: "She was the kid you always wanted to be. She was always on the top of her game."

"Martha was very fun to have around," Dorthy said. "I guess I just can't remember the negative things."

Nobody can remember the negative things because they were all saddened by Martha's short life and violent death. And because there are very few negative things to remember. By all accounts, Martha was a well-adjusted, likable young lady with a lot of talent and no problems. "She was always a very secure kid," Dorthy said. "She didn't hesitate at trying things."

When the Moxleys moved to Greenwich, Dorthy believes that Martha would have preferred to stay in California, but the move was not traumatic. They still had a condo in Lake Tahoe to which they returned in the summer, and every winter Martha went skiing with her California pals. She was also a conscientious letter writer and kept in touch with distant friends.

Martha lived alone on the third floor of the Walsh Lane house. Like everyone else in the house, she had her own bathroom. Dorthy remembered Martha's top-floor room as being "like a little garret." Looking out her window at the back of the house was a big bay window. Tiger and Junior climbed up and down the tree and went through the open window in her room. Michael Skakel told Sutton Associates that on the night she was murdered, he climbed that tree and tried to summon Martha by throwing pebbles at her window.

In Greenwich, Martha made friends quickly. She had her friends from the public school she attended and friends from Belle Haven who attended private schools.

"They were really nice girls," Dorthy said of Martha's friends. "They weren't troublemakers or on drugs or anything."

In her free time, Martha went out with her friends to movies or to play tennis or swim at the Belle Haven

Club. Her first year in Greenwich, she attended Western Junior High School, where her picture was all over the yearbook. Her friends were good students and interested in boys, like all fourteen-year-old girls. She did her artwork and practiced music. And she tutored her classmates in Spanish, since she was a year ahead of them in that subject.

Martha was definitely a leader. Although a new student from another part of the country in a very status-conscious town, Martha was voted the girl with the best personality in her class. A year after arriving in Greenwich, Martha was sports editor of the yearbook, had gained scholastic honors, and won letters for field hockey and basketball. Family friend Rosemary Mein said, "It was one of Martha's strengths that she could adjust to change, and she had done so here."

Martha was also very sensible. Instead of taking her daughter shopping for clothes, Dorthy simply opened accounts at some of the local stores and told Martha to buy what she wanted. If Dorthy didn't like one of her selections, she said she would tell Martha to take it back. "I never had to return anything," Dorthy remembered.

Martha didn't have to be told what to do. And she was very open and honest with her family. It seemed as if she told her mother everything. Sometimes Martha told Dorthy more than she wanted to know.

"She talked constantly to me," Dorthy explained. "I would be in the kitchen and she'd go on and on about things that happened that day, just talk, talk,

talk. I would finally say, Martha, you just have to stop talking because I can't concentrate, I have things to do."

Dorthy knew that her daughter liked drinking beer. John often joked that he was going to give her a case of beer for her birthday. She would drink an occasional beer at home, and while she didn't do it in the house, Dorthy knew that Martha smoked. "We were very open about these things," Dorthy said. "She didn't have to sneak." Dorthy did the laundry, telling her kids, "If you want to hide anything, don't hide it in your dresser drawer, because Mother's in your dresser drawer every week."

The summer of 1975 Martha blossomed. She spent much of her time at the Belle Haven Club, swimming and playing tennis. Fit and tan, Martha was no longer simply "cute." She was now developing into a beautiful young woman.

"She had lost a lot of baby fat and she just had the braces taken off and she really looked terrific," Dorthy said, "so she was getting a lot of attention and loved it."

Dorthy's little girl was no longer a baby. Now she was getting noticed by boys. Like any teenage girl, she enjoyed their attention.

Martha had a boyfriend, Peter Ziluca, with whom she started going out that summer. It wasn't an intense relationship but "one of those puppy love kind of things," according to her mother. Peter would see Martha during the weekend or on holidays, but they didn't go out on dates. There was no set rule against dating, it just never came up. Martha was often busy with her school activities and other friends.

There is a time in every young girl's life when her body outpaces her experience and she is confronted with the realization that some boys are not content with just being friends. For children, adolescence is an exciting, confusing time. For parents, it is thrilling to see their children progress toward adulthood, but also sad to see them lose their innocence. Martha seemed to be handling this difficult period the same way she handled everything else—with ease.

For Martha the autumn of 1975 was a time of change. The difficult transition from awkward little girl to beautiful young woman was almost complete. Martha liked being a girl. "She didn't try to be sophisticated or grow up too fast," her mother said. Growing up is a process that you can't stop. Martha was still the fun-loving kid she had always been, but she was also changing.

Beauty is often a burden, one she seemed to handle well. Chris Gentry, a Belle Haven neighbor who was with Martha the night she died, admitted, "I was always kind of intimidated by Martha." He said Martha and John, "these gorgeous blond California people," were also very friendly.

At Greenwich High, Martha was meeting new friends. She tried out for cheerleading but didn't make it. Although she was a little disappointed at not making the squad, she got over it and started planning to go out again next fall. "She didn't dwell on things,"

Dorthy said, "just talked about it and finally got rid of it and then went on."

Martha was a promising young woman coming of age. She appeared happy with herself and well adjusted socially. She had a wide variety of interests and a lot of friends. She was well off, living in a beautiful house in an exclusive and secure neighborhood with lots of young people nearby. She had a loving, healthy family whose midwestern values survived both California and Greenwich. She was a brilliant student. Her family and friends loved her. Yet Martha Moxley was murdered. Why? Who could have done it?

As Martha changed, so did her relationship with her family. John drove Martha to Greenwich High every morning in his green Dodge Challenger. They were two years apart and hung out with different groups of friends. John was the troublemaker, Martha was the good girl. "I think Martha was always a big pain in the neck to John," Dorthy said, "because she always did things right and John was always wrong."

Martha and John had a normal sibling relationship that had its minor strife, but even their conflicts had been changing.

"When you're fifteen or sixteen years old, all of a sudden you realize you can't hit your sister anymore," John said. Martha had discovered that she could get back at her brother with a well-chosen insult.

Martha's changing relationship with John showed her growing sense of her own power and autonomy. She was a talker and had a sharp tongue. She obviously wasn't afraid of boys, even big strong boys like her brother the varsity football player.

This confidence is clear in her dealing with Thomas Skakel the night of her murder. Thomas made several advances to Martha. She told him to stop. Then they started "fooling around" in the driveway and backyard. The witness accounts are hazy, but it seems that in this pushing and shoving match Martha gave as good as she got. She was last seen falling down behind the wall in the Skakel backyard, with Thomas on top of her.

Of course Thomas was bigger and stronger than Martha. And from witness reports, she eventually responded in some way to his advances. At one point they were seen "making out." But how far did Thomas want to go? And how far was Martha willing to let him? Could this sexual play have led to murder? Or did it make someone jealous enough to kill?

When Martha was first reported missing, the police were not very worried. They interviewed Dorthy Moxley, who told them that Martha and she had not had a fight, and that Martha had not stayed out late before, although the week previous she had been out until three or four in the morning. To the Greenwich officers, it seemed that she was just out late at a party, maybe with her boyfriend. Or she had had a few beers and was afraid to go home. Martha Moxley was probably the least likely runaway in Belle Haven.

When her body was found and the investigation

progressed, detectives began to speculate that although there was no sexual molestation, Martha's murder could have been sexually motivated.

Everyone said that Martha was outgoing, even flirtatious. After speaking with many of Martha's friends and several people who were with her the night she was murdered (including the suspects), Sutton Associates files state: "No one considers her to be promiscuous, or inappropriately preoccupied with sexuality. Rather, her flirtatiousness seems to have been of the 'nice girl' variety, and was indicative of a self-confident and cheerful disposition."

By flirting, Martha didn't do anything wrong. It wasn't her fault that someone couldn't deal with the fact that she was attractive and liked attention. Her life was changing, growing more complicated. She no longer confided so completely in her mother.

Dorthy always felt that Martha could, and did, talk to her about everything, but Martha never once mentioned the Skakel boys. Dorthy believes that Martha met them at the party held by Tory and Holly Fuchs a week before she was murdered. However, it appears that Thomas and Martha had met prior to that date.

According to Thomas Skakel's statements seventeen years after the event, he and Martha had a sexual encounter on the rear lawn of the Skakel property from 9:30 to 9:50 P.M., ending in mutual masturbation to orgasm. From several witness accounts and her diary entries, we know that Thomas had made advances to Martha, not only on October 30 but also on other occasions. We know that there was a fierce, often violent, sibling rivalry between Thomas and Michael. We know that both were sexually interested in Martha.

Once Martha died, Dorthy read her diary. In it Dorthy was very surprised to hear the Skakel boys mentioned, because Martha had never said anything about them to her. One entry is particularly chilling. Martha wrote that she liked Tommy, but she was afraid of Michael.

Her diary entry shows that she did, in fact, like the attention, but it also sounds cautious, even fearful. The Skakel boys' reputations might have alarmed her as well as attracted her. Perhaps Martha had never realized that she was becoming a sex object. Her previous experience was being the object of social and family affection. Now she was an object of possession. Even though she was only a sophomore in high school, Martha was more mature about certain matters, particularly sex, than the boys in her social group. That maturity was not based on experience, just common sense. Teenage boys rarely understand the difference between flirtation and romance. They tend to see all female attention as being sexual in nature, and their own sexual desire seeks immediate gratification.

While Martha was out the evening of October 30, her killer was nearby. Somewhere in Belle Haven, probably close enough to see or even touch her, Martha's killer was fantasizing about her. He wanted her. He even thought of her as his own. He wanted to possess her completely and all to himself. Martha was probably unaware of the feelings she had stimulated until it was too late.

People normally associate victims with being weak. In this case, Martha's strength left her vulnerable. "Martha was a very sharp girl," her mother said. "She wasn't stupid about things." Martha was too smart to be manipulated. She had too much respect for herself to be humiliated and too strong a personality to be bullied into something she didn't want to do.

Martha was a confident young woman, comfortable around her peers and in her surroundings. She didn't feel she had to work hard to fit in. She made friends easily and naturally. The characteristics that make her memory live on actually killed her.

She was sexually attractive to young men and enjoyed their attention, but she made them keep their distance.

Had Martha been a weak person, with low self-esteem and a poor self-image, she might not have been a victim. She was obviously the victim of a rage attack that was most probably sexually based. If the suspect had gotten what he wanted, Martha would probably not have been killed.

If Martha were promiscuous, if she had let boys do what they wanted, she might be alive today. But Martha respected herself. She was a good girl. And that's why somebody killed her.

The next question is: Who could have done it?

12

Profile of a Killer

*A criminal personality profile is an educated attempt to
provide investigative agencies with specific information
as to the type of individual who would have
committed a certain crime.*
—*Vernon J. Geberth,
Practical Homicide Investigation*

Homicide investigators should profile the killer
without having a specific suspect in mind.
The power of a profile is to have the identity
of the suspect anonymous at that point and develop
the profile strictly from the evidence left at the
crime scene. You don't want the profile to be pol-
luted by your own knowledge of a specific suspect.
Instead, you profile a suspect without a face. Then
your investigation will give him an identity.

Profiling is not something you can learn out of
a book. You must have seen enough crime scenes
and apprehended enough suspects to put the two
together. In order to be a good profiler, you have to
place yourself in the suspect's shoes and walk
through the scene as the suspect. How did he commit the murder? Where did he move? What choices
did he have to make? You have to imagine what was

going through his mind during the act. How did he feel? What drove him to do this?

The first thing a detective must do is figure out, as best he can, what the suspect did and where he moved. Once he pieces together the suspect's movements in chronological order, then the detective can begin to understand, or at least ask the right questions.

In this case, we know that the killer picked up a golf club from the Skakel house or lawn, or somewhere nearby. Then he went to the Moxley property. Whether he went there alone or with Martha, we do not know.

He attacks the victim in the curve of the driveway. She is struck with the golf club and falls facedown on the ground. He picks her up by the feet and drags her across the driveway to the Japanese elm, where he continues his attack. Sometime later, he drags her farther beneath the pine tree. There he pulls down her jeans and panties but does not rape her.

Those are his movements, but what do they mean? You need to examine the act closely in order to establish a motive. Once the motive becomes obvious it usually points toward a single suspect, or a group of suspects with a similar connection to the victim.

What was the motive here? The victim was murdered in one location very near the Skakel and Moxley homes. Then she was moved. Her body was hidden under a tree. She was facedown, her jeans and panties pulled down to her knees. At first glance, the scene might appear to be a sex crime, but neither the evidence nor the sequence of events supports that hypothesis.

Had the victim been sexually assaulted, raped, or tortured, then the second site would make some sense—the assailant incapacitates or kills her at one site, then moves her to another location in order to sexually assault her. But the autopsy found there was no evidence of sexual assault. And the fact that there were no bruises, abrasions, or debris on her bare skin indicates that her clothes were pulled down after she was dragged beneath the tree. Sexual assault was not the motive for this murder.

If the victim wasn't sexually assaulted, then why was her body moved? The first site must have been very incriminating to the killer. This indicates that the suspect knew the victim and lived nearby. Had he been a stranger to the area, unknown to the victim, then moving the body to a place of conceal-ment would make no sense. That would only have lengthened the time he spent at the scene and actu-ally increased his chances of being apprehended.

From my reading of the crime scene and facts from the autopsy, the victim lay facedown in the large pool of blood for at least a half hour, maybe longer. This indicates that the suspect returned to the scene to hide the body and confirms that he moved it to delay discovery of the body or take it farther away from where he himself might be found.

The evidence is very conclusive regarding the cause of death. There were several blows to the vic-tim's head with a golf club. Why were there so many blows? Why did the killer stab the victim with the broken shaft of the golf club?

Perhaps this level of violence was inflicted to make sure the victim was dead. Perhaps it was rage. Or could it have been an effort to camouflage the scene by sheer brutality? Surely, no one in Belle Haven could commit such a violent act. At least, that's what the killer wanted the police and the public to think.

Could a killer who was sophisticated and a stranger to both the area and the victim stage a crime scene like this? Perhaps. But this crime appears personal, not random. The most obvious indication of the personal nature of this murder is the method of death and the overkill of the victim. The rage of the attack and the absence of sexual assault would further show that the suspect most probably knew the victim.

If, for instance, the condition of the victim under the pine tree—specifically, the pants and panties pulled below her knees—was staged to make the attack appear to be motivated by rape, then the uncontrolled rage in the murder does not fit. This would indicate careful planning by the suspect, a presence of mind that does not match this crime scene.

Why was her body left facedown beneath the tree? There are four possibilities:

1. An intentional act, resulting from guilt due to the massive damage done to the victim's face.

2. A deliberate attempt to humiliate the victim, as the suspect felt the victim had humiliated him.

3. A ploy to make police assume that the victim's positioning was to allow sexual access from the rear.

4. Or it could just be that he dragged her facedown and left her in that position.

The only indication that sexual assault was a motive is the position of the victim's jeans and panties. What if they were pulled down by accident? We know that the victim was dragged facedown across the driveway, for her face was scraped and showed evidence of gravel particles embedded in her chin, forehead, and nose. This would indicate that the suspect dragged the victim by her feet and probably moved her the same way to her final location under the pine tree.

The golf club was a weapon of convenience. The club was right there within reach when the emotion of rage overwhelmed the suspect. The suspect felt comfortable with the weapon, as other people would feel comfortable seeing him with it. This would not be a weapon that would illicit alarm, such as a pistol; therefore, the victim would have no fear seeing it in the suspect's hand as he approached.

These facts, combined with the lack of defensive wounds, the location of the murder, and the circumstances of the victim's last human contacts, definitely indicate that she knew her murderer.

The question of motive still remains. The victim was not robbed of any jewelry or money. She was a fifteen-year-old high school student and surely not involved in any illegal business schemes or drug trafficking. She was not insured by herself or her parents, which is a common motive in family murders. She was not raped. That leaves just one motive for the crime: emotion. She could have been killed because of lust, love, infatuation, jealousy, envy, or hatred, but the motive was definitely personal.

Five characteristics of the killer:

1. The suspect knew Martha Moxley.
2. The suspect felt very comfortable being in Belle Haven and no doubt was a neighbor.
3. The suspect had an intimate personal attachment to the victim that provoked uncontrolled rage, whether that attachment was based on reality or merely his perception.
4. The suspect either never intended to have sex with the victim or was interrupted before the act.
5. The weapon was no doubt an item that was handy and comfortable to the suspect. The golf club was absolutely a natural item for him to possess, and Martha would not be surprised to see this in his hand.

13

Convenient Suspects

I thought they were hoping that I was a convenient suspect.
And if they could wrap it up quickly, that would be great.
　　　　　　　　　　　　　　　—Ed Hammond

From the first hours after Martha's body was found to this day, the Greenwich police investigated dozens of suspects whom more experienced detectives would have immediately written off. These suspects had no motive, no opportunity, and no connection to Martha or the crime scene, but they were convenient. They didn't come from powerful families and they cooperated with investigators. From day one, the police knew that Thomas Skakel was the last person seen with Martha and that the golf club came from the Skakel house. Still, they wasted valuable time and resources chasing suspects they should have known didn't kill her.

On October 31, 1975, after a brief observation of Martha's body, Captain Keegan went to the Moxley house and interviewed Dorthy for more than two hours. While Keegan went to the Moxleys', detectives Steve Carroll and Joe McGlynn canvassed the neighborhood.

One of the first houses Carroll and McGlynn checked was the Hammond residence, right next door to the Moxleys'. Inside the house twenty-six-year-old Edward Hammond was studying for one of his classes at Columbia's graduate business school. They were suspicious of the young man and asked him to come down to headquarters to give a statement.

The original report, written by Joe McGlynn that same day, states: "Prior to taking the statement, subject was advised of his rights." When I spoke to him in 1997, Ed Hammond said that he was never read his rights, and Steve Carroll corroborated that he wasn't. The Greenwich police never read suspects their rights during interviews. They only mirandized them just prior to arrest. Nobody was ever mirandized during the Moxley investigation, although the police did interview several people whom they considered suspects and were hoping would confess. It's almost a good thing that nobody did confess, because if they had, their statements would not have been admissible in court.

McGlynn's report does not give any reason for the officers' initial suspicion of Hammond. He does report that "because of the nature of the information contained in Mr. Hammond's statement, it was requested by the officers that Mr. Hammond leave the following articles of clothing, which he claimed to have worn the evening of 10/31/75, for processing and examination by the state lab." McGlynn then

lists seven items of clothing. Hammond also allowed
the police to take hair and fingernail samples.

Why did they think Hammond was a suspect?
Here is what the police say: McGlynn and Carroll
knocked on the door of the Hammond residence
that afternoon—no time is given, but we can esti-
mate it was around 3:00–4:00 P.M. While they interviewed Hammond, the detectives asked if he
would show them his room. Hammond walked
them upstairs and gave permission for them to look
around. During his search of Hammond's room,
Carroll found a box of condoms, one of them used.
He also looked out the window of Hammond's bedroom and saw a direct line of sight to the Moxley
yard where Martha was attacked. Based on these
observations, the police thought they had their
man. "We figured he was the perfect suspect for this
sort of thing," Steve Carroll said later.

Dorthy Moxley remembered: "Right after they
discovered Martha's body, they didn't ask anybody
anything, they just zeroed in on Ed Hammond."

At 3:40 P.M. detectives Dan Pendergast and
Mike Powell arrived at the crime scene. Immediately Captain Keegan told them to go interview
Ed Hammond's mother. Steve Carroll had called
Marianna Hammond at work, telling her that Ed
was being taken to police headquarters. She left
work and went to headquarters herself, so Powell
and Pendergast interviewed her there. During the
interview, she recounted her actions and observations the night previous. At 4:00 A.M. that morning

Dorthy Moxley had called to tell Mrs. Hammond that Martha had not come home.

According to the police report: "Mrs. Hammond signed the attached Consent to Search Premises w/o a Search Warrant Form, as did her son William Edward Hammond, both are attached."

In the redacted police report, there are no consent-to-search forms signed by the Hammonds, although there are several similar forms signed by others. I asked Hammond about it, and he stated that neither he nor his mother ever signed a consent-to-search form. Steve Carroll said he doesn't know who did the Hammonds' consent-to-search forms, but figures that Mrs. Hammond must have signed one, because she was the owner of the house. Even if she had, the consent form would not have been legitimate. Ed Hammond was an adult, and his room was his own private dominion.

Whether they had legal consent or not, detectives Pendergast and Powell proceeded to the Hammond residence, where they conducted a thorough search, collecting five bags of evidence. The evidence was booked. Some of it was turned over to the state crime lab, the rest kept at police headquarters.

Later that night and the next morning, police continued their neighborhood canvass. They asked a lot of questions about Ed Hammond. From their interviews, police learned that the young man was something of a loner who was thought to have a drinking problem. This increased their suspicion that he had killed Martha Moxley.

That first day, Hammond was very cooperative.

Although he lived next door to Martha, he didn't know her socially, having only met her once at a party the Moxleys held the previous weekend. He knew that Martha had been missing and saw the activity on the Moxley property when her body was found. Soon a uniformed officer came to the door and asked him a couple of questions, then left. Shortly after that, Carroll and McGlynn arrived. They asked if Hammond would go to headquarters for some routine questioning, and he agreed.

At police headquarters Hammond was interviewed by the detectives and he believes at least one person from the state's attorney office. He said he remembered being questioned by a man named Solomon.

Hammond stated that the police never indicated he was a suspect and he was never read his rights. "It was supposedly an informal interview to help with the investigation," Hammond said. They asked him what he had done the night previous, and he told them he came home from school, did some homework, ate dinner, watched television, and went to bed around midnight.

Hammond told me that at this time, around 4:00 P.M., as far as he knew, the police hadn't been up in his room or asked to search for anything. "They went through my house," Hammond said, "and they took articles of clothing of mine without permission or consent." While the police said that Hammond had given permission and allowed them to search the house in his presence, he denies that permission was ever granted.

Back at headquarters, once Hammond gave the police his statement, the questioning became more accusatory. According to Hammond, the investigators said things like: "We believe you did it, why don't you tell us about it? You'll feel better."

Jack Solomon was leading the questioning. Hammond remembers him saying, "We could understand how it might happen. You were attracted to her, you lost control. . . ."

At the time, Hammond was wearing a sweater that had dog hairs on it from the family Saint Bernard. According to Hammond, Solomon told him, "You know, we can match those human hairs on your sweater to Martha."

"This is ridiculous, those are dog hairs," Hammond responded. "I don't know anything. I didn't do anything."

The police finally let Hammond go, driving him home around 6:00 P.M. When they got back to the Hammond residence, Mrs. Hammond was back at the house and the search had already been concluded.

The morning of November 1, Hammond got a call around 10:00. The police said they had some more questions and asked if he could come back. Hammond told them he couldn't. The next morning, according to the police report, he was asked to take a polygraph. Hammond refused to take the test until he talked to his lawyer. Meanwhile, the police began their background check on Hammond, which was to last several weeks.

They interviewed Hammond's former classmates

and roommates. They interviewed his teachers at
Yale and Columbia. They got his military service
record and did several FBI checks on criminal and
civil records. They checked with the State Department to see if his passport was valid, as if they were
expecting him to flee the country. They continued to
ask the Belle Haven neighbors about him.

On November 13, 1975, Hammond was reinterviewed by Tom Keegan and Joe McGlynn. His attorney was present at the interview, and according to the
police report, "Hammond was again advised of his
rights." Again, Hammond says that he was never read
his rights, and it was not Greenwich police policy to
read a suspect his rights unless he was being arrested.

The next day, Hammond was given a polygraph
test. The results were inconclusive, and the polygraph examiners determined that the test was
affected by the fact that Hammond was on medica-
tion. Hammond agreed to take a second test.

Exactly a week later, he was taken back to
Bethany and given another polygraph. This one he
passed.

After he passed the second polygraph, the
police drove Hammond back to Greenwich.
During the ride, the police seemed more friendly,
even sociable. Hammond sat in the rear seat, and
two investigators were in the front. The man in the
passenger seat suddenly turned around and pulled
an object out of his pocket, showing it to Hammond. "Do you know what this is?"

"No, I don't," Hammond replied.

"This is the golf club that was used to murder Martha." The officer held the golf club head in his hand.

Hammond told them that he didn't know anything about it. He thinks that they were trying to get him to say something incriminating, a last-ditch effort to get him to confess.

On January 28, 1976, after the Skakel family had withdrawn cooperation and Thomas Skakel was the prime suspect, detectives called Hammond's lawyer and said they wanted to talk to him some more. The Hammonds and their lawyer requested an invoice of the property seized by police during their October 31, 1975, search. That invoice was written up the next day. On March 5, 1976, Detective Jim Lunney went to the Hammond residence to reinterview the Hammonds. They "reiterated the same sequence of events which took place on the night in question. They were unable to give any additional information relative and pertinent to the investigation."

This time the Greenwich police considered Hammond a friendly witness. Perhaps if they had treated Ed Hammond and his mother with more respect in the beginning, they might have gotten some valuable information from them. Instead, Ed Hammond was handled like a guilty suspect. When he was cleared, the police hoped he would just forget the searches, interrogations, and polygraphs and now help them make a case against someone else.

Twenty-two years after the investigation, Hammond is still upset by the way he was treated. "I certainly resented the fact that they had gone through the house and searched it without consent. I talked to my mom about this and she didn't give consent," Hammond said. "I thought that the way I was questioned was out of line."

I asked Hammond why he thought the Greenwich police went after him. "I thought they were hoping that I was a convenient suspect," he said. "And if they could wrap it up quickly, that would be great."

That attitude also helped develop another theory of how Martha was killed, a belief that was held by many in the neighborhood back in 1975 and even to this day: Somehow a transient wandered in from the Connecticut Turnpike, found a golf club, and killed Martha with it.

The Turnpike Transient Theory is nothing more than wishful thinking. Even a cursory examination of the crime scene and the autopsy indicates that Martha knew her killer and the initial attack came as a complete surprise. Belle Haven is not the kind of neighborhood where transients wander around. As amateurish as their security force may be, the one thing they can do is keep out people they don't want. I know this from experience. Even if a transient had gotten by the guard posts, he would have been seen by one of the dozens of children and adults who were out at some point that evening.

As impossible as the Turnpike Transient Theory was, police still investigated it. They searched the woods between Interstate 95 and Belle Haven, and followed up any possible witness identification of an unknown person in the area. They found no evidence in the woods, and all the sightings proved to be local residents.

While the Turnpike Transient Theory didn't pan out, the Greenwich police continued to look for convenient suspects, no matter how little connection there was between these suspects and the death of Martha Moxley. At one point or another and for varying lengths of time, all of these people were investigated as possible suspects by the Greenwich police:

- A Bronx man who had been arrested for indecent assault four years prior on the outskirts of Belle Haven.

- A middle-aged female Belle Haven resident who was reported to have "odd behavioral habits."

- A relative of a Belle Haven family who had been arrested for assaulting two females in White Plains, New York, in 1962.

- A "known sexual deviant" in New Rochelle, New York.

- A Belle Haven neighbor who was seen walking on Walsh Lane the night of October 30, 1975.

- A Stamford, Connecticut, man who had been arrested on Halloween for striking a young woman with a baseball bat.

- A Greenwich man who had applied for a job as security officer at the Belle Haven Club after the murder.

- A man who had shot a popgun at some Belle Haven youths.

- A man who had installed drapes in the Moxley house.

- Two Belle Haven female youths who had reportedly sold marijuana.

- A Belle Haven man who someone had said was "a violent person."

- A man who slapped and threw a stick at two Belle Haven children.

- A Greenwich man who had been arrested for removing a gun from his father's room.

- A Greenwich man who had been arrested for a traffic incident on October 30, 1975.

- A Norwalk, Connecticut, man who had been arrested for larceny, possession of stolen goods, and violation of parole.

- A man who had driven his red car in Belle Haven on October 30, 1975. The police had found red paint scrapings on a traffic stanchion that had been hit by a speeding car that evening.

- A Belle Haven resident who had been arrested for breach of peace in 1971.

- A man who called the Moxley house claiming to be an advisor to President Ford and offering to help the Moxley family.

- A Stamford man who was reported to have a section of a golf club in his home. It turned out to be a shoehorn.

- A Stamford man who had been arrested for breach of peace on November 11, 1975, and was carrying a golf club at the time.

- A young Greenwich man who had given Martha a ride home on occasions.

- A Pecksville, New York, man who had attacked a nurse at a veterans' hospital with a baseball bat.

- A Belle Haven man who chased three youths off his property with a golf club.

- A Belford, New Jersey, man who had been stopped for speeding and eventually arrested for assaulting two police officers and resisting arrest. A sixteen-inch length of coaxial cable with what appeared to be human blood was found in the trunk of his car.

- A photographer who had taken pictures of Martha and the Moxley house two months before the murder.

- A New York City man who was arrested for assaulting an eighteen-year-old girl with a golf club in Central Park.

- A Greenwich youth who reportedly "had been going with a girl in the Belle Haven area and had broken off with her recently."

- A Greenwich man who was known to frequent the Belle Haven area. He was friendly with a local family.

- Several full-time employees of the Homestead Inn.

- A part-time employee of the Homestead Inn.

- A former employee of the Belle Haven Club.

- A man who had been picked up hitchhiking on the evening of October 30 and said, "I didn't mean to do it."

- A local boy who had reportedly said, "I know who killed Martha Moxley."

- A part-time gardener who worked on two Belle Haven properties.

- A Syracuse, New York, man who had been involved in an undisclosed incident at the Skakel house in 1970.

- A mentally disturbed New York City man who had made phone calls to the Moxley residence.

- A Greenwich youth who had been arrested on unspecified charges and then threatened that "he would do something on Halloween."

- The former head of the Belle Haven security patrol.

- A local man, known to have a drinking problem, who told the owner of a bar that three youths had come up to him in the bar and told him they were going to kill a girl with a golf club. The man said one of the youths was referred to as "Skakel."

- A young male deaf-mute from New Rochelle, New York, who had killed a girl in early 1974 with a golf club.

- A man who observed a girl matching Martha Moxley's description in the Byram business area late at night on October 25, 1975.

- A relative of a Belle Haven family who drove a cab in New York and was being investigated for domestic difficulties.

- A college student who told John Moxley's girlfriend that he knew who murdered Martha and that the killer moved to California two weeks after the homicide.

- A relative of a Belle Haven family who had been arrested in three different states for sexual abuse of young girls.

While these suspects make up a strange and disparate group, they all have several common denominators: None of them could be placed with Martha Moxley the night of the murder. None of them had motive or opportunity. And there was no physical or witness evidence to tie them to the crime in any way. In short, none of them killed her. Few of them should have been suspects for more than a minute. The Greenwich police had no business investigating any of these people. They would have done better going through a phone book and picking out names at random.

Looking at Teletypes and interfacing with other agencies concerning similar murders is often a useful investigative tool, but you need to find some nexus between your case and other homicides. They don't have to be exactly the same, but there should be some evident connection. And it usually only works in serial killings, which the Moxley homicide was not. In this murder, you have a weapon of opportunity and a rage-based attack, which would indicate some personal connection to the victim.

These suspects, and nearly everyone else investigated in the murder of Martha Moxley, were the objects of suspicion only because they were easy. The Greenwich police hoped that the murderer was somebody who wasn't wealthy or well connected, somebody from outside the neighborhood, but those hopes proved fruitless. Once they realized the suspect probably came from the neighborhood, the police and the Belle Haven community engaged in a witch hunt.

Anybody in Belle Haven who was said to be a little odd was investigated. Sometimes those reports were nothing more than a suspicion from a nosy neighbor or a long-term grudge finally being settled.

In the minds of the Greenwich police, someone who was capable of smoking pot or shoplifting was also capable of a brutal murder, whether or not they had motive, opportunity, or a connection with the victim.

As a result, dozens of innocent adults and children were submitted to polygraphs, harsh questioning, suspicion, and rumors. At least one house was searched without a warrant or permission. Ed Hammond was harassed for months after he thought he had been cleared.

Meanwhile, the Skakel boys, who everybody in the neighborhood knew were violent and wild and who had been with Martha that night, avoided scrutiny until the police were left with no choice but to consider them as suspects. The police didn't determine that the suspect must have come from the Skakel house until the reinvestigation that began in 1991. Only at that time did they stop looking for convenient suspects. By then, the case was already a hopeless mess.

The police spent the crucial early stages of their investigation looking at suspects who met their criminal profile, a profile that had more to do with their own fear and inexperience than any probable connection to the crime. Most of these suspects were able to continue with their lives relatively unaffected by the Moxley investigation. The next suspect we encounter was not so lucky.

14

Suspect: Ken Littleton

Those rich people ruined my son's life.
—Maria Littleton

On October 30, 1975, Ken Littleton spent his first night in residence as a tutor for the Skakel children. Since that night, his life has become a nightmare. In a few short years, he went from being a bright young man with a promising future to a mentally unstable alcoholic with a criminal record.

Despite his problems since the murder, I am convinced that Ken Littleton did not kill Martha Moxley. The fact that she was murdered his first night on the job was just a coincidence. It was a very unlucky coincidence for Ken Littleton, and a very lucky one for whoever did kill Martha.

Littleton's presence in the Skakel house provided the Greenwich police with their most convenient suspect, one whom they investigated longer and with much more diligence than they pursued anyone else. In fact, they still consider Littleton a suspect to this day. Why? Littleton, like the suspects I described in the previous chapter, was not rich, powerful, or well connected. He was merely an educated servant of the rich. He was an outsider.

In the fall of 1975, Ken Littleton was a twenty-three-year-old recent graduate of Williams College. He taught science and coached sports at the exclusive Brunswick School, where three of the Skakel boys attended. Rushton Skakel was looking for a live-in tutor to look after his seven motherless children. He wanted somebody who would be able to help them with their homework, but he also needed somebody physically powerful enough to control the often wild boys.

Ken Littleton was a big, strong, intelligent young man who had played rugby in college and had a good rapport with the students at Brunswick. He had previously baby-sat for the younger Skakel children and knew Thomas, John, and David from school. Rushton hired him to start on the long Halloween weekend. Since Rushton was going away on a trip, the new tutor temporarily moved into the master bedroom on the second floor in the rear of the house, with a terrace that faced Walsh Lane and the Moxley house.

That night Littleton took Thomas, Michael, Rush Jr., John, Julie, Jim Terrien, and Andrea Shakespeare to dinner at the Belle Haven Club. Though Littleton told police that he and the older children had only one beer each, Thomas later admitted to having several beers and two scotches during dinner.

The Skakel party left for the Belle Haven Club about 7:00 P.M. and returned at 8:45. While at least a dozen young people converged on the Skakel residence, Littleton went up to the master bedroom and unpacked. After he finished unpacking, he stayed in the room watching television. At 9:30 P.M., Nanny Sweeney, the Skakel housekeeper, heard dogs barking outside and asked Ken to investigate. He went outside for three to four minutes but saw nothing and only heard the sound of leaves rustling in the wind. Sometime around 10:00, Julie Skakel reported seeing someone she believed was Littleton in the kitchen. At 10:03, Littleton said that Tommy came upstairs and watched *The French Connection* on television with him. "He came up," Littleton told investigators, "approximately twenty minutes before the chase scene." The chase scene began at 10:23 and ended at 10:32. Once the chase scene was over, Tommy left the bedroom. Littleton says he remained in the master bedroom all night until morning.

The next morning, Littleton was out working in the Skakel yard, probably raking leaves. He no doubt saw the commotion by the Moxley house after Sheila McGuire found Martha's body. By that afternoon, according to Jim McKenzie, "[Littleton] was in some sort of semidisbelief himself about what was going on and how did I get myself into this family?"

Along with other Skakel family and household members, Littleton was interviewed by police the

afternoon of October 31. During the early part of the
investigation, Littleton was interviewed like every
other member of the Skakel household and was apparently not considered a suspect. On November 5,
1975, when detectives came to the Skakel house to ask
Thomas to take another polygraph, Littleton was reinterviewed. A pair of dungarees with possible blood-
stains had been found in the Skakel garbage. Littleton
told police that the males attending the dinner at the
Belle Haven Club dressed according to code in jacket,
tie, and trousers.

Shortly after Martha's murder, the Skakel family went on a hunting trip to Windham, New York.
Littleton told investigators that he drove the Skakel
family's camper up to Windham, but others have
said that Littleton drove up in his own car. Either
way, the trip seems to have been an opportunity for
the Skakels to confer away from Belle Haven and the
Greenwich police. At Windham, they also probably
met with their family lawyer and advisor, Tom
Sheridan, one of the founders of the resort.

If Littleton had committed the murder, I doubt
the Skakels would have brought him up to Windham to see how they could help. Since the hunting
trip was most probably a legal confab, Littleton was
brought along because he knew something—or the
Skakels thought he knew something—that was very
important.

Police reinterviewed Littleton again on November 14, 1975. Although the police record does not
describe the content of this interview, it is possible

that since the initial interviews were not taped, and
the November 14 interview was, they went over
previously related information in order to have it
recorded on tape.

On November 20, Greenwich detectives contacted authorities in Massachusetts and requested a
background check on Littleton. A Massachusetts
state trooper reported that "the subject had no criminal record, comes from a quiet family, nothing
peculiar about the family." On December 10, detectives Carroll and Lunney visited Littleton at
Brunswick School. At this interview, Littleton
added to his original statement by relating that at
some point, the precise time redacted in the police
report, he walked outside to check on the Skakel
boys, could not see any of them, and went back
inside the house. Then he checked the interior of the
house and saw David and Steven Skakel in bed. The
five other children were out somewhere.

Once the Skakel family had rescinded cooperation, detectives Carroll and Lunney went to
Brunswick School on February 9, 1976, in order to
obtain a written statement from Ken Littleton.
School staffers told the detectives that Littleton had
left for the day. They called the Skakel residence and
were told that Littleton was in a meeting.

According to the police report, on April 2,
1976, during an interview with Steve Carroll, Jim
Lunney, and Detroit investigators Gerald Hale and
John Loch, Mildred Ix stated that "she felt strongly
that Thomas Skakel was not involved in the fatal

assault of Martha Moxley. . . . [She] felt strongly
that Mr. Littleton should be checked out as a suspect. She could not understand that Mr. Skakel
would keep him in his employ because he didn't
contribute anything to the household." Mrs. Ix also
stated that "girlie" magazines were found in
Littleton's room and he was in the habit of visiting
the Skakel gazebo in the nude. This was the first
time in the police record that Littleton is mentioned
as a possible suspect.

When Carroll, Lunney, and the Detroit investigators tried to interview Littleton at Brunswick on April
5, Littleton stated he wouldn't talk to police without
consulting his attorney, Manny Margolis. Two days
later the police returned to Brunswick, and Littleton
said he would not speak to them, nor would he provide them with a written statement to support circumstantial evidence against Thomas Skakel because
he believed the boy was innocent. "I didn't have anything to hide," Littleton told Len Levitt years later. "I
just didn't think Tommy could have done it." At the
time, Littleton said that he was simply following the
advice of the Skakel family and their attorney.

A week later, Ken Littleton retained attorney
John Meerbergen on the advice of the lawyer for
Brunswick School. When Meerbergen contacted the
police to let them know that he had been retained,
he scheduled an interview between the police and
his client. The interview took place on April 22,
1976. Again Littleton refused to sign a written
statement implicating Thomas Skakel. At the con-

clusion of the interview, Littleton and his lawyer
said they would be available for further questioning.

Littleton left the Skakel house sometime in the
spring of 1976 after a falling out with Rushton,
who refused to pay Littleton his wages until
Norman Pederson, the headmaster of Brunswick,
interceded. "I never understood why [Rushton
Skakel] turned against me," Littleton told Levitt. "I
think he wanted to separate himself and his family
from me when the police began pressuring me."
Why would Rushton Skakel risk alienating the
tutor in such a manner? Could it be that he didn't
know what Littleton knew—if anything?

In the fall of 1976, Greenwich police began to
consider Littleton himself a suspect. On October
18, Littleton failed a polygraph examination. He
told investigators that he failed the test because "he
was upset over his recent criminal activity and
arrest." That summer, Littleton had been arrested in
Nantucket for grand larceny, breaking and entering,
and burglary. He was accused of breaking into stores
and a boat on four separate occasions and stealing a
total of $4,000 worth of items.

Years later, Littleton told Len Levitt that the
thefts were "antics" he committed while intoxicated. But Littleton's arrest nearly a year after the
murder convinced Greenwich police that they had
finally found their man.

Soon after Littleton failed the polygraph examination, Jim Lunney met with Manny Margolis, asking to reinterview the Skakel family about Little-

ton's activities. Margolis said that since most of the
Skakels were away from home, he would ask them
questions that Lunney submitted in writing.
Margolis then acted as a go-between, conducting
interviews with Thomas concerning Littleton and
then passing the information on to the police.

Ken Littleton refused to submit to any more
polygraphs or a sodium pentothal examination. As
police spent the next several months looking into his
background, an interesting picture emerged. Prior to
his employment with the Skakels, Littleton was a
model student and athlete. During the summer of
1976, which Littleton spent in Nantucket, he started
behaving strangely. Eschewing the preppy clothing
that he had usually worn, Littleton dressed in a white
outfit with his shirt unbuttoned halfway down, wearing a shark's tooth around his neck. Walking around
town, he would often look at himself in store windows and fix his hair or flex his muscles. Friends who
knew him the previous summer said that he had definitely changed for the worse.

With their pursuit of Thomas Skakel going
nowhere, the police immediately switched gears.
Now Littleton was the prime suspect. Never mind
that murder and burglary are completely unrelated
offenses. Never mind that there was no indication
that Littleton was capable of murder. Never mind
that there was no known connection between
Littleton and the victim. Ken Littleton was acting
strangely in Nantucket—he must have killed
Martha Moxley.

When parents at Brunswick heard about the Nantucket incident, Littleton lost his job. Headmaster Norman Pederson said that although Ken was a good teacher and got along well with the students, they couldn't have him at Brunswick until he got the matter in Nantucket cleared up. Littleton got a job at St. Luke's School in nearby New Canaan, but he was soon released from that job as well because of police scrutiny.

In May 1977, Littleton was given a suspended sentence for the Nantucket charges and placed on probation. At that time, he refused to submit to a sodium amytal interview regarding the Moxley murder in return for a reduced charge.

As the Greenwich police continued to investigate Littleton, his life took a downward spiral. Littleton moved down to Florida, where he was arrested at least three times for drunk driving, trespassing, and disorderly conduct. During one of those arrests, Littleton gave a false name. After his arrest for drunk driving, Littleton mumbled something about having to speak with the Kennedys. According to the Sutton Associates files, on February 28, 1982, he was found guilty of disorderly conduct in Florida. Three days later, also according to the files, he was found guilty of shoplifting. He got married and divorced. He moved to Canada. He worked at a loading dock. He drank. His mental problems increased. His life grew progressively worse.

Littleton told Sutton Associates: "I attribute [my life's decline] as the environmental cause to my manic-depressive illness. Bipolar is the politically correct term now." He also described to the Sutton investigators an incident in Hull, Quebec, in which he was beaten and robbed and left to die. The beating was so severe, Littleton said, that he was actually clinically dead for several minutes. He suspected that the beating was an attempted hit on his life ordered by the Skakel family. There is no indication in the Sutton Associates files that they investigated this allegation.

During his time in Florida, Littleton contacted David Moxley at least twice. Once he called and expressed condolence for Martha's death, then said he would be willing to undergo a sodium pentothal test. Littleton later claimed he was drunk when he made the phone call. He also wrote Mr. Moxley a letter, again expressing his condolences but offering no pertinent information. These contacts with the victim's family show sympathy, but are they indicative of guilt? Littleton obviously felt bad about what happened to Martha, but he didn't seem to be able to do much about it.

As recently as a few years ago, Littleton was a regular visitor to his alma mater, Williams College, where he would hang around with the undergraduates and tell them stories about the murder that occurred while he lived in the Skakel house. One Williams student remembered him as an odd, even bizarre character trying to relive his glory days on campus.

Meanwhile, back in Greenwich, the investigation into Martha's murder grew colder and the heat on Littleton increased. When Frank Garr and Jack Solomon reinvestigated the case, they treated Ken Littleton as the prime suspect, and they were not alone in their suspicions.

In July 1993 investigators from Sutton told Len Levitt that they had evidence they hoped could shift the focus of the investigation to Littleton. They were even more emphatic to Dorthy Moxley, saying they could prove that the Skakels didn't kill her daughter. Unfortunately, Sutton Associates' investigation into Ken Littleton did exactly the opposite by pointing more suspicion on the Skakels themselves.

During an interview in Boston with a Sutton Associates investigator, Littleton stated, "The only person I remember seeing that night was Tommy. You're probably interested in this, because I give him an alibi for a certain period of time." He then went on to relate basically the same story he told police. What is interesting about these initial statements is that Littleton isn't at all concerned about establishing an alibi for himself, only Thomas.

While being quite candid in most areas discussed with Sutton, some of Littleton's answers were cryptic, even coy. When the investigator asked Littleton whom he believes committed the murder, Littleton said, "No comment." The investigator asked if he believed one of the Skakels was responsible. Littleton once again answered, "No comment."

Even without naming who he thinks killed

Martha, he casts suspicion on Michael, who had been with Martha earlier that evening but avoided scrutiny for so many years because of his apparent alibi for the assumed time of death. In his Sutton interviews, Littleton questioned whether Michael in fact went to the Terriens' along with Jim Terrien, Rush Jr., and John. Littleton also stated that he thought the murder occurred after 10:30 P.M., opening up the timeline and making it possible for Michael to have committed the murder. Littleton went on to theorize that Martha could have been lured from her house or could have been having a sexual encounter outside the house, and then was murdered sometime around 11:00 P.M. to 12:00 A.M. He made these statements before it became public knowledge that Thomas and Michael had changed their stories.

When the investigator pushed a little harder, Littleton admitted that when Thomas left the master bedroom, he could just as easily have gone out to meet with Martha again. Why, if Ken Littleton believes Thomas is innocent or is trying to protect him, would he make these statements? Perhaps because he's telling the truth, even if he's not telling all that he knows.

During the last twenty-two years, there have been rumors, speculation, and even loosely based fiction (*A Season in Purgatory*) that suggest Littleton could have been paid off to hide the truth. I can understand the dramatic possibilities of using such a scenario, but the fact is that from the beginning,

Littleton actually caused trouble for Thomas Skakel.

In his initial police interviews, Littleton said that when he checked Thomas's room sometime after 9:30 P.M., he wasn't there, contradicting Thomas's original statement that he had left Martha at 9:30 by the back door and gone inside. Thomas's story about doing a homework assignment on Abraham Lincoln, the Puritans, and log cabins was also contradicted by Littleton's initial interviews. When police asked Littleton if Thomas had any such homework assignment, Littleton said he didn't know about it. If Littleton were covering up for Thomas, he probably would have answered differently.

Although Littleton did offer statements that cast suspicion on Thomas, he says he is convinced that Thomas didn't kill Martha. When Littleton was asked to sign a statement that implicated Thomas Skakel in the murder, he refused based on his belief that Thomas did not kill Martha. Steve Carroll said that during questioning about Thomas, Littleton blurted out, "I'm not going to help you build a case against Tommy!" At the time, Littleton was still employed by the Skakels, but, even after he left the Skakel house, Littleton still refused to implicate Thomas in any way. At the same time, he continued to offer information that casts suspicion on the Skakels, particularly Michael. He talked about Michael's violent behavior and told the Sutton investigators that he thought the boy was on drugs. He questioned Michael's alibi of going to the Terriens' and offered his opinion that the murder happened much later. He also discussed scenarios in which Michael at least had the opportunity to murder Martha.

How much does Littleton know? That is anyone's guess. The Sutton files make it apparent that he knows more than he told the police. Considering the way he was treated by the Greenwich police and investigators for the state's attorney office, it's no wonder he won't tell them everything. The fact that he cooperated with them at all indicates that he has nothing to hide.

During their reinvestigation of the case, detectives Jack Solomon and Frank Garr worked hard to implicate Littleton. Littleton cooperated by submitting to another polygraph, which he failed, and by talking to the detectives without his attorney present.

Thinking that he could be a serial killer, Solomon and Garr hoped to connect Littleton to a string of unsolved homicides in Massachusetts, Florida, and Maine. Solomon and Garr's suspicion of Littleton as a potential serial killer was disclosed by Sutton Associates. During a meeting with the Skakel investigators, Solomon and Garr told them that they were looking into the other unsolved murders and hoped for a connection to Littleton. At one point, Solomon told the Sutton investigators, "What do we have to do to prove to you that Littleton is our man?"

The investigation went nowhere. Instead of trying to connect Ken Littleton to murders in other states, they should have tried to come up with at least one piece of evidence that connected him to the murder of Martha Moxley. They couldn't. Garr and Solomon collected blood and hair samples from Littleton. As of this writing, no samples from Littleton were matched to trace evidence at the crime scene.

Although Littleton remains a suspect to this day, the only tangible evidence police have against him is the fact that he failed two polygraph tests.

Frank Garr said, "It's interesting that in 1976 Littleton submitted to a polygraph examination and failed it. And then, eighteen years later he takes another polygraph examination and fails again. I mean, that's *interesting*."

If Littleton is a paranoid, psychotic, bipolar alcoholic, then how could Garr expect him to pass any kind of polygraph? It would be impossible to get a reliable polygraph reading from him. The very fact that Littleton's stability is open to question is reason enough not to polygraph him.

With Littleton still the prime suspect and the Connecticut investigation going nowhere, John Moxley suggested that he interview Littleton. At first the police were resistant, but John didn't give up. Eventually the police endorsed the idea. They sat down with John and prepped him for the interview. They also offered him whatever resources they had available.

Littleton was no longer represented by John Meerbergen, who now served as attorney for the town of Greenwich. He retained Boston lawyer Carol Ball because he was dating one of Ball's best friends.

Initially, Ball had been reluctant about John's proposed interview. When John first tried to contact Littleton, Ball set down several conditions: no recording devices, no contemporaneous notes, and John would have to answer any questions Littleton asked. John agreed to all the conditions. During their conversation, John could tell that the lawyer was uncomfortable. Finally he said, "What happens if, during the middle of this he breaks down and says, 'I did it. I killed your sister.' What are we going to do?"

There was a very long pause. John could tell that his question really knocked her for a loop. Then she got back into defense lawyer mode and said, "We'll deal with that if it comes. But he didn't do it."

A few days later, Ball wrote to John, "My client Ken Littleton has agreed to your request to meet out of sympathy for your family and based on his belief that you and he are both victims of the individual who killed your sister so many years ago and of the bungled investigation which followed."

John flew up to Boston on June 10, 1994, and met with Littleton and Ball in the lawyer's office. After eighteen years, here he was, one of the prime suspects in his sister's murder. Here was the guy who had failed the polygraph test, who had behaved so strangely since the incident.

Littleton's appearance and demeanor confirmed everything that John had heard about him. "He's a very, very strange guy," John said. He felt that Littleton appeared very paranoid, and it didn't seem like an act. Several times during the interview, Littleton broke down sobbing.

John asked him: "Why haven't you been able to convince anybody that you don't have any involvement in this? Stand up naked to the world and clear yourself. Why won't you do that?"

Littleton had no answer. When he was arrested in Nantucket for larceny, Littleton had the opportunity to plea-bargain his charge down from felony to misdemeanor, on the condition that he give a sodium pentothal interview to the Connecticut detectives. And he wouldn't do it. He told John Moxley, "I wasn't going back to Connecticut for the naked light bulb treatment."

John asked: "What about your career? You went to a good college, you're a bright, articulate guy. If you're innocent, you have nothing to hide."

All Littleton could offer was the excuse that a felony record would only keep him from getting public school credentials and he didn't want to teach in public schools anyway.

John said: "Ken, that's the exact kind of thing that makes people believe you've got something to hide."

Littleton couldn't give him an answer.

John asked repeatedly: "Why can't you convince anybody that you didn't do it?"

This was the question that bothered Littleton the most. He would say, "I didn't do it. What can I do to convince you?"

John said, "Take a polygraph test."

But Littleton had already taken polygraphs on two separate occasions and failed them both.

"Do you know who did it?" John asked.

"I don't know who did it," Littleton responded.

John stated that Littleton was very upset about the turns his life had taken. "He said it was conspiracy against him," John recalled. "He said a big part of it was the Skakels, a big part of it was the police, the media, why would they be coming after me?"

John didn't believe that Littleton had any involvement, but he did feel that Littleton had been intimidated in some way.

"It was unique in my life to be in a room with somebody where I was asking questions that would make a grown man cry," John said three years later.

When John left the lawyer's office, he said, "Littleton was the happiest guy in the world." He walked John two blocks to the corner and shook his hand, saying, "Thanks for coming up."

As for John: "When I left there I felt that I had been in the presence of a true wacko."

According to Sutton Associates files, Littleton has "a genetic and sociocultural predisposition to bipolar mood disorder stemming from stressful occurrences." They also stated that Littleton is a serious alcoholic who in the mid-1990s was recovering in a twelve-step program. If the police made suspects out of every person who lived in Belle Haven in 1975 and wound up having psychiatric or substance-abuse problems, they would have had a lot of work on their hands. What the police were unable to do was link any of Littleton's behavior directly to the crime under investigation.

"He is mentally ill. You people made him crazy," Littleton's mother, Maria, told one reporter, referring to state investigators.

Ken Littleton is obviously a troubled man, but none of his mental, emotional, or substance-abuse problems connect him to the murder of Martha Moxley. Whether the Moxley murder and investigation created these illnesses or merely exacerbated existing problems he already had is not for me to determine. I do know that constant suspicion and pressure can illicit some very bizarre behavior in people. Littleton has not acted differently from many policemen I have known who cracked under stress.

To this day, Frank Garr and the Greenwich police still consider Ken Littleton a suspect. In treating Littleton as a hostile suspect, they lost a valuable source of information, probably the one person outside the immediate Skakel family who knows the most about the events of October 30, 1975. The police should have treated him with trust and respect. Even if they thought he was a suspect, they had no good reason to treat him like one. They should have groomed Littleton instead of grilling him. Then maybe he would have been more forthcoming, and the investigation might not have taken such a toll on him. They might even have solved the case.

Why I don't think Ken Littleton committed the crime:

1. Littleton had no connection with Martha. From the crime scene and body we know that the victim knew the suspect. Ken Littleton didn't know her. She didn't go to school at Brunswick (an all-boys school) or nearby Greenwich Academy. She might have met him once at the Skakel house when he was baby-sitting, although there are no indications that they did meet. Instead, the police clung to this possibility because it was the only known connection they had between the victim and the man they wanted to be her murderer.

2. Littleton has an alibi. He can account for his time the night of the murder better than anyone else in the Skakel house. While the kids were running around outside, driving friends home and returning at all hours, Ken was in the master bedroom unpacking. Then he spent the rest of the evening watching *The French Connection*. While other suspects have had trouble with their alibis, Littleton has always stuck to the same story.

3. Littleton has cooperated with authorities and apparently never worried about prov-

ing his own innocence. In all of his contacts with police and private investigators, Littleton seemed more concerned with the innocence or culpability of Thomas and Michael than his own involvement.

4. Littleton had no motive. The murder of Martha Moxley was a rage-based attack by someone who knew her and who wanted to be or was sexually involved with her. As detectives investigated his background, they found that as a big, good-looking guy, Littleton never had trouble with women. However bizarre some of his behavior may have been in the years following the murder, he does not show a propensity toward extreme physical violence.

5. Littleton had no opportunity. He wasn't familiar with the house or the neighborhood. If the murder occurred shortly before 10:00 P.M., how could he have gotten back inside the Skakel house and been calm, clean, and composed at 10:03 when Thomas walked into the master bedroom to watch television?

6. Littleton had no money, no powerful family behind him, no clout. If Littleton had murdered Martha Moxley, he would not have gotten away with it.

15

Suspect: Thomas Skakel

Tommy was bad . . .
—*Steve Carroll*

Though they won't say it publicly, many in the Greenwich police and the Connecticut state's attorney office apparently believe that Thomas Skakel killed Martha Moxley.

When Thomas passed a polygraph on November 9, police focused on other possible suspects. Then, on December 11, Geoffrey Byrne and Helen Ix came forward with their eyewitness reports of Thomas and Martha engaging in sexual horseplay. While it is not known why they waited so long to give this account, both Ix and Byrne repeatedly stated that they did not think Thomas could have killed Martha.

By the time Ix and Byrne came forward, there were no clues supporting the Turnpike Transient Theory, Ed Hammond had been cleared, and no one was looking closely at Ken Littleton yet. The police seem to have come to the conclusion that Thomas was the murderer by process of elimination. They chased convenient suspects and came up empty. It always came back to Tommy, the most inconvenient suspect they had. He was the only one seen with the victim near the assumed time of death, and the murder weapon came from his house. In addition to these clues, Thomas's medical history, emotional difficulties, and disciplinary problems, all indicated a troubled and possibly violent young man.

As discussed earlier, his medical problems began at the age of four, when he fell from a moving car. The impact resulted in linear fractures on both sides of his skull. According to Sutton Associates, several doctors have concluded that this injury caused mental and emotional problems.

By all accounts, Thomas was a high-strung child. Susan Yuzna, a former nanny of the Skakel family, wrote that "Tommy Skakel was the most disturbed child I have ever met."

A boyhood friend described a home movie he has of a birthday party. All of his friends are sitting at the table, except for Thomas, who is running around like a madman.

Thomas was "definitely manipulative," said one former classmate. He could be charming at times to get what he wanted from someone. If he didn't get what he wanted, he wasn't charming at all. "You either played his game or you didn't play with Tommy," the classmate said.

When he didn't get what he wanted, Thomas would throw temper tantrums. Despite a prescription for the drug Dilantin to control his hyperactivity, Thomas remained a wild and often uncontrollable boy. Even Rushton Skakel confirmed this in his statements to the police.

This is not a complete picture of Thomas Skakel. He is also described as being somewhat shy, well-liked, and a good athlete. I believe that these other descriptions, the "quiet Tommy," are the result of his being in a place or situation where he did not feel comfortable. At Belle Haven, Whitby, and Windham, Thomas Skakel lived a life sheltered by wealth and power. The people who describe him as being "nice" or "quiet" are often people who did not know him very well or only saw him when he was on good behavior.

Among the people who misjudged Thomas Skakel are members of the Greenwich Police Department. Despite the history of trouble the Skakel boys had caused, the Greenwich police at first refused to believe that Thomas could have committed the murder.

Since they began by thinking he could not have done it, the first police interview of Thomas Skakel was very casual, even though they knew he was the last person seen with Martha. When the police realized that the golf club came from the Skakel house and suspicion began to focus on Thomas, he and his family had already been interviewed several times. During each interview, Thomas probably learned more about the investigation than the police learned about him.

The afternoon Martha's body was found, Thomas attended a field hockey game at Rye Country Day School in Rye, New York. He was wearing a big red cowboy hat and joking around. Witnesses say that they felt he could not have behaved that way if he had just murdered Martha. Thomas attended Martha Moxley's funeral, where he stood apart from his friends and family. After the funeral, Dorthy Moxley came up and gave him a hug.

On November 3, detectives Brosko and Lunney requested Rushton Skakel's permission to give Thomas a polygraph. Both Rushton and Thomas agreed that he would take the test. In the state of Connecticut, you are considered an adult at the age of seventeen. Thomas was seventeen at the time, so his parent's permission was not necessary. I'd like to think the Greenwich police knew the law and were just giving Rushton a courtesy. Even then, they were treating Thomas with more deference than they treated Ed Hammond. I wonder what would have happened if Rushton had simply said no. I imagine the Greenwich police would have just walked away, considering the polygraph a dead issue.

The polygraph was administered that same evening in Bethany. Thomas was given three tests, all inconclusive. Rushton and Thomas were driven back to their home and arrangements were made for another test to be taken. Captain Tom Keegan said that Thomas had not been sleeping, "He was too washed out, like a wet rag." While the polygraph examiner felt that Thomas failed the polygraph because of his physical condition, the detectives felt it was because he had something to hide.

Thomas was given a second polygraph on November 9. Although he passed the test, the polygraph examiner's report is not included in the police record—even though every other polygraph report is. And the daily police reports make no mention of Thomas being taken to the examiners. If these documents exist, why were they redacted? Did Tom Keegan edit them out of the released police record because he thought they might be used as evidence for Thomas's defense? Didn't he know that complete and unaltered police records must be provided to the defense on discovery?

Keegan himself admitted to Len Levitt that Thomas passed the polygraph. Levitt obtained tapes of the polygraph interview and stated that the questioning was not thorough or well framed. "It went like this, 'Is your name Thomas Skakel? Did you kill Martha Moxley?'" Levitt said. During the polygraph, Thomas was never asked what time he left Martha. His lawyers frequently state that he passed two polygraphs but have not furnished documentation to support that claim.

Just because Thomas was submitted to polygraph examinations doesn't mean he was under great suspicion. After all, the Greenwich police gave polygraphs to at least a dozen people, many of whom they cannot have seriously considered suspects. Once Geoffrey Byrne and Helen Ix told police about the sexual horseplay, the police began to change their minds about Thomas.

The investigators developed a hypothesis about the murder: Thomas wanted to have sex with Martha. She refused. As she started walking, then running home, Thomas chased her. He picked up a golf club along the way. Trying to stop her, he hooked her with the club. Unfortunately, he hit her on the side of the head and knocked her down. Once he had her down, he began a maniacal attack. When the golf club head snapped off, he stabbed her in the neck with the broken shaft. With the shaft still in her neck, he stood on it and snapped it off. Then he took the piece of shaft out of her neck—without leaving any fingerprints—and dragged her body underneath the tree. Her body safely hidden from view, Thomas pulled down her pants and panties. He still wanted to have sex with her. Something stopped him. Perhaps he was interrupted by someone. Or else he could not perform.

This hypothesis raises a lot of questions. The two most important ones are: How could the Greenwich detectives' attitude toward the suspect change from "Tommy Skakel, good ballplayer" to "maniacal attacker" in less than two months, with no new evidence but the Ix and Byrne statements? If Thomas was the murderer, how did he pass a polygraph?

The Greenwich police felt Thomas's medical and psychological history could prove that he was capable not only of murder but of blocking out any memory of it. During interrogations, Thomas would reportedly draw a blank whenever injuries to Martha were discussed. They believed Thomas had a violent fit accompanied by a blackout, and his medical and psychological history would show that he was prone to such attacks.

Psychological and medical records can be rich sources of information and even evidence, but they only show the potential or predisposition to commit an act. First you have to establish evidence that the person committed the crime; then such records can be useful to ascertain motive. Once you establish probable cause to believe the suspect committed the act, it would be possible, even easy, to obtain a search warrant for his records.

On December 16, Detective Jim Lunney received an authorization letter to obtain Thomas's hospital, medical, psychological, and school records. The detectives were able to obtain some important information from a neurologist who treated Thomas after his head injury in 1965. On January 20–21 that path of investigation was shut down when Chris Roosevelt and others convinced Rushton to rescind cooperation and hire a lawyer to represent Thomas. Once Manny Margolis came on board and formally withdrew cooperation of the Skakel family, the Greenwich police investigation was effectively over.

The Greenwich detectives had built their investigation on voluntary cooperation. They didn't know how to investigate uncooperative suspects. During the months when the Skakel family had been cooperating, the Greenwich police had missed their opportunity to make a case against Thomas.

Once Margolis cut off access to his client, detectives Steve Carroll and Jim Lunney still tried to interview Thomas whenever they could. "If we saw him on the avenue," Steve Carroll recalled, "we would always make a point to ask him questions, even try to badger him, that was our job."

On April 14, 1976, Jim Lunney saw Thomas celebrating his eighteenth birthday at Boodles, a local bar. Lunney was with a Detroit homicide investigator brought on to advise Greenwich on the case. Lunney walked up to Thomas and asked him to come into a private room and talk. There he told the boy, "I may be on this case for a hundred years, but I'm going to prove you did it or you didn't do it."

In the spring of 1976, Thomas spent two weeks in Ireland, staying with his aunt Pat Skakel Cuffe. His family claimed that the trip had been planned long in advance, but it was a rather convenient hideout for the young suspect. While it was widely reported that he had taken off to Switzerland, I found no evidence supporting those claims. After returning to the States, Thomas left Brunswick School and tried to attend a school in New York, but parents objected to his presence. He ended up graduating from Vermont's Vershire Academy in 1977.

Thomas enrolled in Elmira College in upstate New York, but had to leave the school in June 1978 for academic reasons. He moved to New York City, where he briefly attended the New School for Social Research in spring term 1979. During the early

1980s, he was living and working in Los Angeles. He traveled throughout the world, in Europe, Africa, and Latin America, and contracted malaria in Mexico. At one point, he claimed to be an environmentalist, working to save the Borneo rhino and Cuba's ivory-billed woodpecker.

In May 1989, Thomas married Anne Maitland Gillman, a Boxford, Massachusetts, native who worked for the retail clothing firm Banana Republic. The two settled down in Pound Ridge, New York. Thomas had a New York real estate license but had trouble getting clients. Instead, he worked in New York City for Harco International, a trade corporation with big-time political and financial connections.

Harco International was founded by Harvey Hamment, a power broker between the Soviet government and American business interests. Hamment's mentors were former CIA chief Bill Casey and his law partner Gerald Dichtler. The company's personnel included several high-ranking military and espionage retirees, as well as businessmen with extensive foreign ties. As one former Harco associate I will call Jay Edgar described it, "Harco was at the time a hotbed of activity of trade with Russia." The company was in a good position to profit from the recent collapse of the Soviet Union.

Although in his early thirties, Thomas was an errand boy around the office. He was obviously connected and not just through the Kennedys. "It was almost like the fact that he was an erstwhile Kennedy cousin was a blemish," Edgar said.

Edgar went on to describe that he "got the feeling at the time that they really protected Thomas, and were overprotective of him." Company officials were careful about to whom Thomas talked and often questioned associates about their dealings with him. "It almost felt as if Tommy was there because he needed a safe place to make a living," Edgar said, "where people wouldn't screw with him, where he would be protected, and where there was enough inherent clout around the office that he wouldn't be aggravated."

He socialized with Thomas a few times and thought it was odd that Thomas's attractive wife was kept at home and never came into the city with him. Whenever he and Thomas went out, company officials made sure Edgar kept an eye on him.

He describes Thomas as "a nice kid, a little bit nerdish." Thomas had a tendency to drink too much, and when he drank he loosened up a little. Even then Thomas was still very reserved and did not talk openly.

"It was almost like the kid was a little snakebit," Edgar said. "I think his dad probably grabbed him by the scruff of the neck and tossed him in the office and said, stay there, do what you're told, keep your nose clean, don't talk too much."

While in New York, Thomas socialized with his family, including cousins John Kennedy Jr. and William Kennedy Smith. In 1991 when Smith went on trial for rape, the Martha Moxley murder was back in the spotlight. Soon the Skakel family had hired

Sutton Associates. The medical and psychological data and conclusions, doctor's reports, memos, and interview statements in the following pages come from the Sutton files.

One of the first things Sutton did was contact their former FBI colleagues at the Academy Group to develop a profile of the murderer. As a result of that profile, Sutton concluded that "the probable offender shares many obvious characteristics with Tommy Skakel (as well as other leading suspects)." These characteristics include: "the offender was between fourteen and eighteen years of age, resided within easy walking distance of the victim's residence, was in the same socio-economic status as the victim, had regular interaction with the victim, would have experienced strong sibling rivalry tendencies, would have experienced behavioral problems both at school and at home and was under the influence of drugs and/or alcohol at the time of this crime."

The Sutton Associates files contained the following comment: "It seems that Tommy and his brother Michael were exceptionally difficult children who suffered from remarkably similar behavior disorders." In 1971, when Thomas and Michael were twelve and ten, respectively, they were both sent to see Dr. Ellen Blumingdale, a psychologist. This was prompted by the temper outbursts that both boys had displayed and their constant fighting with each other.

In an interview with the Sutton investigators,

Rushton Skakel Jr. stated: "Mom had no control over Tom. If he got mad, there was nothing she could do about it." When Rushton Sr. was home, "father would wallop him," Rush Jr. said. When their father wasn't home, which was often, the family would threaten to call Mr. Phelps, a neighbor who was big and powerful, to handle Thomas.

"At times I think Tom brought mother to tears," Rush Jr. said. When their parents were away, "things would get out of hand. You could depend on Tom acting up.

"Father began to drink much more intensively after Mother's death," Rush Jr. told the Sutton Associates. "This appears to have become progressively worse. He was in High Watch Sanitarium for two weeks in February 1976 after an intensive drinking bout." Rush Jr. described Thomas as doing "a fair amount of drinking," although he did say that Thomas was often more easygoing when intoxicated. He also characterized Thomas as being "generally impatient and impulsive," according to a document in the files.

After the Skakels had rescinded cooperation, the Greenwich police hired Dr. M. Hale, from the Yale University School of Medicine, as a consultant. The police gave Dr. Hale access to the few medical records they had of Thomas, mostly pertaining to his head injury as a young child. Without any contact with the subject, Dr. Hale made the following diagnosis: "Tommy might be inflicted with an organic neurological problem that could have resulted in a violent outburst that could have resulted in the brutal murder of Martha Moxley."

Hale based his theory on a report written by Dr. Camp, the neurologist who examined Thomas at age eight. Camp's report indicated that at age four Thomas fell from a moving car. Thomas struck his head, suffering a linear left-parietal fracture of the skull. He was unconscious for ten hours and hospitalized for two weeks.

Immediately after the accident, there were changes in Thomas's personality. Dr. Camp described Thomas as becoming introspective and less happy, subject to temper tantrums and outbursts of anger: "He would rant and rave, be extremely noisy, and on one occasion put his fist through a door. . . . On another occasion he pulled a phone out of the wall."

The Skakel family hired Dr. Stanley Lesse of New York City to supersede Dr. Hale's findings in the event of a trial. Tom Sheridan controlled most of the information given to Sutton Associates, providing full reports in some areas but writing digests and memos concerning more sensitive data. In a memo dated January 9, 1979, Sheridan wrote: "I have the distinct impression at this writing that Dr. Hale is being used by the Greenwich police to scare Mr. Skakel and entrap him into admissions which might implicate one or more of his sons. In any event, Mr. Skakel didn't fall for that trap and did follow a very reasonable approach of consultation with Dr. Lesse."

When Thomas first visited Dr. Lesse, the doctor asked him why he was there. Thomas answered that "he was a suspect as far as Martha Moxley's murder was concerned and that there was a desire to rule out any possibility of an organic or psychological problem that could have precipitated violent behavior that might have resulted in her death." Whether Thomas used such clinically precise language or not, he knew why he was there. He was aware of the significance of this examination. He also was aware of what kind of responses he should be giving. Dr. Lesse conducted several interviews and examinations, including a "truth serum" test, giving Thomas a dose of nearly half a gram of sodium amytal dissolved in water.

Based on his own observations, as well as Thomas's medical records, Dr. Lesse wrote a report dated May 11, 1976. In the report, Lesse stated that "Tommy was a problematic and often unruly child," affected by the death of his mother and the alcoholism of his father. The doctor's conclusion, which the Skakels and their lawyers used as "proof" that Thomas did not kill Martha, reads as follows:

1. This patient does not have epilepsy, nor does he evidence any organic brain defects.

2. The patient does not manifest significant referential or paranoid behavior patterns. There is no evidence of any malignant sociopathic trends.

3. I could not document after repeated interviews, including a sodium amytal interview,
   that Thomas Skakel was responsible for the
   death of Martha Moxley.

4. I do not find any evidence that Thomas
   Skakel is a psychosocial risk to his family or
   to his community.

While the Sutton Associates were not given the
sodium amytal transcripts, they did have notes from
Lesse's other interviews with the suspect. Thomas's
answers to Lesse do not dramatically differ from what
we know of his statements to the police, except they
give us a few pertinent details that, in light of other
information, turn out to be fairly revealing.

"The patient was questioned as to his conversation with Martha Moxley. 'I spoke to Martha for
five minutes. Maybe it was two minutes, maybe
more.' He was asked 'What did you speak about?'
'I can't remember what we talked about. I remember when we broke up, she asked whether I wanted
to meet later and go out hacking. I told her I
couldn't because I didn't have time and I had
homework to do.'"

As we know, there was no homework assignment that night. Nor, if there had been, was there
much chance that Thomas would go inside and do
homework after drinking several beers and cocktails
and fooling around with a pretty girl.

According to Tom Sheridan's memo: "Tommy

functioned poorly in school, and lacked motivation for his scholastic endeavors. . . . Some degree of Tommy's disinterest in academic achievement is attributed, by Dr. Lesse, to a general lack of emphasis placed on scholastic endeavors by the Skakel family."

In his interview with Lesse, Thomas stated: "After I gave Andrea the keys, I went up to my room. I spent about five minutes with the group before going up to my room. I studied English, reading something about log cabins. We were studying the Puritans. I studied for about five minutes. Then I needed a book that was in the guest room. I was on the third floor and that was downstairs. I was in the guest room for about five or ten minutes and I brought the book back to my room. After another five or ten minutes I went down to Dad's room to watch television with Ken and then I went back up to sleep."

About Martha, Thomas is clearly evasive, even trying to point the blame at his brother. He says: "I never knew her. She was a good friend of Michael's. I met her two or three times before that." When asked, "Was she a sexy girl?" Thomas replied, "She did not appear to be a very sexy girl to me." Dr. Lesse asked, "Was she pretty?" Thomas answered, "She was kind of pretty. She was quiet in her own way."

If Thomas were not somehow culpable, why would he feel he had to lie about his own sexual feelings toward Martha? Her diary entries prove that he was making sexual advances. Any photo from the period shows that she was a very attractive girl. Not only did Thomas deny any sexual interest in Martha herself, but he also denied any kind of sexual activity, from intercourse to masturbation.

At times during the interview, Thomas tried to sound like a prude.

> Dr. Lesse: What sort of questions were you asked at the police station?
>
> Thomas: They questioned me about a lot of things. They questioned me about whether I had any sexual feelings or sexual desires or any sexual activity with Martha or whether I approached her sexually. I didn't like that because that's not like me or my family. They questioned me in pretty hard terms, terms that we don't commonly use. They questioned me many times with regard to the details of what had taken place and what I had done.

Dr. Lesse commented: "He was questioned intensively with regard to strong sexual desires directed towards girls or to Martha Moxley. I could not elicit any evidence of strong feelings towards the murdered girl."

The doctor believed Thomas was being truthful and even tried to support the Turnpike Transient Theory: "The patient did mention that there had been some kind of prowler in the area some time prior to October 30th."

Whoever analyzed the doctor's report for Sutton viewed Lesse's conclusions with skepticism. They felt that either Dr. Lesse was "tainted by a sympathetic disposition toward the patient which inhibited his ability to notice obvious inconsistencies" or else that "Tommy, to some degree or another, successfully deceived Dr. Lesse."

One thing is certain: Thomas was afraid of the sodium amytal needle. "As the needle was inserted, he became extremely apprehensive once again, began to whimper and at times cried openly, 'Please take it out, please take it out!' He held his body rigid and had to be reassured that nothing would go amiss."

Was Thomas afraid of the needle? Or was he afraid of the truth?

The next doctor to examine Thomas did not know who he was or whether he might be connected to a murder. Lesse arranged for the boy to undergo a battery of psychological tests under the pseudonym Thomas Butler, at Presbyterian Hospital's Division of Psychology on March 15, 1976. The tests would be administered by Patrick de Gramont, Ph.D. We can assume that he was operating under more objective conditions than Dr. Lesse, and his findings bear that assumption out.

Gramont found Thomas "to be a well-behaved and congenial young man. . . . He worked hard at his tasks, and appeared to enjoy his success." However, when Gramont analyzed the test results, he "arrived at some grave conclusions with regards to Tommy's state of mind, emotional development, and capacity for impulsive and dangerous behavior." Gramont also seemed to corroborate Dr. Hale's organic-neurological impairment theory.

The psychologist administered Bender-Gestalt designs—a series of cards containing abstract designs the subject is asked to copy onto a blank sheet of paper. The test measures visual-motor perception and can indicate both emotional and developmental problems.

Thomas's results "suggested constriction, depression, and low self-esteem, with possible impulse control problems associated with a need of structure." In the figure drawings, Thomas drew a healthy and content middle-aged man, while the female figure "is poorly executed and looks ill at ease and somewhat menacing."

Gramont noted both immaturity and impulsiveness in the test results:

> Thomas has had a good deal of difficulty adjusting to the demands and responsibilities of adolescence, and his judgment and reality-testing are highly erratic at this time. His outward adultlike manner is, in his words, a "mask," and inwardly, he feels, at times, very much like a passive, helpless child. As such, he experiences a profound sense of inadequacy, and an inability to assert himself sufficiently to survive in a competitive society. While suspicious of the motives of others, he

is easily led, and unable to establish his own needs and goals. The material also suggests that this passive orientation is a defense against the expression of a great deal of underlying resentment and hostility. And that grandiose fantasies and antisocial acting out appear to be the only release available to him, at a time when he feels so very unsuccessful and unaccomplished in his life.

Gramont commented, "His low esteem and repressed drive are particularly evident in sexual confusion."

During sentence completion tests, used to assess the patient's attitudes toward family and peers and reveal anxiety and/or guilt, Thomas was asked to finish various sentences. These are some of his responses:

"Usually he felt that sex . . . 'made him unhappy.'
"After he made love to her . . . 'he got drunk.'
"My sexual desires . . . 'are very low.'
"As a child my greatest fear was . . . 'mother.'
"When she refused him, he . . . 'slapped her.'
"A man would be justified in beating a woman . . . 'who did not do as he said.'"

Gramont: "He appears to have little insight into the extent of his underlying resentment and hostility; nor does he appear to fully recognize the relationship of these feelings to both his unresolved guilt feelings over his mother's death three years ago, nor to the resentment that underlies his guilt feelings."

Other tests suggested "psychosexual confusion, based on an identification with mother, in addition to the conflicted feelings of anger and guilt." This lead Gramont to conclude: "Thomas's anger is apparently readily released in relation to women."

During the evaluation, Thomas had an IQ tested at 113. The Greenwich police believed he was slow, even mildly retarded.

Gramont's test results and commentary led a Sutton analyst to comment: "Dr. Gramont has presented a series of objective findings which, especially in light of speculation surrounding Tommy's involvement in the murder of Martha Moxley, are somewhat alarming. . . . It seems odd, then, how little attention Dr. Lesse paid to Dr. Gramont's findings."

Sutton Associates themselves interviewed Thomas Skakel on October 7, 1994. By then, he was running a bed-and-breakfast in Stockbridge, Massachusetts, where he still lives with his wife and two children. During the interview, Thomas broke down sobbing and told the investigators that he hadn't left Martha Moxley at 9:30 P.M. Instead he had spent an additional twenty minutes or so with her behind his house.

According to the Sutton investigators' notes from that interview:

> They began an extended (twenty minute) kissing and fondling session which includes

mutual fondling (breast, vagina, and penis), and is concluded when both masturbate partner to orgasm. At this point (approximately 9:50 P.M.), both Martha and Tom rearrange their clothes and Martha says good night. She is last seen by Tom hurrying across the rear lawn towards her house. Tom stated that he did not open Martha's brassiere; however, he did fondle her breasts while his hand was under her outer garments and shirt. He further stated that he opened Martha's pants, slightly pushing them down. He fondled her vagina without pushing her panties down. Thomas Skakel stated he soiled his clothing (underwear) when Martha brought him to orgasm, using her hand on his penis. He stated that upon leaving Martha, he re-entered his house, but never changed his clothing or showered.

During the same interview, Thomas said that prior to the encounter he had a brief conversation with Martha while he was standing at the kitchen door and she was outside in the driveway. He said that he told her to wait inside the house for him.

Under hypnosis, Julie Skakel stated that at 9:30, "I could see Martha walking around the back fence and about the same time that Tommy closed the door, Andrea tried to get in the front door, but she couldn't, so she rang the doorbell. I could see Tommy slowly walking through the kitchen."

Julie placed Martha outside by the back fence when Thomas said she was inside waiting for him to answer the front door. Thomas's story seemed to imply that Martha's waiting for him indicated she was a willing participant in a sexual encounter.

During a subsequent interview on February 6, 1995, Thomas changed his story again. This time he said he didn't tell Martha to wait for him inside. Instead, when he came back from giving Andrea the keys, he walked back through the house and looked to his left. Martha was standing inside, and Thomas claimed to have been surprised to see her. When asked why she was waiting there, he replied, "Maybe she wanted more of Tommy."

During the October 1994 interview, Thomas said there was initially some friction between Martha and him. She forcibly rejected him twice. In the February 1995 interview, he said only that he had asked Martha if she wanted to "make love" and she had said no.

His alcohol consumption that evening is also in question. Ken Littleton told the police in 1975 that he and the older Skakel children (including, presumably, Thomas) each had one beer at dinner. In the first Sutton interview Thomas said he had four or five beers at dinner and then another beer at home, before he was with Martha. In the second interview, he said that in addition to a total of five or six beers, he also had two scotches at dinner. Seven to eight measures of alcohol within three hours is a lot of booze for a seventeen-year-old boy.

There are several other minor discrepancies between the two interviews. In October 1994, Thomas said he didn't go to the Terriens' because he was tired. In February 1995, Thomas said he did not remember why he decided not to go. Of course he didn't want to admit that he stayed behind because he wanted to be with Martha. That would reveal interest and intention, which Thomas would rather not disclose.

In the first interview, Thomas said that he did not recall speaking to Mrs. Moxley in the early-morning hours of October 31. In the second interview, he said that he remembered the conversation.

Just when did Thomas learn that Martha was missing? Julie stated that Mrs. Moxley first called sometime around 1:15–1:30 A.M.

Julie related: "I went upstairs and asked Tommy where she was, when the last time he had seen her. He said the back door, and then he had to study for a test. He was tired. So, I went back downstairs and told Mrs. Moxley the same thing."

At 1:30 A.M. Thomas already had his back-door/homework alibi ready. Was he merely embarrassed about their sexual encounter? Or did he know that something had happened to Martha?

During the February 1995 interview, Sutton investigators keyed on these discrepancies but did not get satisfactory answers. Their files stated: "Tommy could offer no clarification. Generally, his responses would be limited to 'I don't know,' or else he would not reply at all."

Steve Carroll noted the same evasion in his police interviews with Thomas. "Every time anything came up about Martha, he would draw a blank," Steve said. "And it was so obvious, because his whole demeanor would change."

Thomas's medical and psychological condition as described in the Sutton files clearly indicate that he was a troubled young man. But was he capable of murder? I believe that his continued denials and evasions, combined with his family's lack of cooperation with authorities, shows some level of complicity.

If Thomas Skakel was not involved in the murder:

1. Why did he change his story after seventeen years?
2. Why did he lie to the Greenwich police in numerous interviews and statements?
3. Why did his father rescind cooperation?
4. Why is he willing to endure nationwide suspicion of being a murderer rather than cooperate with authorities?

16

Suspect: Michael Skakel

. . . But Michael was a lot worse.
—*Steve Carroll*

While his brother Thomas was a suspect from day one, Michael Skakel has avoided scrutiny and suspicion. Michael is two years younger than Thomas and was fifteen years old at the time of Martha Moxley's murder. He was with Martha that evening, having met her a half hour before Thomas showed up. He was known to have some sort of romantic involvement with her. Michael would have been considered a suspect, but he appeared to have an alibi that covered the presumed time of death. Once that alibi is called into question, or the time frame of Martha's murder is expanded, then Michael becomes a very strong suspect.

In a family known for being undisciplined and out of control, Michael Skakel was the wildest of them all. The anecdotes about his dangerous behavior are endless. Neighbors, friends, police, and

investigators recount such stories as Michael skate-
boarding down the stairs, skiing and driving like a
maniac, drinking, fighting with his brothers,
threatening other members of his family, and
killing animals.

Michael had a hair-trigger temper that could
be set off easily. He was high-strung and hyperac-
tive. When told he couldn't do something, he
would often throw a fit. After his mother died,
Michael became even more difficult and more violent. Rushton would have to sit on Michael to get
him under control, or call in his neighbor Mr.
Phelps.

His father often had no other choice than to let
Michael get away with bad behavior. At a local
sporting goods store, Michael would walk right in
and take things. The owner would call Rushton
and tell him what Michael had just stolen. His
father, then, would say to put it on the bill.

Michael was feared in the neighborhood and
even in his own family. According to the Sutton
Associates files, Tom Sheridan noted that Rushton
Skakel told him "Julie is frightened to death of
Michael." He had a violent and antagonistic sibling
competition with his older brother Thomas.
Squabbles between the two brothers frequently
became violent.

The Greenwich police knew about Michael's
reputation for wild and violent behavior. Several of
them thought he was capable of murder. Why
wasn't he considered a suspect?

On October 30, 1975, at around 9:00 P.M., Michael, Martha Moxley, Geoffrey Byrne, and Helen Ix were listening to music in the Skakel family Lincoln parked in the driveway. Martha and Michael sat in the front seat. Helen and Geoff were in the rear. At approximately 9:15 P.M., Thomas came out of the house to retrieve a cassette tape from the car. He encountered the other kids and began talking to Martha. Soon he entered the car and sat next to Martha. Thomas put his hand on Martha's leg. Martha told him to stop it. There is no record of anything Michael said or did during this time.

Around 9:30, Jim Terrien, John Skakel, and Rush Skakel Jr. came from the house and told everybody to get out of the car. John and Rush were going to drive Jim back to the Terrien house on Cliffdale Road, some twenty minutes away, and watch *Monty Python* there. Michael decided to go with them. He asked Martha to come along, but she declined. Thomas said that he would stay at home. Michael reportedly got in the car with his brothers and cousin. The Skakel Lincoln took off.

Embarrassed by Martha's flirtation with Thomas, Helen and Geoff decided to go home. As they walked together through the Skakel backyard, they saw Martha and Thomas continuing their sexual roughhousing.

At approximately 9:35 P.M., Fred Sibley, a young busboy at the Homestead Inn, was walking home down Field Point Road. A black Lincoln came screeching around a corner, nearly hitting Fred. As he jumped out of the way, the Lincoln tires squealed and the car fishtailed down the road. A white male passenger inside the car shouted "Asshole!" as they drove away. When I interviewed him in 1997, Fred could not recall how many people were in the car.

Michael was reportedly at the Terriens' until 11:00 P.M. He said he returned home at 11:20 P.M., went right up to bed, and fell asleep until the next morning.

Sometime after 9:30 the next morning Dorthy Moxley walked across Walsh Lane to the Skakel house. She knocked at the back door off the sunporch. Moments later, Michael opened the door. Dorthy asked if he or anyone had seen Martha. Michael said, "No." Dorothy noted that Michael looked pale, disheveled, and hungover, as if he hadn't slept the night previous.

When Martha's body was found, Michael was at home. As the crowd of neighbors, police, and media converged on 38 Walsh Lane, Rush Skakel Jr. told investigators years later, "Michael seemed to be the most curious one. He was going nuts. He was in an obnoxious mood."

Michael was outside in front of the Skakel house when Peter Coomoraswamy walked up and told him, "They found Martha. Sheila was the one who found her." Peter and Michael sat on the lawn and watched the activity. Michael spoke to reporters from *Greenwich Time,* the Associated

Press, and the *New York Times,* telling them that the last time he saw Martha was with his brother Tommy, at 9:30 the night before. This is the first time Thomas was placed with Martha that night, and it made all the papers the next morning. Largely on the basis of Michael's statements to the press, Thomas Skakel was the prime suspect, at least in the public's mind.

A *Greenwich Time* reporter on the scene described Michael as "an exuberant, freckled-faced lad." At one point a reporter walked up to Michael and asked, "Is it true your mother was a steak choke victim?" Michael burst out crying. He was out of control when Great Lakes Carbon attorney Jim McKenzie arrived at 5:15 P.M. "My first reaction to him was that he was the wildest of the group," McKenzie said. "I can't say he was in control. . . . He obviously had to be calmed down a little. He was a little hyper."

Detectives Jim Lunney and Ted Brosko were in the Skakel house by 3:00 P.M. Julie Skakel was the first to be interviewed by police. Michael was the second. He related that at approximately 9:10 P.M., Martha, Helen, and Geoff came to the back door of the Skakel house. He directed them to another door, then let them inside. They walked through the kitchen and out the side door into the driveway. Then they got into the car. He said they were sitting and talking in the car when Thomas came out, sat in the car, and started talking to them.

The police report does not quote Michael giving his alibi. It is not known when that alibi was first established, but Michael was eliminated as a suspect because of it. He wasn't given a polygraph, as one detective stated, "because we had no reason not to believe him." His brother John Skakel was given a polygraph and passed. Presumably, John was asked about the trip to the Terriens'. Since John passed the polygraph, police felt that the alibi covered Michael, Rush Jr., and Jim Terrien as well.

Early on, the Greenwich police had reason to suspect Michael's alibi. On November 5, 1975, detectives Steve Carroll and Jim Lunney interviewed Jim Terrien's sixteen-year-old sister Desneiges, trying to pinpoint the time the boys had left the Skakel residence. Desneiges said that when she went to bed at 10:00 P.M., her brother and the Skakel boys were not at the Terrien house. She heard their voices later that evening, but she was asleep and didn't know what time it was.

Dorthy Moxley phoned the Terriens sometime after midnight the night Martha was killed, and Jim's mother Georgeann Terrien answered. She had no knowledge of the Skakel boys being there, and after searching the house and grounds, couldn't find her son. Jim Terrien later told Sutton Associates that he had been with a married woman and would disclose her name only if he were subpoenaed.

Although the police did not consider Michael a suspect, they continued to get indications that perhaps they should take a closer look at him.

On March 9, 1976, the Skakel family gardener,

Franz Wittine, was reinterviewed by detectives Steve Carroll and Jim Lunney. By this time, Wittine had quit working for the Skakels and was now living in upstate New York. He told the police that he felt "everyone in the household had been treating Michael Skakel as if he knew something." He said that Michael's brothers and sister "were being exceptionally nice to Michael since the incident of Oct. 30, 1975." This was just a "gut feeling" on Wittine's part.

Early in the morning of March 5, 1978, Michael was driving the family Jeep on a local road in Windham, New York. As Michael drove near the scene of an accident, a responding police officer signaled him to stop. Instead, Michael nearly ran the officer down. He fled the scene, and during the ensuing chase ran the Jeep into a telephone pole. The car was wrecked, but both Michael and his passenger were unharmed.

Michael was arrested and charged with driving without a license, speeding, failure to comply, and driving while intoxicated. This was not the first time he had been in trouble in Windham. The Skakel family, and Michael in particular, had raised a lot of hell in the ski resort. Neighbors would constantly complain about the Skakel boys. Whenever something happened, their father or Tom Sheridan would bail them out.

For example, a former ski instructor at Windham said that one of the Skakels attacked a female ski-lift attendant when she tried to take an

illegal lift ticket from him. Despite the fact that
the incident was reported to the resort management, apparently nothing was done about it.

After his arrest for the March 5, 1978, accident, Michael pled guilty to all the charges except
the DWI. The case was held in abeyance. Later that
afternoon, a plane arrived at the local airport and
Michael was handcuffed and transported by two
attendants and a doctor to Elan, a private treatment
center and school for troubled youths in Maine.

Tom Sheridan had worked out the deal in
which the case was dismissed on the condition that
Michael attended Elan for at least six months. A
memo Sheridan wrote at the time and quoted in
the Sutton files stated that Michael was under "the
influence of heavy drinking or smoking pot or a
combination of both." He further wrote:

> The facts relating to the pleading and dis-
> position of those charges in Windham are
> not pertinent to this memo. . . . What
> should be noted, however, is the fact that
> in my interviewing of Michael on that
> occasion, he was obviously a disturbed per-
> son and hooked on either booze or pot. He
> showed little or no remorse for having
> nearly killed the companion in his car and
> when confronted with the potential prob-
> lem of a subsequent conviction for drunken
> driving, his only comment was, "Next
> time I won't get caught."

At the time, according to family sources, Michael was "plagued with serious emotional problems" and living "a reckless and drug-fueled existence." A friend of Michael's told me, "I just don't think his dad knew what the hell to do with him."

If Sheridan and the Skakels thought Elan would straighten Michael out, or at least keep him out of trouble, they were wrong.

The Elan School calls itself "an educational boarding college-preparatory and general academic school for adolescents with emotional, behavioral, or adjustment problems." That's a fancy way of saying Elan is a rich kid's reform school. Many of the students have severe emotional and/or substance abuse problems. The treatment methods are controversial. The cost in 1978 was $30,000 a year. Elan made so much money that its owner, Joe Ricci, became a millionaire in his thirties. He now owns Scarborough Downs racetrack, and has run unsuccessfully for governor of Maine.

When Michael first arrived at Elan, he was immediately taken to a trailer for a three-hour taped interview. In this interview, Michael was repeatedly asked why he thought he was there. He said something happened, but he wouldn't be specific. Whenever the interviewer pressed Michael for details, he would laugh.

At several points during the interview, Michael described a girl with a golf club embedded in her chest. Whenever he brought this up, he would laugh. The interviewer asked, "What are you laughing about, Michael? Here we have a young lady who has a golf club embedded in her chest, and you're laughing. What's so funny about that?"

Michael wouldn't answer.

"How did she die?"

Michael wouldn't answer.

"What happened?"

He just laughed.

The interviewer was convinced that Michael knew something, but he couldn't get him to admit anything.

That interview was not the only time Michael's involvement in the Moxley murder came up at Elan. A man I will call Lou Phillips phoned the *Unsolved Mysteries* tip line on February 15, 1996. According to the transcript, which was passed along to Frank Garr, Phillips said that he lived in the same house with Michael in Elan for two years during the late seventies, when both were there for drug and alcohol treatment. He further claimed that Michael had admitted to several people that he killed Martha Moxley with a golf club. According to Phillips, Michael made the confession in group therapy, saying he had killed her because he was drunk.

A document from the Sutton files claims, "Reportedly, Michael once even confessed to the murder of Martha Moxley in a therapy session while a patient at the Elan treatment center. He quickly recanted." The source of this information is unclear, and could be Lou Phillips, although it is not unreasonable to assume that Sutton and the Skakels had other sources at Elan.

A former Elan staffer told me: "Elan was probably a good place to hide, but Michael Skakel definitely didn't come there to seek treatment." Michael didn't want to cooperate, and what should have been a treatment center became a prison for him.

One week after he was initially admitted in March 1978, Michael attempted his first escape from the facility. He was taken into custody after a wild chase by Elan staffers. Michael successfully escaped on November 15, 1978, traveling to Boston and then on to New York before being returned to Elan by his brother Rushton. On November 29, 1978, he escaped yet again, remaining at large for nearly three weeks. Once again, he was returned to the facility by Rushton Jr.

After one of Michael's escapes from Elan, he was represented by attorney Bernadette Coomoraswamy, a Belle Haven neighbor who is now a federal judge.

The Sutton files stated that Michael was in Elan as late as 1991, but he did not stay there continuously. Starting in 1978 and continuing for at least the next ten years, Michael was shuttled around among numerous institutions, including Elan. Residence in these facilities not only kept Michael out of the house, and supposedly out of trouble, but also kept him shielded from investigators seeking to find out about his possible involvement in the Moxley murder.

In 1987 an informant I will call Batman met Michael Skakel at Father Martin's rehab facility in Aberdeen, Maryland. Michael was in Father Martin's for drug and alcohol treatment. Batman was there for a heroin and cocaine addiction. Batman became good friends with Michael, who told him his father had sent him away in the middle 1970s because of something that happened. Michael said he ended up in abusive treatment facilities for as long as two years in places like Maine and other locations in New England and throughout the country because his father wanted to keep him out of trouble and away from everyone.

"Michael was very reclusive, angry, and strong," Batman said. "Michael said that his family would kill him if he gave out certain information."

Batman remembered Michael telling him, "Something happened back home and the police were involved. Since then I've been in a whole lot of facilities. The police want to talk to me. So my family keeps moving me from one place to another because the police can't track you down."

Michael said that when he got out he planned to hit the talk-show circuit exposing abuse in rehabs.

"He was always angry when he talked about his family, used a lot of four-letter words," Batman said. "He really hated his dad for what he did to him."

Michael would take that anger out in violence. According to Batman, during a volleyball game

Michael spiked the ball and injured another patient. Instead of offering an apology, he reportedly said, "I haven't felt that good since I killed cats with a golf club."

At St. Martin's, Michael never had any visitors. During family week, he was one of the only patients who didn't have some family members come see him. Since the patient lists at such facilities are confidential, he didn't get any other visitors, like the Greenwich police. Batman said that's why Michael was shuttled in and out of different rehabs: "Once you sign into a facility like that it's pretty hard for the law to get you because they can't divulge information about patients."

Michael finally got out of the institutions in his early thirties. In the mid-1990s he graduated from Curry College, a Massachusetts school with a special program for students with learning disabilities. He got married and moved to Cohasset, Massachusetts, where his wife, Margot, worked as a golf pro at the local country club. Michael got a job as a driver for his cousin Michael Kennedy during his uncle Ted's 1994 reelection campaign. After Teddy won reelection, Michael went to work for a Boston real estate firm, but that didn't last.

He went back to work for Michael Kennedy, who served as head of Citizens Energy, a nonprofit energy company founded by Joe Kennedy II. According to company documents, Michael Skakel served as director of international programs for Citizens Energy, overseeing the implementation of the company's programs throughout Africa, Latin America, and the Caribbean.

In February 1996, Michael visited Cuba with his cousin Bobby Kennedy Jr. and a delegation from Citizens Energy. Meeting with Fidel Castro, Michael suggested that the Cuban leader turn an abandoned nuclear reactor into "the Atomic Hotel and Nightclub." Castro laughed, "It's a good idea. It has a wonderful view and plenty of clean water."

Things went sideways for Michael Skakel when he got friendly with Michael Kennedy's baby-sitter, a teenager with whom Kennedy was having an affair. Because of his "desire to help others," according to a Kennedy family source, Michael Skakel tried to discourage the affair. He befriended the girl and her parents. Once the mother found out about the affair, she reportedly attempted suicide, and Michael was there to talk her out of it. He also acted as messenger among the baby-sitter's father, Michael Kennedy, and Victoria Gifford Kennedy. The baby-sitter's father gave Michael Skakel several of Michael Kennedy's letters to his daughter. Michael Skakel gave those letters to Victoria in order to confirm the relationship existed. According to Michael Skakel, Victoria destroyed the letters without reading them.

Michael told fellow attendees at an AA meeting all about the affair. When the story broke in Boston newspapers, Michael was a source. Michael also spoke to the Norfolk County DA who was investigating the case, telling the DA that Kennedy committed statutory rape.

The Kennedys had another sex scandal. The baby-sitter and her family did not press charges. Michael Kennedy checked into an Arizona clinic for treatment of sex addiction. And Michael Skakel had to find a new line of work. He started lobbying for a settlement from Citizens Energy. Reportedly, Skakel got a package worth a quarter of a million dollars to work "freelance" for the company.

On New Year's Eve 1997, Michael Kennedy suffered a senseless accident on the slopes of Aspen Mountain. Despite warnings from the local ski patrol, he and his family were playing an improvised game of football on the ski slopes on the last run of the day. He ran headlong into a tree and died of massive head and spinal injuries.

The baby-sitter incident is pertinent in this case because Michael Skakel might have been jealous of his cousin, hoped to get him in trouble, and possibly get the girl for himself. Or, if he was sincerely trying to help her, his actions could have been motivated by unresolved guilt about a teenage girl who was killed in 1975.

Could Michael have killed Martha Moxley? While most aspects of the Academy Group profile fit both Skakel boys, a few pertinent details fit only Michael. The Academy Group believed the killer was sexually inexperienced, a habitual window peeper, and an emotional loner. These characteristics describe Michael more than Thomas. The younger Skakel's subsequent statements fit the profile even better.

In his January 9, 1979, memo Tom Sheridan noted that he felt the Greenwich police were using Dr. Hale "to scare Mr. Skakel and entrap him into admissions which might implicate one or more of his sons."

Note that Sheridan said, "one or more of his sons." Evidently he felt that more than one Skakel boy could have been involved in the murder. In another memo, dated June 6, 1978, Sheridan speculated that Michael could have killed Martha "and doesn't know it and possibly somebody else, i.e. Tommy, could have hidden the body."

There has always been speculation that two suspects participated in the death of Martha Moxley. Whether the crime involved one or two people, there are indications that the initial attack and the movement of the victim's body occurred in two stages, separated by a significant period of time.

First Martha was attacked in the driveway. Then she was dragged across the driveway and assaulted near the Japanese elm, where most of the blows were delivered. She lay there long enough to bleed out several pints of blood. Then she was dragged beneath the pine tree.

The Greenwich police believed that the murder occurred all at once, sometime between 9:35 and 10:00 P.M. They did not consider that it would have taken time for Martha to bleed enough to create the large pool of blood near the Japanese elm. They thought only one suspect was involved.

All that changed when Michael Skakel's statements to Sutton Associates became public. On August 4, 1992, Michael told Sutton investigator Willis Krebs that he had lied to police about going to bed after returning home from the Terriens' at 11:20–11:30. Instead, he had gone back out and was near or at the murder scene between 11:40 and 12:30. Len Levitt published his article about Michael's change of story on December 4, 1995. Coming more than twenty years after the murder, this revelation no doubt took the police off guard. Now Michael's 9:30–11:20 alibi didn't matter. Or at least it shouldn't have.

After Levitt's article ran, Frank Garr contacted Steve Carroll and told him that he now considered Michael a possible suspect. While they discussed various motives—sexual connection with the victim, possible jealousy, and sibling rivalry with his brother—Garr's prime reason for suspecting Michael was the fact that he had changed his story. With all this, Garr and Carroll still determined that yes, Michael could have done it, but he just wasn't there. They couldn't budge from their belief that the murder occurred between 9:35 and 10:00 P.M.

Here is Krebs's digest of Michael's statement:

Upon leaving the house, he ran towards Walsh Lane and after passing the Moxley residence, turned right into a driveway, walked to the end and approached a ground floor window of the house. Michael stated that he had been at the house on other occasions to look at the woman who resided therein (name unknown). This woman, on many previous occasions, would not be wearing clothing. On this occasion the woman was lying on a couch wearing some sort of night garment. After looking into this window for a short period of time, he walked to the Moxley's house, climbed a tree and looked into the room he thought was Martha's. He yelled at the window, "Martha, Martha," but there was no response. Michael then stated that he masturbated to orgasm in the tree. After climbing down, he stopped near a street light on Walsh Lane. Michael stated that he felt "someone's presence" in the area where Martha's body was eventually discovered. He yelled "into the darkness" and threw something at the trees. Still fearing what was there, he ran back to his house. He crossed in front of his house, and, finding all the doors locked, climbed to the second floor. He entered his room through his bedroom window. He felt he was out of the house between thirty and forty-five minutes, arriving home at sometime around 12:30 A.M. Once in his room, he went to sleep.

This isn't just Michael changing his story a little. He is stating that he knowingly lied to the police nineteen years prior on the very material issue of his whereabouts, quite possibly at the time of Martha's murder.

Let's examine his story more closely: Michael left the house at approximately 11:40 P.M. He ran past the Moxley house and peeped on a usually naked woman he regularly visited late at night. First, why did he run? Secondly, why was he very careful to describe that he was on Walsh Lane in front of the Moxley house? In my opinion, Michael's visit to the woman's house only gave him a reason to be seen running by the Moxley house.

It is very possible that the house where Michael regularly peeped was not another neighbor's but the Moxleys'. At 11:40 Dorthy Moxley was downstairs in the television room, wearing a nightgown and sleeping on the couch, just like the woman Michael described in his statement. Did he regularly peep on Dorthy, or was it Martha? Michael is careful to say that he didn't know if the third-floor window was Martha's. The Moxley house was huge. If Michael had not known that window was Martha's, he was very lucky to have chosen the right one. My reading of his statement indicates that Michael knew where her room was and had climbed that tree before, possibly to peep on her. But he can't admit that.

Michael's statement carefully accounts for his presence near the crime scene. The streetlight at the west end of the Moxley drive and Walsh Lane is the very area Michael described. Standing at that location, you can directly see the French doors and balcony of Rushton Skakel's bedroom, where Ken Littleton was staying the night of October 30, 1975.

The once loyal Littleton was no longer controlled by the Skakels. Michael could have seen him on the terrace or through the French doors. He could think, or be even certain, that Littleton saw him. Who knows what Littleton saw? Maybe Littleton doesn't even realize what he saw himself.

Michael described to Sutton Associates how he was disappointed that the woman he usually peeped on was wearing clothing. He then walked to the Moxley house, climbed a tree, and looked into the room he thought was Martha's. He yelled, "Martha, Martha," but received no response. While sitting in this tree, outside a room he was not sure was Martha's, Michael began masturbating, eventually reaching orgasm and ejaculating.

Even for Michael Skakel, this is strange behavior. Why would he make these embarrassing admissions nineteen years after the murder? Because he could have been seen on the Moxley property, he wanted to appear as if he thought Martha was still alive at that time, and most importantly he had to account for any of his semen that mysteriously turned up.

The murder occurred in 1975, when DNA was just three letters. By 1994 DNA fingerprinting was state of the art. Michael had to account for any genetic evidence that might be on the victim. If he was in a tree near her room, or next to the crime scene throwing something, a defense lawyer could argue that was why his semen was found on her dead body.

After climbing down from the tree, Michael specifically remembered stopping by a streetlight on Walsh Lane. The only streetlight in the area is the one directly between the crime scene and the rear of the Skakel house. That's twice that Michael put himself under that light. He thinks he was seen by someone.

While standing under the light, he felt some-one's presence in the area where Martha's body was found. He yelled into the darkness and threw something at the trees. Michael now said that fear-ing what was there, he ran back to his house. Once again Michael placed himself where he could have been seen, where he could have been heard yelling, and, of course, where he could have been seen mak-ing a swinging motion with an object.

Finally, Michael said that the doors were locked when he returned at 12:30 A.M. and he had to climb up to his second-floor bedroom window. Several people I have interviewed said that the doors were never locked in the Skakel house. Why would Michael have to climb inside?

If Michael had either killed or just moved Martha, he might not want to chance being seen by someone in the lighted house. At the very least, he would have blood spatters on his clothing and shoes. Walking into the house from the dark, he could not be sure that he wouldn't track in blood.

It's the same reason O. J. Simpson stopped under the light at his front door. That was the first time he realized he was leaving a blood trail.

In his own interviews with Sutton Associates, Ken Littleton clearly cast suspicion on Michael. He described Michael's sadistic behavior and speculated about whether Michael used drugs. Littleton recalled the weekend at Windham just after Martha's murder. Michael used a shotgun to shoot small animals. On another occasion, Michael bludgeoned a squirrel to death with a golf club. Littleton said he was sickened by Michael's behavior.

Littleton also cast doubt on Michael's alibi. "Are we sure Michael was in the car?" Littleton asked. The Sutton investigator attempted to press Littleton, but he would only say, "I have a definite feeling in my mind that the murder was committed after 10:30 at night." When asked why he made this statement, Littleton simply answered, "Because."

Maybe Littleton wasn't sure. Or maybe he made himself sound less certain than he actually was. He could have been afraid to tell everything he knew, so he dropped little clues to the investigators, hoping they would independently discover the facts.

When Littleton suggested that Michael might have gone out and thrown pebbles at the Moxley house, the investigator asked Littleton: "Did you see him [Michael] throwing pebbles at the window?"

Littleton answered, "No."

The investigator followed up with, "Would you tell us if you did?"

Again Littleton answered, "No."

Other information cast doubt on Michael's alibi. John Skakel was interviewed under hypnosis on May 4, 1993. As John relived the events of October 30, 1975, the interviewer repeatedly asked him where Michael was when he and Rush were at the Terriens'. John could not place Michael with them. While he did say that somebody else was with them, he couldn't identify the person as Michael. This same line of questioning was followed in separate interviews with John, receiving similar results. During an interview with the Sutton investigators, Julie Skakel stated, "No way did Michael go to the Terriens'."

Did Michael go to the Terriens'? It doesn't matter. Even if Michael's alibi is solid, he still could have killed Martha after he returned.

According to the Sutton Associates files, Julie and John Skakel heard noises downstairs around 11:30 P.M. the night of the murder. The commotion was so loud that Julie got out of bed and went to the top of the stairs to check. John heard "something going on in the mud room" and "the sound of the back door." Steven Hartig, a neighbor of the Skakels', heard noises in the area of Walsh Lane at about the same time.

According to the Sutton documents, Michael's psychological and emotional difficulties are even more significant than his brother's. Most of the tests and reports provided to Sutton Associates were filtered through Tom Sheridan. Why weren't they given raw data concerning Michael, the same way they got Thomas's reports? Was this omission intentional?

Tom Sheridan's digest of Elan staffer Anna Goodman's report on Michael quoted in the Sutton files stated: "Both boys are impulsive personalities. Both have very poor ego development and a bad self-image. Both are sexually immature and blocked emotionally. Both have alcohol and possibly drug problems. Both are very likeable and outstanding athletes. Both are lost, personally disorganized and have no life plan. Their only point of departure is in the fact that Tommy feels loved by his family and Michael does not."

After testing Michael extensively, Dr. Sue Wallingford-Quinlan concluded that he suffered from "a severe agitated depression, a sense of being over-whelmed by a sense of evil and the futility of life. The depression is possibly of psychotic proportions but the protocol was too guarded to be certain. Mental functioning is clearly fragile. Extent of pathology is evident in borderline features: 1) intrusions of personal concerns into intellectual functioning, 2) primitive fantasy content, e.g. mutilated bodies, masked, distorted figures, concerns about bodily integrity and deformity, 3) inadequate capacity for attachment to other people."

By "borderline features" Dr. Wallingford-

Quinlan is referring to borderline personality disorder, "a pervasive pattern of instability of interpersonal relationships, self-image, and affects, and marked impulsivity." According to the *Diagnostic and Statistical Manual of Mental Disorders,* borderline personalities are easily bored and often engage in reckless and self-destructive behavior. They experience intense fears of abandonment and react with inappropriate anger when they feel they have been abandoned. They often idealize lovers and make excessive demands on them. When those demands are not met, the borderline personality can quickly switch from idealizing the person to devaluing them, frequently lashing out with anger and rage. According to one expert in the field, "Once the rage is acted out, borderline personalities frequently describe actually seeing themselves committing the act, disassociating themselves and even looking down on themselves during the act, but are unable to stop it." After viewing Michael's psychological records, the expert told me: "This is a person who once triggered, would most probably lose all control."

Dr. Wallingford-Quinlan continued:

The core of the depression is the feeling of being helpless, of being buffeted and brutalized by external forces. He sees himself as the helpless victim. There is also a great fury inside him focused primarily in hatred for his father. This anger is very frighten-

ing and he has inadequate defenses to deal
with it except for avoidance and inhibition
of behavior. There is some trend toward a
more paranoid stance in which projected
anger and fear that other people see him as
crazy combine to produce interpersonal
distancing and disparate resistance to
manipulation by external forces.

He feels he has no control over his life and
he resents his father for that. Lack of a feeling of control leads him to act out, sometimes violently.

Tom Sheridan's digest of Anna Goodman's Elan
report states: "Michael has 'started to talk about a
lot of things that bother him which he blocks out
most of the time.' In a distraught state, i.e. crying
off and on, he talked about feeling that 'he always
had to be a certain way because of who he is.' Anna
Goodman, then, interprets this to mean that
because he is a Skakel he had to do things (many of
which were dangerous, i.e. drinking and fast driving) so people would accept him."

Michael's personality, psychological profile,
and past acts show a violent, troubled young man
who has the capacity to murder, but what about
motive?

Michael and Martha were the same age. Martha
knew Michael longer than she knew Thomas. Her
diary clearly stated that both Skakel boys were

romantically interested in her. She also said that while she liked Thomas, she had to be careful of Michael. Several sources have confirmed that Michael and Martha had some sort of romantic relationship. Some of these sources even refer to Michael as Martha's "boyfriend" or "ex-boyfriend." Michael's aunt Sue Reynolds told Manny Margolis, "Martha Moxley was at one time Michael's girlfriend." According to Sutton Associates, "This is a confirmation to Margolis. It has been reported to him by others."

The Sutton files contained the following anaylsis:

> We have found considerable evidence to show Michael had been involved in a relationship with Martha Moxley. According to one source, Michael and Tommy even fought over her. Along the blurry lines of teenage romance, Michael was known to be Martha's boyfriend for some time. Coupled with our extensive knowledge of just how vehemently they fought with each other, this information suggests Michael had more than ample reason to [be] extremely upset when Tommy was carrying on with Martha by the side of the house just before 9:30 P.M.

Sutton Associates stated that Thomas and Michael's "early relationship was distinguished by an intense, exceptionally explosive rivalry."

What would have happened if Michael, already under the influence of alcohol and possibly drugs, saw his girlfriend, Martha Moxley, making out with his older brother Tommy?

"Martha's friends reportedly left shortly after this point because they found Martha's behavior to be embarrassing," notes a document in the Sutton files. "Clearly, her activity with Tommy was purposefully demonstrative. It seems likely, as well, that Martha's young friends were disturbed by the inherent awkwardness of watching Martha blatantly and immodestly courting the affection of her ex-boyfriend's older brother in her ex-boyfriend's presence. We know practically nothing of how Michael reacted to all this, and it is a glaring omission. For certainly, he had a reaction, and it may have been extreme."

Michael told the Sutton Associates interviewer that he did not consider Martha Moxley to be a flirt. "By all other accounts, many of them emphatic and coming directly from her good friends, Martha Moxley was a relentless flirt."

We know that he saw Martha and Thomas together, first sitting in the car, where Thomas touched her leg and made other advances that she rebuffed. Minutes later, Michael saw them in the driveway engaging in horseplay and eventually making out. However initially resistant Martha might have been to Thomas's advances, she did eventually give in to him, and Michael saw it. How can he say that she wasn't a flirt? Why would

Michael downplay her flirtatiousness unless he had something to hide, like being enraged by it?

Sutton Associates asked Michael when he first heard that Martha was dead. He couldn't remember. As a document in the files concludes: "One reason why Michael may not have been able to pinpoint the time when he was made aware of Martha's death, could be because he knew she was dead before anyone else."

Throughout the investigation, several people who knew both brothers well stated that Michael was more capable of murder than Thomas.

According to the Sutton files, Rushton Sr. "conceded that Michael could be capable of [the murder]." Michael's aunt Sue Reynolds spent a lot of time in the Skakel house following the murder. A Tom Sheridan memo notes that Sue Reynolds "is persuaded 'that Tommy had nothing to do with the crime.' On the other hand, she has 'very negative vibrations with reference to Michael.' Michael is deeply involved in alcohol and not under control— 'he is capable of anything.'"

Mildred Ix told Dorthy Moxley, "I just don't think Tommy could do it. But Michael, I'd give you Michael in a minute."

Why I believe Michael Skakel was involved in the murder of Martha Moxley:

1. His psychological profile reveals a severely disturbed youth with violent tendencies,

substance-abuse problems, and an often explosive sibling rivalry with his brother Thomas.

2. He reported seeing the murder weapon "embedded in her chest," a detail only someone present at the scene would know.

3. After seventeen years, he changed his story, placing himself at the murder scene and other areas where the killer might possibly have been observed.

4. He lied to the Greenwich police in 1975 about his actions and movements the night of October 30–31.

5. He doesn't remember when he first heard that Martha was dead.

6. According to a fellow patient, Michael once confessed in a therapy session to the murder of Martha Moxley. He quickly recanted.

17

Hypothesis of a Murder

The following is what I think happened on the
night of October 30, 1975. Relying on the
evidence and witness statements from investigations into the case, I will try to get into the minds
of suspects and witnesses in order to help me, and
the reader, understand who killed Martha Moxley.

At 9:15 P.M. Martha Moxley, Thomas and Michael
Skakel, Helen Ix, and Geoffrey Byrne are sitting in the
Skakel Lincoln listening to music. Martha is in the
front seat between Thomas and Michael. The two
brothers are both interested in and competing for
Martha. In this tense situation Thomas places his
hand on Martha's leg in a sexually suggestive manner.
Martha reacts, raising her voice and demanding that
Thomas take his hand off her. He complies. A few
minutes later, Thomas touches her again. Again, she
tells him to stop. Michael is sitting on the other side
of Martha. Angry and jealous, terrified that Martha

has abandoned him, Michael struggles to control his emotions.

Around 9:30 P.M., the group is chased from the car by Jim Terrien, Rush Jr., and John Skakel. Jim Terrien needs a ride home, where the boys are going to watch *Monty Python*. Thomas says he will go with them. Michael also says he will go. He asks Martha to come along, but she refuses. Thomas looks at Martha and changes his mind. He'll stay home, too. Michael doesn't want to go, but in front of his friends, brothers, and cousin, he doesn't want to seem too bothered by the fact that Martha won't go with him.

Along with Jim Terrien, John, and Rush Jr., Michael gets into the Lincoln. Geoffrey Byrne and Helen Ix start to walk home, leaving Thomas and Martha alone. As they leave, their friends see Thomas and Martha making out and engaging in horseplay by the edge of the driveway. Driving away in the Lincoln, Michael sees them also.

Now that they are alone, Martha and Thomas go further. They start kissing and petting on the back lawn. After a few minutes, Thomas and Martha realize it is too cold to be rolling around on the ground. Martha is ready to go home, but Thomas convinces her to come into the house. Reluctantly, Martha follows Thomas inside. Walking and talking like burglars on the job, Thomas whispers to Martha "Stay here" as he points to the guest room.

Thomas walks upstairs to his father's room,

where Ken Littleton is watching television. Thomas does not know Littleton well enough to be sure he would not come looking for him later, so Thomas makes an appearance. After sitting with Littleton through *The French Connection* chase scene, Thomas makes an excuse to leave. He announces he has homework to do and is going to his room.

Of course, Thomas does not go to his room. Instead he returns to Martha, who is waiting for him in the guest room. It is now about 10:35 P.M.

Martha and Thomas resume their sexual encounter, laughing, playing, touching. Meanwhile, at the Terriens' Michael is in a very different mood. Sitting with his brothers and cousin several miles away, his imagination runs wild. He visualizes Martha having sex with Thomas. The more he imagines, the angrier he gets. Martha lied to him, she embarrassed him, she hurt him. She abandoned him, just as he knew she would, just as his mother had, just as every woman ever did. His older brother Thomas always got what he, Michael, wanted. Feeling slighted, insignificant, once again mistreated by those he thought loved him, Michael slowly works himself into a rage.

At approximately 11:00 P.M., John, Rush Jr., and Michael get into the Lincoln and leave the Terriens'. On the ride home, Michael sits in the backseat in total silence.

While the three boys drive back to Belle Haven, Ken Littleton checks Thomas's room. He cannot find him. New in the house and probably uneasy about asserting his authority, Ken simply shrugs it off and returns to the master bedroom.

At approximately 11:20, the Lincoln pulls into the driveway. Thomas and Martha are startled by the noise of the car. After a moment they both realize the others are back.

Thomas instructs Martha to be quiet as he peeks from the door and watches Michael, John, and Rush, Jr. enter the house and walk up the stairs to their bedrooms. When he doesn't find Thomas upstairs, Michael decides to go back downstairs to look for him. It is now about 11:30 P.M.

After waiting a few moments, Thomas tries to sneak Martha out of the house. From the top of the stairs, Michael watches Thomas holding Martha's hand as he leads her through the house. When they reach the back door, Michael catches up to them. He is angry and accusatory. Thomas reacts aggressively. The long-smoldering rivalry between the two boys quickly ignites.

Martha is embarrassed and sickened by the confrontation. The two brothers seem to be fighting over a toy. As they exchange vicious threats, Martha slips out the back door.

The commotion by the back door does not go unnoticed. Julie Skakel hears male voices downstairs at 11:30 P.M. She goes out to look down the staircase and recognizes her brothers fighting again. David Skakel also hears raised voices, and as he strains to listen, he looks at his clock-radio. It is now 11:33 P.M.

Tired of Michael's ranting, and satisfied that he at least has got what he wanted, Thomas runs up to his room.

Michael is left standing by the back door. He feels the rage build inside him. He has no sense of right or wrong, no empathy, no guilt. He doesn't care about anyone or anything. There is only his anger; it knows no boundaries and demands satisfaction. He looks about the room and focuses on a golf club that has been a source of release so many times. He grabs the six iron and walks out the back door.

As his eyes adjust to the darkness, Michael sees a figure walking across the backyard. The figure turns its head and looks in his direction but continues walking. He recognizes Martha. Michael runs to her, stopping her near his family's pool.

Martha tells Michael she wants nothing more to do with him. She tells him she resents his possessiveness and the stupid rivalry with his older brother. Then she turns and walks toward her house.

Michael has just heard his worst fears confirmed. He is overwhelmed with rage, not just jealousy of Martha but rivalry with Thomas, hate for his father, resentment of his lost mother, and a thousand other emotions that no one, not even he, understands. Running to catch up with Martha, he crosses Walsh Lane and momentarily loses sight of her as he passes under the bright streetlamp at the edge of the Moxley driveway.

Ken Littleton has heard voices downstairs and

now outside. He walks out onto the terrace outside the master bedroom to investigate. He looks toward the pool, scans the backyard, and stares into the streetlamp on Walsh Lane. Again he hears voices. He strains to hear, but they are too far away.

Michael stops Martha again just a hundred feet from her front door. Martha is losing patience with him. Her normally sweet personality is now taking an edge. She loses her temper, berating Michael for his behavior and making no excuse for choosing Thomas over him. As Martha takes control of the situation, Michael feels his own control, however slight it once was, slipping away.

Martha turns her back on Michael and just walks away. To Michael, this is the most spiteful thing she could do. She doesn't even care enough to fight with him. He doesn't matter, not to her nor to anyone else. He never did. Everybody hates him, nobody has ever loved him. He is an empty void, insignificant, ignored, unloved, abandoned. His mounting anger turns into a blind rage. He does not think, or even feel anymore. He simply acts.

Michael holds the golf club in his hand. His grip tightens. He swings the club reflexively as he has many times before, but this time he hits a human being.

Martha drops instantly. She lies facedown near the driveway. Her body does not move. Michael pokes at her with the club, but she does not respond. He does not feel any compassion for her lying inert on the ground. Michael's only fear is getting caught.

Michael grabs Martha by her feet and drags her facedown across the gravel driveway. The light from the streetlamp allows him to watch her head bounce on the rough drive. As he continues dragging Martha toward the small Japanese elm tree, he looks beyond Walsh Lane and sees Littleton standing on the terrace. Michael cannot tell if Ken sees him, but that's something he can deal with later.

Near the little tree, he stands over Martha. Her body begins to move. She is still breathing. Michael's first thoughts are not how to help but how he can finish her off. Michael looks around for the golf club until he realizes that he dropped it on the other side of the driveway.

Michael runs to find the golf club. When he returns, he finds that Martha is very much alive. Michael strikes Martha once or twice, then waits for some indication that she is dead. She continues to move and breathe.

She is still beyond his power; she won't even die when he wants her to. Michael strikes again and again, each blow coming harder and faster. Seeing himself beat her, as if he were physically removed from his own body, Michael is enraged that Martha will not die. He is completely out of control; the blows are savage. Eventually the club head breaks off and is flung toward the circular drive. The shaft snaps in several pieces, one falls by Martha's head.

Blood is now visibly pooling under her head. Michael is astonished that Martha is still moving slightly. He takes the broken shaft and drives the jagged end through her throat, leaving it in her body. Martha is finally motionless. She is dead.

Michael steps back and looks at what he has done. Something drips from his forehead into his eyes, and as he wipes it away he sees that it is not sweat, but blood. Michael runs toward his house, stopping in the cover of well-groomed shrubbery to think about what he will do next. It is about 11:50–11:55 P.M.

Standing in the bushes, Michael begins to feel the onset of shock. He is shaking uncontrollably and is sick to his stomach. It is beginning to dawn on him what has happened. There is nothing he can do now—except make sure he does not get caught.

How will he cover his tracks? Michael looks out toward the Moxley house and sees her body lying near the tree. He can't leave her there. Someone could see her from the street.

He walks back toward the body and sees Martha lying facedown in a large pool of blood. The remaining portion of the golf club shaft is sticking out of her body. Michael ponders the sight and feels a surge of power and dominance. For once, he is in charge.

Michael knows that he cannot leave Martha here. He grabs her by the feet just under the front of her ankles. His hands wrap around the bottoms of her blue jeans. He quickly moves backward, dragging Martha with him. The sloping lawn causes Martha to swing on the damp grass, and her blood-soaked head leaves a zigzag path through the leaves.

Michael holds on tight to Martha as he moves faster onto level ground. At one point, her loose-fitting jeans slip off her waist, exposing her panties. Michael looks at her bare skin. He is uncontrollably aroused.

Looking over his shoulder, Michael spots a pine tree near the far edge of the yard. He maneuvers Martha's limp body toward the tree and pulls her under its low-hanging boughs.

To most this sight would be a horror, but to him this is a conquest. Michael touches her still-warm body. He pulls her pants and panties well below her knees. Michael feels stimulated looking at his victim, helpless and staged in humiliation. He masturbates while staring at Martha's ravaged body. Once he ejaculates, he runs back to his house.

When Michael is about to walk in the back door, he realizes he has blood on his hands and clothes. Having gone in and out of his second-story window many times to evade detection by his father, Michael climbs up the trellis and through his bedroom window. Inside he strips off his clothes and cleans away all evidence of the murder from his body. It is now 12:30 A.M.

Michael goes to bed and lies awake the remainder of the night. He hears the phone ring but pretends not to notice. He hears voices downstairs—his sister Julie, his brother Thomas. They're looking for Martha. Michael knows what happened to her. He wonders if he will get caught. It is now 2:00 A.M.

PART V

Anatomy of a Murder Investigation

18

Timeline

No matter how outrageously bizarre
the lead is, I follow it to the end.
—Tom Keegan

OCTOBER 30, 1975

8:45 P.M.—Thomas, Michael, Rushton Jr., John, and Julie Skakel, Jim Terrien, Andrea Shakespeare, and Ken Littleton return from the Belle Haven Club.

8:55 P.M.—Martha Moxley, Michael Skakel, Helen Ix, and Geoffrey Byrne sit in the Skakel car listening to music.

9:15 P.M.—Thomas Skakel joins group in car, sitting next to Martha.

9:15–9:30 P.M.—Thomas and Martha leave Skakel car and" make out" in driveway.

9:30 P.M.—Jim Terrien, Rush Skakel Jr., John

Skakel, and Michael Skakel all reportedly
leave to go to the Terriens' house on
Cliffdale Rd.

9:30 P.M.—On their way home, Helen Ix and
Geoff Byrne see Martha and Thomas
falling behind fence.

9:30–9:35 P.M.—Nanny Sweeney hears noises
outside, asks Ken Littleton to check.
Littleton exits back door for three or four
minutes, hears nothing suspicious.

9:35 P.M.—According to Thomas Skakel's
interviews with the Sutton Associates in
1994–95, he and Martha begin sexual
encounter fifty feet into rear yard of Skakel
residence.

9:50 P.M.—Helen Ix hears her dog Socks barking.

9:50 P.M.—Julie Skakel reportedly sees someone in bushes by kitchen.

9:50–9:55 P.M.—According to Thomas Skakel,
he and Martha end their sexual encounter.
Martha runs across Skakel lawn toward
her house.

APPROXIMATELY 10:00 P.M.—Robert Bjork, resident of 101 Otter Rock Drive, observes

vehicle parked outside his house. He goes out to investigate and sees the vehicle is an unmarked police car manned by a Belle Haven security guard.

10:03–10:17 P.M.—Thomas enters master bedroom where Littleton is watching *The French Connection*.

APPROXIMATELY 10:30 P.M.—Steven Skakel hears the Ix dog barking and female laughter from "either Helen or Martha."

10:32 P.M.—*French Connection* chase scene ends. Thomas leaves bedroom.

11:00 P.M.—Rushton Jr., John Skakel, and Michael Skakel reportedly leave Terriens' to return to Skakel residence.

11:20 P.M.—John Moxley returns home. His mother informs him that Martha has not come home yet. He drives around Belle Haven looking for her.

11:20 P.M.—According to Thomas Skakel, Rushton Jr. returns home, goes to sleep on floor in Thomas's bedroom.

11:25 P.M.—Julie Skakel hears noises downstairs in Skakel house.

APPROXIMATELY 11:30 P.M.—Neighbor Steven Hartig hears noises near Walsh Lane.

11:33 P.M.—John Skakel hears noises downstairs in Skakel house.

11:40 P.M.—Michael Skakel reportedly leaves his house and begins "peeping" in neighborhood.

OCTOBER 31, 1975

12:30 A.M.—Michael Skakel reportedly returns home from Moxley residence.

2:00–3:00 A.M.—Dorthy Moxley calls neighbors looking for Martha.

3:35 A.M.—John Moxley goes out to search for Martha again.

3:48 A.M.—Dorthy Moxley calls Greenwich police to report that Martha is missing.

4:00 A.M.—Dorthy Moxley calls Skakel residence. Julie Skakel asks Thomas when and where he last saw Martha. He says 9:30 by the back door.

SOMETIME AFTER 4:00 A.M.—Patrolman Daniel Merchant responds to Moxley house.

Along with Dorthy, Merchant searches the
entire Moxley residence and a small cottage in the rear of the house. Then two
Greenwich patrol cars conduct motorized
search of Belle Haven area.

6:00 A.M.—John Moxley returns home from
second search.

6:15 A.M.—Franz Wittine goes out to walk
Max, the Skakel family dog.

9:15 A.M.—Juvenile officer Dan Hickman
interviews Dorthy Moxley over the phone.

9:45 A.M.—Hickman and Jones conduct an
hourlong motorized search in the Belle
Haven area.

BETWEEN 9:30–10:00 A.M.—Dorthy Moxley
goes to Skakel residence, talks to Michael.
Without looking or asking, he says
nobody knows where Martha is. Dorthy
asks Franz Wittine to look in camper
for her.

12:15 P.M.—Martha's body is found by Sheila
McGuire.

12:30 P.M.—Hickman and Jones receive radio
transmission from police headquarters.

Upon contacting headquarters, they proceed to Moxley residence with lights and sirens going. Hickman and Jones arrive at Moxley residence, park in driveway, and view the body. They both notify headquarters.

12:45 P.M.—Chief of Detectives Tom Keegan and detectives Carroll and McGlynn arrive on scene.

TIME UNKNOWN—Lowell Robertson identifies body.

TIME UNKNOWN—Dr. Richard Danehower examines body.

1:15 P.M.—Dr. Coleman Kelly arrives at crime scene.

1:15 P.M.—Dorthy interviewed by Tom Keegan until 3:00 P.M.

3:00 P.M.—Detectives Carroll and McGlynn interview Ed Hammond.

3:00 P.M.—Detectives Brosko and Lunney interview Julie and Michael Skakel.

4:00 P.M.—George Skakel and John Pinto drive off in Skakel family camper.

4:00 P.M.—Detectives Brosko and Lunney interview Ken Littleton.

4:00 P.M.—Connecticut State Police Crime Laboratory is contacted and requested to respond to Moxley residence.

TIME UNKNOWN—Connecticut Chief Medical Examiner Elliot Gross informs Captain Keegan that he has a heavy caseload and cannnot view the body at the crime scene. He instructs Keegan to bag Martha's body and take her to the morgue.

4:30 P.M.—Rushton Skakel Jr. leaves for Dartmouth.

APPROXIMATELY 4:30–5:00 P.M.—Connecticut mobile crime lab arrives.

5:15 P.M.—Jim McKenzie arrives by cab at Skakel residence.

5:30 P.M.—Detectives Brosko and Lunney observe golf club in a storage bin in the Skakel residence. The golf club apparently matches the pieces found at the crime scene. They are not able to obtain permission to remove the golf club.

5:30 P.M.—Martha's body removed from crime

scene and taken to morgue at Greenwich Hospital.

5:40 P.M.—Thomas Skakel is taken to police headquarters for questioning.

6:00 P.M.—Detectives Brosko and Lunney interview Helen Ix and Geoffrey Byrne.

8:00 P.M.—Rushton Sr. returns home.

9:00 P.M.—Franz Wittine drives Jim McKenzie back to New York City.

10:30 P.M.—Thomas Skakel returns home from police headquarters.

NOVEMBER 1, 1975

9:30 A.M.—Directed by Captain Keegan, Greenwich police, along with gas company personnel, begin searching for the missing club handle.

10:00 A.M.—Dr. Elliot Gross arrives at Greenwich police department. He views videotapes and photos of the crime scene, then proceeds to the scene, where he takes his own photos.

12:40 P.M.—Dr. Elliot Gross conducts autopsy
on Martha Moxley at Greenwich Hospital.
He concludes that Martha was killed by a
golf club.

TIME UNKNOWN—Captain Tom Keegan tells
reporters, "We don't have a heck of a lot to
go on. This is going to be a long one."

NOVEMBER 2, 1975

Greenwich detectives take golf club matching
the murder weapon from Skakel home.
They ask Rushton Sr. if he knows Ed
Hammond or ever invited him to golfing
parties. Meanwhile, Captain Keegan
directs a search of the crime scene and
neighborhood for the missing piece of the
murder weapon.

5:55 P.M.—Chief Stephen Baran issues a press
release concerning the missing portion of
the murder weapon.

6:00 P.M.—Captain Keegan dispatches a
nationwide Teletype concerning the missing portion of the murder weapon.

NOVEMBER 3, 1975

> 7:15 P.M.—Thomas Skakel is taken to
> Connecticut State Police in Bethany for
> polygraph test. Results inconclusive. He
> agrees to take another test and is returned
> home at approximately 1:00 A.M.

NOVEMBER 4, 1975

More than five hundred people attend the
funeral for Martha Moxley held at First
Lutheran Church in Greenwich.

NOVEMBER 9, 1975

Thomas Skakel takes a second polygraph and
reportedly passes.

NOVEMBER 10, 1975

Detective Lunney conducts a background
check on Ken Littleton.

NOVEMBER 15, 1975

Detectives Brosko and Lunney reinterview the

Skakel family, Andrea Shakespeare, Jim Terrien, and Helen Ix.

NOVEMBER 21, 1975

Ed Hammond takes second polygraph test and passes.

NOVEMBER 24, 1975

Greenwich police chief Stephen Baran asks the Neighborhood Cleaners Association in New York City to report any bloodstained clothing brought into member establishments.

DECEMBER 2, 1975

Police contact fifty-five cleaners in the lower Fairfield County area asking them to report any bloodstained clothing brought into their establishments.

John Moxley takes polygraph examination and passes.

DECEMBER 6, 1975

While arranging for John Skakel to take a
polygraph examination, Detective Jim
Lunney asks Rushton Skakel if any members of his family and/or household staff
had ever been confined in a mental insti-
tution or similar facility. Mr. Skakel
responds in the negative.

DECEMBER 9, 1975

John Skakel takes polygraph examination
and passes.

DECEMBER 11, 1975

10:00 A.M.—During reinterviews with detec-
tives Carroll and Lunney, Helen Ix and
Geoffrey Byrne describe Thomas and
Martha engaging in horseplay at the
Skakel back door at approximately 9:30
P.M. on night of the murder.

6:30 P.M.—Detective Lunney searches the
Skakel's Windham residence with
Rushton's permission.

DECEMBER 12, 1975

Greenwich police receive autopsy report from
Elliot Gross.

DECEMBER 13, 1975

Detectives Carrol! and Lunney reinterview
Thomas Skakel at length and obtain hair
samples from him.

DECEMBER 17, 1975

Dorthy Moxley takes polygraph test—results
are inconclusive.

JANUARY 16, 1976

Greenwich police obtain written permission
from Rushton Skakel Sr. for Thomas's
medical, school, and psychological records.

JANUARY 20, 1976

Greenwich detectives are contacted by Chris
Roosevelt and told that he would not release
Thomas's Whitby School records without

personally speaking to the Skakels. According to the police report, he stated that if Thomas was arrested, he would be defended by a battery of lawyers who would claim the boy was temporarily insane.

JANUARY 22, 1976

Rushton Skakel formally withdraws permission to release Thomas's records. Later that day, he collapses at the Ix house and is checked into Greenwich Hospital complaining of chest pains. In an interview at the hospital, Rushton informs detectives Carroll and Lunney that he has retained Manny Margolis as criminal attorney for Thomas.

JANUARY 25, 1976

David Moxley sets up meeting between Greenwich police and his colleague John McCreight.

JANUARY 28, 1976

Detectives Carroll and Lunney request permission to reinterview Ed Hammond.

JANUARY 30, 1976

Manny Margolis informs Captain Keegan that
he has advised the Skakel family not to
speak to the police.

FEBRUARY 4–7, 1976

Detectives Carroll and Lunney travel to Detroit,
Michigan, to brief members of the homicide squad of Detroit Police Department on
the Moxley investigation and receive their
advice.

FEBRUARY 9, 1976

Detectives Carroll and Lunney go to
Brunswick School in an attempt to obtain
a written statement from Ken Littleton.
Littleton is not available.

FEBRUARY 18, 1976

Greenwich police meet with Skakel family
advisors Father Thomas Guinan and Father
Mark Connolly concerning medical and
psychiatric tests they would like to have
performed on Thomas Skakel.

FEBRUARY 25, 1976

Greenwich police meet with Rushton Skakel,
Manny Margolis, and Father Connolly
concerning the tests they want Thomas to
take. Skakel says he would make a decision
after conferring with Margolis.

MARCH 3, 1976

Manny Margolis informs the Greenwich police
that his client would not comply with
their request for medical and psychiatric
testing.

MARCH 5, 1976

Ed Hammond and his mother are reinterviewed. This time Hammond is treated as
a witness, not a suspect.

MARCH 15, 1976

Dr. Stanley Lesse arranges for Thomas Skakel,
using the pseudonym Thomas Butler, to
be given a series of psychological
tests by Dr. Patrick de Gramont at
Presbyterian Hospital in New York City.

MARCH 16, 1976

Greenwich detectives brief homicide investigators from the Nassau County Police Department on the Moxley case.
According to the Greenwich police report, the Nassau detectives determine that the investigation was conducted "competently and professionally."

MARCH 25, 1976

Donald Browne tells reporters that the police are "apparently being frustrated by the refusal of a particular family, which could supply pertinent information to assist or cooperate" in the investigation. He refuses to identify the family.

MARCH 28, 1976

BETWEEN 4:00 AND 5:00 P.M.—Rushton Skakel appears at Moxley residence with drink in hand, having just been at an AA meeting. He tells David and Dorthy Moxley that Thomas had undergone some type of examination and the result of the examination proved negative. David Moxley urges Rushton to turn these test results over to the Greenwich police. Skakel says that his lawyer advised against it.

MARCH 31, 1976

Commander Gerald Hale and Inspector John Loch of Detroit homicide arrive in Greenwich to advise and assist in the Moxley investigation.

APRIL 2, 1976

During an interview by Hale and Loch, Mildred Ix states that Rushton Skakel told her that he had arranged for Thomas to be submitted to a series of psychiatric examinations. He also told her that the tests showed Thomas was not involved in the murder. Robert Ix says that he had also heard about the tests but didn't put much faith in them. Mildred says that Chris Roosevelt told Rushton not to allow the police to see Thomas's Whitby file because it contained a doctor's report stating that the boy was subject to blackouts. She also describes an act of vandalism that Thomas had committed after a fight with his brother Michael. Mildred feels strongly that Ken Littleton should be checked out as a suspect.

APRIL 5, 1976

Greenwich police seek to interview Ken
   Littleton at Brunswick School. He says he
   won't talk to police without first checking
   with his attorney, Manny Margolis.

APRIL 7, 1976

Ken Littleton refuses to talk to Greenwich
   police. He also refuses to sign a statement to
   support circumstantial evidence against
   Thomas Skakel, as he believes him innocent.

APRIL 13, 1976

Attorney John Meerbergen informs the
   Greenwich police that he has been retained
   by Ken Littleton.

APRIL 15, 1976

Captain Keegan and Detective Lunney meet
   with an unidentified witness "for the purpose of ascertaining information on the
   behavior of Ix and Bjork dogs on the night
   of the murder." The witness "stated that all
   indications given, the Ix dog witnessed

part and/or all of the murder. He further
stated he would be unable to state if the Ix
dog knew the attacker." Keegan, Lunney,
and the witness proceed to the Bjork
house, where they walk the Bjork springer
spaniel to the area where Martha's body
was found to see if he picks up a scent.
"Investigators followed the dog and he
traveled toward the McGuire residence,
then to the Keefe property and then he
returned home."

APRIL 16, 1976

Captain Tom Keegan and Detective Jim
Lunney check with the Animal Control
Division of the Greenwich Police
Department for any complaints involving
the Skakel dog, Max. Nothing on file.
They next go to the Ix residence, where
they check to see if the household clock is
accurate. "At this time, the clock was
approximately two (2) minutes fast."

APRIL 22, 1976

Ken Littleton reinterviewed by Greenwich
police with his attorney present.

APRIL 30, 1976

Thomas Skakel admitted to Greenwich
Hospital for hemorrhagic gastritis.

MAY 11, 1976

Dr. Stanley Lesse submits a full report on
Thomas's medical and psychological
tests to the Skakel family and their
attorneys.

SEPTEMBER 2, 1976

Jacob Zeldes, lawyer for the Moxley family,
meets with Captain Keegan and Detective
Lunney. He has been in contact with the
Skakels and their attorneys, and it was
agreed that Zeldes will obtain the services
of a doctor who will confer with the doctor
who examined Thomas.

OCTOBER 18, 1976

Ken Littleton takes a polygraph examination,
which he fails. He tells investigators that
he had been arrested that summer for
burglary and larceny in Nantucket,

Massachusetts. He says that he is willing
to submit to further testing, but will have
to talk with his attorney.

OCTOBER 19, 1976

Littleton tells police that he has been advised
by his attorney not to submit to any further testing.

OCTOBER 21, 1976

Detective Lunney meets with Manny Margolis
for the purpose of obtaining interviews
with Skakel family members on the subject of Ken Littleton. Margolis is given a
list of questions, which he will try to get
answered by the Skakels.

OCTOBER 30, 1976

Detectives Carroll and Lunney conduct
overnight surveillance at the crime scene.

NOVEMBER 9, 1976

Manny Margolis tells Detective Lunney that he

has conducted an interview with Thomas
Skakel on the subject of Ken Littleton.

NOVEMBER 12, 1976

Detectives Carroll and Lunney begin extensive
background investigation on Ken
Littleton.

MARCH 3, 1977

Jacob Zeldes informs detectives Carroll and
Lunney that he has retained psychiatrist
Dr. Robert Davies of Yale–New Haven
Medical Center to meet with Dr. Stanley
Lesse and evaluate the material that
Manny Margolis makes available concern-
ing his tests of Thomas Skakel.

MAY 1977

Ken Littleton is given a five- to seven-year suspended sentence for the Nantucket
charges. He refuses to submit to a sodium
amytal interview concerning the Moxley
case in return for reduced charges.

DECEMBER 12, 1977

Captain Keegan and Detective Lunney travel
to Vermont, where Thomas Skakel is now
attending school, to gather background
information.

DECEMBER 14, 1977

Keegan and Lunney travel to Boston to meet
with Ken Littleton's probation officer
and conduct further background
investigation.

MARCH 5, 1978

Michael Skakel is arrested in Windham, New
York, on charges of unlicensed operation,
speeding, failure to comply, and driving
while intoxicated.

JUNE 1978

Thomas Skakel expelled from Elmira College
for academic reasons.

OCTOBER 17, 1978

Connecticut governor Ella Grasso authorizes a
$20,000 reward for information leading to
the arrest and conviction of the murderer
of Martha Moxley.

OCTOBER 28, 1978

Greenwich police meet with a psychic who
states that she has been having a dream
about the Moxley homicide for three years.

OCTOBER 30, 1978

Detective Lunney conducts overnight surveillance at the crime scene.

MID-NOVEMBER 1978

Michael Skakel escapes from Elan and is
returned after a few days.

NOVEMBER 29, 1978

Michael Skakel escapes from Elan again.

DECEMBER 12, 1978

Michael Skakel is returned to Elan.

OCTOBER 30, 1979

Detective Lunney conducts surveillance at the crime scene.

OCTOBER 30, 1980

Detective Lunney conducts surveillance at the crime scene.

JULY 31, 1981

Greenwich police contact a second psychic, whom Dorthy Moxley had met in Hot Springs, Arkansas.

SEPTEMBER 27, 1981

"Psychic Sue" comes to Greenwich, where Detective Lunney conducts her on a tour of the crime scene and surrounding areas.

JULY 13, 1982

Len Levitt and Ken Brief, editor of *Greenwich Time* and the *Stamford Advocate*, request that all police records on the Moxley investigation be made public.

JULY 20, 1982

Chief of Police Tom Keegan denies the request.

AUGUST 6, 1982

Levitt and Brief formally request the documents be made public under provisions of the state Freedom of Information Act.

OCTOBER 4, 1982

Chief Keegan requests permission to review and edit Len Levitt's article prior to publication. His request is denied.

OCTOBER 30, 1982

Detective Lunney conducts surveillance at the crime scene.

DECEMBER 9, 1982

Hearing is held by the Connecticut Freedom of
Information Commission regarding the
Moxley police report. During that hearing,
Donald Browne admits that a confession
by the murderer is the most likely way the
case will be closed.

JANUARY 5, 1983

Detective Lunney contacts Ken Littleton by
telephone. Littleton, who now lives in
Canada, says he has been talking to Len
Levitt to give his side of the story. He also
says he is willing to undergo tests to prove
his innocence, but doesn't trust the
Greenwich police or Connecticut state's
attorney.

MAY 11, 1983

Freedom of Information Committee decides
that Chief Keegan is to conduct an examination of the Moxley file and decide which
documents can be disclosed, and then
make those documents public.

SUMMER 1983

Len Levitt's article is written, but Ken Brief, editor of the *Time* and *Advocate*, refuses to publish it.

MAY 10, 1991

William Kennedy Smith is charged with rape in Palm Beach, Florida.

JUNE 2, 1991

Levitt article runs in *Greenwich Time* under headline "Moxley Murder Case Still Haunts Greenwich."

AUGUST 9, 1991

The Moxleys increase the existing reward to $50,000 and establish and fund a toll-free tip line to assist in an announced reinvestigation of Martha's murder by Frank Garr and Jack Solomon.

SOMETIME IN 1991

The Skakel family and their attorneys hire Sutton Associates.

OCTOBER 1993

Dr. Henry Lee submits his findings to the
Greenwich Police Department in a six-
inch-thick report.

JANUARY 5, 1994

Jack Solomon admits that the reinvestigation
has turned up "nothing substantial right
now that would lead to any arrest." He
blames the Skakel family for not cooperating.

JANUARY 21, 1994

Dr. Henry Lee says his forensic science laboratory has "done everything we could do"
with the available evidence.

SEPTEMBER 30, 1994

Frank Garr retires from the Greenwich Police
Department to work as inspector for
Donald Browne's office. He takes the
Moxley case with him.

OCTOBER 1995

Frank Garr admits: "Nothing in the way of
investigation has been done probably in
the last year."

NOVEMBER 3, 1995

Dorthy and John Moxley host a dinner at the
Belle Haven Club to thank those who
worked and supported them in the investigation.

NOVEMBER 26, 1995

Len Levitt's *Newsday* article describes how
Thomas Skakel changed his story and
admitted that he lied to police about his
actions the night of the murder.

DECEMBER 4, 1995

Len Levitt's *Newsday* article describes how
Michael Skakel changed his story and
admitted he lied to the police about
his actions the night of the murder.

JUNE 19, 1996

Dorthy and John Moxley double the reward to
$100,000 for one year.

OCTOBER 1996

Frank Garr takes evidence to Washington for
the Defense Department to perform
advanced DNA tests.

OCTOBER 24, 1997

State attorney Jonathan Benedict says a decision will be made early next year whether
anyone will be arrested for the
murder of Martha Moxley.

19

Homicide 101

*The investigation of murder necessitates a certain tenacity
and perseverance that transcends the ordinary investigative
pursuit. Homicides are solved because the detective cares.*
—Vernon J. Geberth

The techniques of homicide investigation are
universal and have not changed that much in
the last fifty years. Two homicide textbooks
that I still find very useful were written in the
1940s. There have been advances in forensic science
and legal requirements governing crime scene technique and the handling of evidence, but the basics
have remained the same.

The reason homicide investigation has not
changed dramatically is that the basics work. By
sticking to the established procedures of crime scene
investigation, evidence collection and analysis, witness interviews, and suspect interrogation, homicide
detectives can solve even the most challenging cases.

It is 12:45 P.M. on October 31, 1975. You are a detective in the Greenwich Police Department. You have

never been to a homicide scene before, but you have gone to homicide school and studied several text-books on the subject.

The responding officers have already arrived at the Moxley residence. When they arrived, they knew that a body had already been found, most probably Martha Moxley. They had the following responsibilities:

1. Determine if the victim was in fact deceased. If not, render first aid, and if necessary, notify emergency medical personnel.

2. Establish if the suspect was still at the crime scene, and arrest him if he was.

3. Protect the crime scene. Establish a perimeter large enough to encompass all areas where the suspect and victim might have been. Protect any obvious evidence and notify detectives about its presence.

4. Start a crime scene log documenting the time and nature of their arrival, their subsequent actions, and any discoveries.

Even if the responding officers did not know what to do, they would at least "freeze" the crime scene, preserving it as they found it and taking no other action aside from protecting the scene. Then they wait for the detectives to arrive.

You arrive on the scene with your partner and a detective supervisor, in this case the captain of detectives. The three of you check in on the crime scene log that one of the responding officers is handling. Then the detective supervisor:

1: Immediately assigns a detective team to the case and allows them to investigate the murder without any interference. As administrator in charge of detectives, the detective supervisor's main role is to protect his detectives from any distractions and obstacles that might affect their proper handling of the investigation.

2: Notifies the Connecticut State Crime Lab promptly, so they can arrive in time to process the scene calmly and under proper conditions. During this notification, he demands that a qualified medical examiner or deputy coroner respond to the crime scene. Once the lab arrives, he makes sure that his detectives work closely with the lab criminalists, directing their collection of evidence and noting their own observations of evidence and body condition.

The captain has assigned you and your partner to the investigation. As lead detective, you now take control of the crime scene and begin taking detailed notes. The first thing you do is interview the responding officers who first observed the body.

Before doing a walk-through of the crime scene, you ask the officers if a suspect was arrested or seen by witnesses. Once that issue is addressed, you follow the most informative officer in retracing his observations and discoveries at the crime scene. You ask the following questions: What did they see, do, and think? Where is the body? Who initially discovered the victim? Was anything touched or disturbed?

Once the preliminary walk-through is completed, you have a feeling for the crime scene and begin to organize and prioritize your observations. The Moxley scene has some specific concerns, including:

1.   This is a very affluent community and will generate spectators and the media.

2.   The crime scene is entirely outside and must be processed as quickly as possible. You have roughly four hours of light remaining. If not done so already, the Connecticut state crime lab should be notified immediately and a request made for them to respond as soon as possible.

3.   Considering the choice of weapon and the location of the victim, just one hundred feet from her home, the victim was most probably killed by someone she knew or someone who lived in the neighborhood.

4. If the suspect lived in the neighborhood, he could be watching the activity at the Moxley home.

Given these concerns, you immediately expand the crime scene perimeter so the activity of detectives and criminalists will be more difficult to observe. You close off Walsh Lane to all but police traffic. The entire Moxley property is secured. You position officers on Otter Rock Drive and Field Point Road. You order an officer to take down the license plate number of every car in the area and have the Belle Haven security do the same for every car entering the neighborhood. Then you order all known witnesses or possible suspects taken to the police station, where they are to be separated and made comfortable, awaiting eventual interviews. Once you have done your preliminary investigation, you will interview the witnesses. If you have a suspect in mind, you will wait to interrogate the suspect until you have gathered enough evidence and information to make that interrogation effective.

Right now, you don't know who the suspect is and you don't need to know. Determining who the suspect is, or who it might be, is not something you do in the initial investigation. You collect the evidence, you analyze the scene, then you make conclusions about the identity of the suspect based on what you have learned.

Delegating all responsibilities that you do not have to perform yourself, you direct available detectives and experienced uniformed officers to assist with a neighborhood canvass and interview witnesses who are not important enough to be taken to the station. As some of these officers may not be experienced or confident enough to perform those responsibilities independently, each specific function should be explained and assigned before the crime scene investigation can begin. Less valuable officers are directed to physically secure the crime scene. Considering that this is an outdoor location, you position officers throughout the Moxley property and all points of entry and egress.

During your interview with the responding officers, you learned that the golf club shaft was present in the victim's head. This is a very important piece of evidence and should be carefully guarded at all times. Since you assigned an officer to watch the body closely, the weapon is still there.

As you begin to process the body, your movements are very cautious near it, and you advise others to be careful as well. You direct the detective criminalist to photograph the body from every possible angle with both color and black-and-white film.

Once the scene is photographed you simply look around, closely observing everything in and around the body. You spend time taking in the scene and trying to imagine what happened there: how the victim was dragged underneath the tree, where the suspect stood, and what he might have touched.

The impact of being physically there with the victim will tell you much more than photos. Your senses are heightened, you can smell and feel the scene. You take detailed notes of every observation and thought as it strikes you. This opportunity will never be available again and you make the most of it.

You note the observable wounds, any signs of postmortem lividity, rigor mortis, and the position of the body. You draw sketches of the body with measurements and as much detail as possible.

The body yields one obvious and immediate clue: the remaining shaft of the golf club still embedded in the victim's body. You note the exact position of the club and any identifiable markings, including the monogram ANN SKAKEL. You note that the Skakels live across the street and that the family includes several young boys, but this is not the time to be chasing suspects.

Moving out from the body to examine the rest of the crime scene, you follow the zigzag trail of blood on the grass and leaves that leads from the victim's location under the pine tree toward the Japanese elm. This indicates that a single suspect dragged the victim to the pine tree. If it were two suspects, she would have been carried and not left such a trail. She was most probably held by her feet while the suspect walked backward. As he lost his bearings, he adjusted his direction repeatedly, accounting for the zigzag tracks.

Following the path leads you to the ground adjacent to the Japanese elm. Here is an eleven-inch portion of the golf club shaft lying in a three- to four-foot pool of blood. The pool of blood indicates that the victim had been lying there for some time. Once the autopsy is performed and her injuries are closely examined, you will be able to determine approximately how long she lay there. The eleven-inch piece of shaft in the blood pool indicates that the majority of the attack took place at this location, due to the significant blood loss and the presence of at least a portion of the murder weapon.

The asphalt driveway close to the Japanese elm shows traces of what appears to be human skin and blood. This would indicate that the victim was dragged across the driveway to the site where the majority of the attack took place.

Forty feet to the east you find an eight-inch por-tion of the shaft and the head of the golf club, which identifies it as a Toney Penna–model six iron. The location of these pieces of the club are in direct line with the swinging motion that the suspect would have had to use to inflict the injuries to the victim at her location by the Japanese elm. At this point, you reach the tentative conclusion that these two pieces of the murder weapon broke off during the attack and were cast forty feet away. Your conclusion seems to be corroborated by the fact that the victim has several wounds that appear to match the shape of the golf club head, but there were only a few specks of blood at the location where the club head was found. If the attack had occurred here, there would be more blood nearby.

The medical examiner arrives and performs an

initial examination of the body. He gives you preliminary indications of the time of death based on
the condition of the body. Now you have some idea
when the crime occurred. This information is crucial in understanding the rest of the evidence. It is
also essential for effective interviewing of witnesses
and suspects.

You check to see whether the criminalist has
collected all the evidence and the photographer has
documented every piece of evidence and its collection. Once those jobs are complete, and only then,
do you evaluate the case thus far and plan the next
move.

The golf club apparently came from the Skakel
house. Dorthy Moxley has already told juvenile officers that Thomas Skakel was the last person
reported seen with Martha Moxley. This connection
must be pursued.

You decide to expand the crime scene even further to include the entire Skakel property. You order
the Skakel house evacuated and secured. Then you
go to write a search-warrant request. Even if the
Skakel family gives you permission to search, you
insist on clearing the house and obtaining a formal
warrant.

You write a powerful affidavit for a search warrant on the Skakel house. Even though you have
never written a search warrant before, you follow the
examples in your detective's manual. There is ample
probable cause even under Connecticut laws, which
require a warrant to be granted only under the con-

dition that there is indication the search may provide an "instrumentality of the crime" and not "mere evidence." The judge grants your search warrant and you lead a team of detectives in a search of the Skakel house.

Here is some evidence you might find:

1. The complete set of Toney Penna golf clubs—minus the six iron.

2. Evidence of blood from the shower, sinks, laundry facilities, shoes, clothes, floors, carpet, and furniture.

3. Trace evidence of Martha Moxley in areas of the home where her presence could not be accounted for: strands of her hair in the shower or sinks; her hair on shoes, belt buckles, watch bands, and clothes belonging to Skakel family members; fiber evidence matching Martha's clothes the night of her death.

4. Any written reference to Martha Moxley: letters, diaries, journals, notes, or doodles. Evidence of any written material focused on a person who could be Martha.

The writing and service of the warrant will take four to six hours, and the collection of evidence will take about the same amount of time to complete.

By about 10:00 P.M. you are ready to sit down with the members of the Skakel family who had any contact with the victim the night before.

Your serving the search warrant will be very effective during the interrogation of the Skakels. In an investigation, the evidence usually speaks for itself. Then the suspect, confronted by the evidence, seals his own fate. The ability to produce incriminating evidence taken from a suspect's home is extremely useful in an interrogation. If a suspect claims during a taped interview that Martha was never in the Skakel house, and you have already collected hair and fiber evidence from the guest room, this is the kind of leverage that can turn an interrogation into a confession.

During the first interviews, you look for the suspect to act somewhat differently from other members of the household. Once this person is singled out, you will turn the interview into an interrogation. There's no reason to turn up the heat yet. You simply let the suspect explain whatever he feels he needs to explain. You provide him with the opportunity to try to talk his way out of it.

The suspect doesn't know what evidence, if any, he left at the scene or at his house. He doesn't know what evidence, if any, was recovered during the investigation and search. Even if you failed to find one piece of evidence in the house, during interrogation the suspect will attempt to make statements that cover possible evidence he thinks might be found. He will try to build a cover story that you can dismantle with the knowledge you now possess.

At some point during the interrogation, as you begin to bear down on the suspect, you advise him of his constitutional rights. If he waives his rights, then you press ahead with a strong interrogation, using the evidence, other witness statements, and his own statements against him. At the very least, he will make incriminating statements and show awareness of his guilt. You might even get a confession.

If the suspect requests an attorney and the interrogation is stopped, you have good reason to believe that your suspect has something to hide. Then you have to build a case against him without his cooperation. Even if he does confess, you still should continue with the investigation. Either way, after the first day of the case you will:

1. Attend the autopsy on November 1, whether or not you got any sleep the night before.

2. Obtain search warrants for phone records of the Skakel residence and the offices of Great Lakes Carbon. Phone calls made prior to 12:30 P.M. could show possible knowledge of Martha's death before the body was officially found. Phone calls made after that time could also yield important circumstantial evidence.

3. Obtain flight records for the Great Lakes Carbon corporate jet on October 30–31. Find out where Rushton Skakel was, who he was with, how and when he found out about the murder, and why he returned to Greenwich.

4. Obtain medical records of all possible suspects through search warrant or subpoena.

5. Obtain blood and hair samples from all possible suspects, either voluntarily or by search warrant.

6. Obtain voluntary hair samples from everyone who was close to the victim's body under the pine tree.

7. Request a polygraph examination of the suspect. Attend the polygraph and make sure the examiners ask a wide range of pertinent questions.

8. Control all the reports and their copies. Advise your fellow detectives of the progress and specific direction of the investigation.

9. Say nothing to the press except: "There has been a murder of a fifteen-year-old girl and the investigation is in progress." Make sure that no other police or officials talk to the press.

If the Moxley investigation had followed these guidelines, they probably would have had an arrest within a few weeks, or even days. This isn't hindsight or expert detective skills, just basic police procedure and common sense.

20

Legal Smoke Screens

I am absolutely convinced that Thomas Skakel is innocent.
I will not discuss my reasons for saying this.
—Manny Margolis

Even if the police investigation had been conducted properly, the successful prosecution of the Moxley murder would have run into interference created by lawyers on both sides. The Skakel family lawyers did their best to make sure that the case was not prosecuted. They got a lot of help from their counterpart in the state's attorney office.

Don Browne was the first lawyer in the Moxley case. He served as Fairfield County state's attorney at the time of Martha's murder and has held on to the case for nearly twenty-two years. When his jurisdiction was changed, Browne took the case with him. Even when he retired, Browne was named a special prosecutor if the Moxley case ever went to trial.

When the Skakels rescinded their cooperation, the Greenwich police met with Browne to seek his help in setting up a meeting with Rushton Skakel and Manny Margolis. That is what the police report states, but the meeting had another agenda. The police basically took their case to Don Browne and said: Look, everything points to Tommy Skakel. You convene an investigative grand jury, they bring in a true bill, then we indict him. A true bill states there is enough evidence and probable cause to bring in an indictment. It eliminates a preliminary hearing, and the case goes straight to superior court. Browne said no. He didn't want to try the case and lose because they would not have another chance. If Thomas was found not guilty, that was it—end of the case.

In the meantime, Browne publicly blamed the Skakels for not cooperating. In late March 1976, he told the Associated Press that the police were "apparently being frustrated by the refusal of a particular family, which could supply pertinent information to assist or cooperate" in the investigation. He stated that the family "have apparently been advised not to assist in the probe." In that statement, Browne also made his first public comment about a grand jury, saying that he did not intend to call a grand jury in the Moxley case, basically confirming what he already told the Greenwich police. He apparently did not want to try the case. Didn't he think there was enough evidence? Didn't he think he could win?

Browne brought so much heat on the Greenwich police with his comment that five days later he had to qualify his statements, telling *Greenwich*

Time: "With a continuing objective look at what the Greenwich Police Dept. has done, I have assured [the community] that this investigation is proceeding in an intelligent, competent and appropriate manner."

By 1982 the Moxley investigation was basically put to rest because Ken Littleton was not a viable suspect and they could not investigate Thomas any further without his cooperation. There is no state law against police talking consensually to a suspect without advising him, but the police had been warned by Margolis that they would be accused of harassment if they continued to badger him. Meanwhile, Don Browne continued to tell the police there was not enough evidence for a grand jury. "We were held off with hopes of the grand jury and that never materialized," a Greenwich detective said.

If they had known that Browne was never going to take the case to a grand jury, the Greenwich police probably would have arrested Thomas, according to Steve Carroll. Don Browne had advised them that an arrest probably was not a prudent move because there was not enough evidence.

When Steve Carroll and Jim Lunney were working the case, making it three detectives, including Keegan, against at least four Skakel family lawyers, the Greenwich detectives frequently went up to Bridgeport to meet with Browne. In those meetings, the police gave Browne all the information they had. Once Steve Carroll asked, "Why not convene a grand jury?"

"Don't tell me how to do my job!" Browne responded. He turned to Tom Keegan and said, "I don't want him up here anymore."

Carroll believes that "Browne doesn't intend to indict and never has. That's why he's so hypersensitive." For a political animal like Don Browne, a grand jury should be the perfect fallback. If they indict, then there must be enough evidence. If they don't indict, then he is off the hook. Why won't Browne do it?

As a state, Connecticut does not have investigative subpoena power—the ability to compel witnesses to testify before a grand jury in a case where an arrest or indictment is not impending. When prosecutors run out of other options, they can call a grand jury of one. A superior-court judge considers the evidence, hears testimony, and can recommend that an arrest be made or a civilian grand jury impaneled.

The problem with a grand jury of one is that in order to compel witnesses to testify, they have to be granted immunity. Browne and Solomon have told the Moxleys that they wouldn't ask for a grand jury of one because by doing so they would have to grant someone immunity and they wanted to make sure that they had the right person. Despite the fact that they were pursuing the wrong suspects—Thomas Skakel and Ken Littleton—by judicious use of immunity they could compel knowledgeable witnesses to testify and gain useful new information that could lead to the real killer.

As far back as March 1976, Browne has been

saying that he does not intend to convene a grand jury. At each stage of the investigation—the 1991 reinvestigation, Henry Lee's 1994 survey of the evidence, the Sutton Associates revelations, new rounds of DNA testing—Browne has promised to consider a grand jury and then refused to convene one.

The Moxleys have repeatedly urged Browne to convene a grand jury, and he has always put them off. "What was frustrating to us," John Moxley said, "is that Don Browne always said, we're going to do it next January, and that was three Januarys past."

When the Sutton Associates revelations came to light, Browne stated: "I certainly hope these investigators will produce existing authenticated reports so that the investigation may be pursued, assisted by them." In other words, he wanted Sutton to give everything to the police.

Because of his firm's client relationship with the Skakel family, Jim Murphy could not volunteer information to authorities. He did tell Len Levitt that if he were subpoenaed, he would turn over everything he had. In other words, he was virtually asking Browne to call a grand jury and force him to testify. Browne refused, as he had done from the beginning. While publicly hoping that the Sutton Associates information would be authenticated, Browne was refusing to use his own legal authority to do it himself, even though the potential witness was eager to testify.

After my informant Batman called the *Unsolved*

Mysteries tip line and provided information about Michael Skakel, Don Browne contacted him. Batman now says that when he told his story, Browne said to him: "Okay, are you lying to me? Don't be lying to me."

"Why would I lie to you?" Batman asked incredulously.

If Browne treated a possible source of valuable information in that manner, why did he do so? I've used snitches before who were junkies, thieves, and murderers. I'll talk to anybody if it might help solve the murder of an innocent young girl. And Batman is actually a good guy. Why won't Don Browne work with a confidential source who wants to help?

Perhaps Browne was suspicious of Batman because he had already been so intimidated by the Skakel lawyers and others that he didn't know whom to trust or believe anymore. If he did call a grand jury today, he would probably try to indict the wrong suspect. And that's possibly how the Skakel lawyers planned it.

The Skakel family lawyers might have been involved in the Moxley case even before Don Browne. They were certainly called in a few hours after Martha's body was found, if not sooner. Jim McKenzie arrived at the Skakel house at 5:15 P.M., having taken a train from Grand Central in Manhattan and then a cab from the Greenwich train station. The trip takes approximately one hour, (longer if he took a local or had to wait for a train to depart). Cab rides to and from the train stations add at least another fifteen minutes total, which means McKenzie would have had to leave his office around 4:00 P.M. at the latest.

McKenzie arrived at 5:15 P.M. He spoke to Michael, but Thomas was not home. When Thomas came back from the field hockey game, McKenzie took him aside before letting him speak to police. McKenzie told me that he didn't give Thomas any legal advice. He said, "I thought about . . . whether I was going to get into the criminal law capacity here of client relationship." While he decided not to represent Thomas in any criminal capacity, McKenzie did ask the boy if there was anything he wanted to tell him. Thomas said no, and McKenzie allowed the police to take him to headquarters.

Although McKenzie said he wasn't at the Skakel house to represent anybody criminally, he could have assumed that role if necessary. That's why he was sent there. If he didn't need to play the criminal attorney role, he could serve as information gatherer and report back to Rushton and the senior attorneys. Any information he did gather could be protected by attorney-client privilege.

McKenzie never talked to the police, and he never talked to reporters, aside from telling them to get away from the house. He never went to the police station. He is never mentioned in any police reports. No official with whom I spoke even knew who he was. For twenty-two years, McKenzie's role in the Moxley case had been kept secret, until I read his name in the Sutton Associates files and figured he must have been an attorney.

Other lawyers involved in the case were more prominent. Chris Roosevelt was a Skakel family friend and former Justice Department attorney who sat on the board of the Whitby School and served as the school's counsel. He said he told Rushton Skakel to hire a criminal lawyer.

Great Lakes Carbon attorneys Joe Donovan and Tom Hayes gave Rushton Skakel extensive legal counsel on the Moxley case. Donovan attended several meetings with Rushton and the police and was there at the Ix house when Rushton collapsed with chest pains shortly after rescinding cooperation. Donovan was, in effect, the family attorney on the matter until Manny Margolis was hired.

Manny Margolis is said by many to be one of the top criminal attorneys in the state of Connecticut. Margolis has certainly been effective in this case, at least in keeping his client from being prosecuted.

Tom Sheridan is an attorney in general private practice in New York City. Michael Skakel has been his legal responsibility since at least 1978, when he helped resolve the Windham incident, and probably earlier. Sheridan is not a criminal attorney, but on several occasions has said that he represented Michael Skakel concerning the Moxley murder. He had to say that he represented Michael in order to claim attorney-client privilege concerning the sensitive information he controls regarding the boy. Sheridan is now "semiretired." In December 1997, he stated he no longer represented Michael Skakel and didn't know who had taken over his case.

While the Skakel lawyers sheltered Michael, they defended Thomas. Tom Sheridan even appeared to be blaming the victim when he told Sharon Churcher of *Penthouse:* "Tommy was horsing around with Martha before she was killed, but that's because she was a vivacious girl and she thought he was pretty cute."

The Skakel attorneys have been anticipating a prosecution for some time now, but they haven't just been on the defensive, building a potential defense for their clients. They have also taken the offensive, protecting their clients from investigation and scrutiny and creating or releasing information that would cloud the issue of their guilt in an attempt to preclude any possible prosecution.

The Skakel family hired Sutton Associates following the renewed attention the Moxley case had received, and the reinvestigation announced by Connecticut authorities. According to Tom Sheridan in *Penthouse,* "The Kennedy family has been saying, 'Why in God's name aren't we fighting back? Well, now we are. . . . We'll spend a few bucks to put the record straight and clear Tommy's name.'"

When the firm was first hired, Len Levitt was approached by Tom Sheridan, Jim Murphy, and Willis Krebs, a retired lieutenant from the New York Police Department working for Sutton. The lawyer and investigators told Levitt that the purpose of their investigation was to gather information in the event that Thomas was arrested. At the same time, they said that they didn't think he would be arrested and that authorities would most likely prosecute Ken Littleton.

Sutton did its best to make that possible.

"Our original objective was based on the premise that Kenneth Littleton committed a homicide," Jim Murphy told Levitt, "and that Connecticut authorities were serious about prosecuting him."

When Sutton attempted to cast suspicion on a suspect outside the Skakel family, Connecticut investigators went for the bait. Frank Garr and Jack Solomon even met with the Sutton Associates and Skakel lawyers several times. Garr and Solomon's stated objective of the meetings was to glean information about the Skakels' investigation. Instead, Garr and Solomon apparently gave the Skakels and Sutton more information than anyone gave them. Garr and Solomon told them that while the Greenwich police had focused on Thomas as a suspect, they believed Littleton was the killer. They also said that they believed Littleton had killed other young women.

"What do I have to do to convince you that Littleton is our man?" Solomon told the Skakel lawyers at one meeting, according to a document in the Sutton files. The memo continued: "Believing that if Littleton was indicted his defense lawyer would certainly 'be dragging in' members of the Skakel family into the case, Sheridan was motivated to prepare for such a potentiality."

Sutton did extensive background investigation

on Ken Littleton and turned much of it over to the Connecticut authorities, who had already gone over most of that ground themselves. The private investigators began to suspect whether Garr and Solomon were sincere in their suspicion of Littleton, or whether they were simply playing along in order to gain Sutton's trust and cooperation.

"Certain allegations [Garr and Solomon] made regarding Littleton's supposed guilt seem to have been without merit," A Sutton analyst concluded. "Solomon alluded to developments in the investigation which, at this point, seem to have been misleading or entirely false."

Frank Garr knew about Sutton Associates from the beginning. In addition to his meetings with them attended by Solomon, he also accompanied at least one former Greenwich police officer on an interview with the Sutton investigators.

Dominick Dunne gave Frank Garr a copy of the Sutton Associates files in the winter of 1997. Yet apparently Frank had talked to hardly any of the people I interviewed whose names I got from the files. And none of the leads I followed showed any of Garr's tracks. Just what exactly did he do with the Sutton files?

On several occasions after Len Levitt's 1995 articles ran, Frank Garr said that he was going to follow up on the Sutton Associates disclosures. Steve Carroll ran into Frank at a funeral at St. Mary's in Greenwich and asked him if he had confirmed anything, specifically Thomas's and Michael's change of stories. According to Carroll, Frank just shrugged his shoulders.

Frank Garr told Dorthy Moxley that the Sutton Associates files were just "scenarios." Dorthy was "dumbfounded" when she heard that Frank had the documents and apparently hadn't done anything with them.

When Sutton Associates found out that I had their files, they called me and tried halfheartedly to threaten me with a lawsuit. They knew they had no legal leverage over me, and soon our conversation turned to the subject of a possible grand jury.

"My thinking all along," Jim Murphy told me, "was that if the Greenwich authorities had at any point wanted to find out the results of our investigation, they should have gotten a grand jury together, they should have tested the privilege and saw whether or not it existed."

Once again, Jim Murphy was virtually begging to be subpoenaed.

"If you were the case detective on this thing," Murphy continued, "you would have turned everything upside down and you would have dragged my ass before a grand jury as soon as you could."

Murphy clearly wants to break the privilege, give the information he has to the proper authorities, and no longer be held by this privilege. The only way he can do this is by being subpoenaed by the grand jury.

After the Sutton revelations were made public, the Moxleys asked Browne whether he could convene a grand jury and get the whole story from the Sutton investigators. Browne said he didn't know whether that information was privileged or not. So the Moxleys hired their lawyer, Jack Zeldes, to do research into the issue and write a study of his findings. I don't know why Don Browne could not have come up with the answer himself, or why the Moxleys had to pay for research on an issue that any junior attorney should know. Zeldes concluded that since Tom Sheridan hired Sutton Associates and Sheridan was not Thomas Skakel's lawyer, the information was not privileged. Using that reasoning, since Tom Sheridan was Michael's lawyer, then Michael's statements would be privileged.

I would argue that since the information was generated by interviews with outside investigators and then passed through at least two other sources—the author of the report and Dominick Dunne—it can no longer be privileged. Once the information is out, the privilege no longer matters. Dominick Dunne did not have any privilege commitment to the Skakel boys. And I certainly don't.

Privilege is not an issue here. Tom Sheridan and Manny Margolis know that. Sutton Associates tried to claim that the information was privileged because its leaking compromised the firm's reputation.

Jim Murphy said that the Skakel attorneys are threatening him with a lawsuit over breach of contract and confidentiality. He also threatened to take me to court, but he hasn't and he won't. Just as the

Skakel attorneys won't ever sue him. They won't sue him because he did just what they wanted. Is it possible that they actually wanted him to leak the boys' stories?

As far as the Skakel lawyers were concerned, hiring Sutton Associates was not a search for the truth but the first step in a legal defense. Although they appear to be analyzing the evidence objectively, or even prejudicially against the Skakel suspects, the detective agency was only able to analyze what evidence they were given, in other words, evidence the Skakel lawyers wanted them to have.

When Sutton were first hired, Tom Sheridan stated that the assault took place just after 9:30. "Tommy was talking to another of his friends at the front door, so he could not have seen the assailant," he said in his *Penthouse* interview.

After Henry Lee was brought onto the case, Sheridan and Margolis met with Lee and other Connecticut officials. Lee told the Skakel lawyers that he was planning to perform DNA tests on evidence collected at the crime scene. If there was a chance the Skakel boys left DNA stains on Martha or nearby, they now had to account for this possibly damaging evidence.

They could not go public and just change the stories they gave to the police nineteen years prior, but they could change their stories and then hire investigators to discover the new information through independent professional channels other than the police. The Skakel attorneys had to realize that Littleton could make absolutely incriminating statements about Michael and/or Tommy. The lawyers had to prepare for that possibility. What better way to change your alibi than at the hands of a skilled ex-FBI agent who finally gets to the truth?

Let's take a closer look at the boys' changing stories and see what they really tell us:

The sexual encounter Thomas Skakel described would account for his semen, hair, skin, and possibly even blood being on Martha's clothes or body. The story Michael told about masturbating in the tree would account for his semen possibly being on her. And his movements and actions from 11:40 to 12:30 that night placed him all over the Moxley property and Walsh Lane—everywhere he might have been seen.

The times of the two stories neatly overlap. Thomas said that the sexual encounter began at 9:30 and ended at 9:50. By the end of that encounter, Michael was at the Terriens'—if he went there. Thomas's story could cover Michael's possibly killing Martha before 10:00 P.M. And it accounts for his own presence on the rear lawn with Martha during that period of time, engaging in activity that a witness might think was some kind of violent act.

Through questioning of Ken Littleton and the other Skakel children, Sutton raises suspicion as to whether Michael went to the Terriens' in the first place. If Michael didn't go to the Terriens', then he could have killed Martha at any time between 9:30 and 12:30. If he did go to the Terriens', then he either could have killed her before he left—which is improbable, because he would have been covered in blood on the way to the Terrien house—or he could have killed her after he returned at 11:20.

On the other hand, Thomas could have met back up with Martha after establishing his presence in the house by watching twenty minutes of television with Ken Littleton and then saying he was going to bed. He could have gone back out after 10:30 and killed Martha then.

Do you see how confusing it gets? Instead of clarifying who killed Martha and how he did it, the Sutton revelations only cloud the issue. Is that what the Skakel attorneys intended, and why they hired the investigators in the first place?

During Thomas's second interview, when he gave further details of the sexual encounter, Manny Margolis stopped the interview. Sutton wanted to talk with Thomas again, but Tom Sheridan would not allow another interview. He also told Sutton that a written report being prepared by the agency would not be needed. Once the stories were leaked to Len Levitt, Sutton had already served its purpose. However much the Skakel lawyers might have wanted Thomas's and Michael's new alibis out, they certainly were not prepared for the files to be given to Dominick Dunne.

The Sutton Associates revelations made Michael a suspect for the first time. Now even the Greenwich police were thinking he might have killed Martha. Meanwhile, Manny Margolis said that he would consider allowing Thomas Skakel to be questioned by authorities if someone else was indicted in the case.

Are the Skakel lawyers playing a shell game with the suspects? For a long time, Thomas and Michael have been represented by separate counsel, in the event that both of them are accused of the murder. The state's attorney office was already confused and frustrated by the facts in the case and unwilling to indict or convene a grand jury. The Sutton Associates revelations have only made them more confused and more frustrated. While the boys' newest statements make it more apparent that at least one of them could be involved in the death of Martha Moxley, the chances of a prosecution seem even more remote.

The Skakel attorneys have a copy of the autopsy and possibly other confidential police records. Skakel money, power, and connections have intimidated the Greenwich police and the state's attorney office. For twenty-two years, the investigation has been at a standstill.

"So long as this police department wants a Skakel as a prime suspect," Tom Sheridan said, "we are not going to talk to them any further."

And as long as the Skakels refuse to talk to the police, Connecticut authorities have an excuse for why they haven't prosecuted.

21

It Can't Happen Here

If you live the lie, you must believe it.
—Fox Mulder

The people of Greenwich are living a lie. They think that by moving out to an exclusive suburb and sheltering themselves with money, and all the things and people money can buy, they can avoid, or at least ignore, human depravity. They are wrong. Greenwich may be richer, prettier, and safer than most other places on this earth, but it is not immune to evil. In fact, the massive state of denial under which the town seems to operate is a form of evil itself.

Not everybody in Greenwich shares that attitude. A lot of people spoke to me, many under the promise of anonymity. Some people even stopped me on the street and gave me encouragement. A secretary at the police headquarters said, "My money is on you." Working in the police department, she knows firsthand what I was up against.

One Greenwich local explained public opinion

this way: "The Skakels know more than they're telling. If that's the case, and everybody's innocent, then why are they not talking? The difference is, at the upper-class level, it's kind of a joke. Among the blue-collar guys, it's yeah, 'The prick sonofabitch got away with it.'"

In the fall of 1975, Belle Haven was the richest neighborhood in the richest town in the richest country in the world. With all of the guard booths and security patrols and off-duty policemen working on the side, Belle Haven residents couldn't protect themselves from murder. When Martha Moxley was killed, they didn't know how to react.

The day Martha's body was found, toilet paper still hung from the trees, and some mailboxes were still filled with shaving cream, reminders of the innocent hijinks that went on the night she died. "We thought we were safe in our community," said one Belle Haven resident. "But I guess we weren't."

After the shock wore off, and the reality sunk in that the killer did not just wander in from the turnpike but was probably in their midst, Greenwich residents became even more afraid. "Everybody was jumpy. People were getting paranoid," according to one detective.

Even to this day, people are afraid. One person who spoke to me under the condition that I not use her name said, "I'm scared to death and still am. It's still unsolved. Somebody's out there and I'm afraid."

The easiest way for Greenwich residents to deal with the fear of crime is to deny that it ever happens.

Despite the fact that the town consistently ranks near the top of Connecticut municipalities in per-capita spending on police, their police department—in 1975 and still to this day—is woefully inexperienced, ill trained, incompetent, and naive.

Their naïveté was particularly apparent in the Moxley case. Dan Hickman, one of the first officers to arrive on the scene and an attender of the autopsy, got sick at the sight of blood. Another officer who helped bag the body vomited at the crime scene. Tom Sorenson, the Greenwich criminalist, had difficulty processing the scene because he had a daughter the same age as Martha.

"Who ever heard of a fifteen-year-old girl being murdered for no apparent reason in an area where there is so little of this type of crime?" Chief Stephen Baran asked. "Why would anyone want to murder a fifteen-year-old girl for? We have not come up with a definite motive for this murder. The motive in most criminal acts is quite apparent but there is no indication of the usual motives in this case."

Baran and the Greenwich police seemed to expect that they would find clear and understandable reasons for Martha's murder. They were not trying to get into the head of the suspect; they wanted to make sense of the act for themselves. A murder didn't fit into their own minds, limited by a sheltered and comfortable existence. So they didn't even try to understand it.

Such naïveté was exploited by the crude application of power by interested parties. That power was exerted by the Skakels and their attorneys, of course, but it also came from other local sources who wanted the incident over with and forgotten as soon as possible.

One Sunday morning well into the investigation, Chief Stephen Baran asked Steve Carroll and Jim Lunney to come into headquarters. From there they went to town hall, where a meeting was held between the two detectives, Baran, First Selectman Rupert Vernon, and the president of the Belle Haven Association.

Vernon, who basically served as police commissioner, introduced the detectives to the president of the Belle Haven Association and said, "We'd like you to tell him where you are on this case."

Carroll and Lunney looked at each other in disbelief. They were working an open homicide case, where too much information had already been released.

"We can't jeopardize the case by telling you anything," the detectives said.

"No, no you don't understand," Vernon replied. "He's president of the Belle Haven Association."

"We can't tell you anything and we think it's wrong for you to call us in and tell us to do this," Carroll said, and then the two detectives walked out of the meeting.

Power loves a vacuum and it found one in the Moxley case. No one took charge in the beginning. No one took charge when the Sutton Associates files dropped on their desks. To this day, people still refuse to take responsibility. Since the state's attorney office was involved from day one, the Greenwich police have found a convenient excuse why the case has never been prosecuted—they blame the DA. And the state's attorney office blames the Greenwich police. When they're together, they blame the suspect for not cooperating, or me for investigating a cold case.

The Moxley murder was not an isolated case, in which normally competent investigators were stymied by money and power. In Greenwich, unsolved homicides are business as usual. Other than self-solvers, I could not find a single homicide in nearly fifty years that the Greenwich police have actually solved.

On September 5, 1984, the body of thirteen-year-old Matthew Margolies was found in a wooded area near the Byram River, where he had been fishing. He had been stabbed repeatedly with a boning knife, then asphyxiated and buried in a shallow grave. The boy had been dead for five days before his body was discovered. As many as six Greenwich detectives investigated the case but got nowhere. Peter Robbins, newly promoted captain of the detective division, said the investigation had been frustrated by a lack of cooperation among local residents.

By 1986 the Greenwich police were forced to admit that the Margolies investigation was at a standstill. While Robbins made repeated claims that he did not need outside help, Chief Tom Keegan

hired Vernon Geberth to evaluate the investigation.
Geberth wrote an eighteen-page report and submitted it to the department. When *Greenwich Time* asked for a copy of the report, the Greenwich police refused to release it. After five years of legal battles, the state Freedom of Information Commission finally ordered the department to release Geberth's report.

The report stated that there was a "clear lack of effective coordination" in the early stages of the investigation.

- No detective had been assigned to check the initial missing person report, and six days of early investigation were lost.
- Only one detective assigned to the investigation actually viewed the crime scene.
- No one briefed officers when they arrived on the crime scene.
- There was no crime scene or assignment log.
- Officers were given assignments, but those assignments were not explained to them.
- Sensitive information was released to the press.
- Then-captain of detectives William Anderson was singled out for his "desire to personally 'take charge' of the investigation."

While Geberth did say that the Greenwich police "conducted a professional and exhaustive investigation," the report clearly showed that the lessons of the Moxley case had not been learned.

Tom Keegan was in charge of this one, too. He had become chief of police in early 1982. His predecessor, Chief Raymond Grant, had been forced out by First Selectwoman Rebecca Breed, who then "ramrodded" Keegan into the post, according to one former selectman.

After less than two years on the job, Keegan received a 105–14 vote of no confidence from his officers, who complained of Keegan's lack of respect for officers and unfair use of his disciplinary powers. Keegan defended his administration by pointing out that the department was writing more traffic tickets than ever before. Breed stood by her chief, calling the vote "outrageous and intolerable."

Breed was defeated in the next election for first selectman, but Keegan stayed in office until 1986. Upon his retirement, the police union issued a statement to "express its joy, due to the announcement of Chief Thomas G. Keegan's retirement."

Keegan moved down to Myrtle Beach, South Carolina, where he ran as a Republican for a seat in the state House of Representatives. Keegan won his first election in 1988 and every one since. He was reelected again in 1997.

Many people have speculated that the Moxley murder was covered up by corrupt police officials. After his investigation, Len Levitt concluded "it wasn't a cover-up, it was a screwup." I would take it further and say the Moxley case was a cover-up of a screwup.

Certainly the Skakel money, power, and connections obstructed the investigation, intimidated the police, and confused the prosecutors. I believe the Greenwich police and Connecticut state's attorney office genuinely wanted to solve Martha's murder. They just didn't know how and refused to admit it. Now they have realized they made mistakes and are afraid that someone—a defense attorney, a journalist, or an experienced homicide detective—might uncover those and other mistakes they don't even realize they made. That is why they don't want to go to trial and why they don't even want to talk about it.

Corruption comes in many forms. Sometimes it is a payoff. Other times it is simply fear, laziness, selfishness. Everybody has his reasons for not solving the Moxley case, or not helping those who could have. There are always reasons not to do something, and cowards will turn those reasons into excuses.

One of the worst forms of cowardice is silence. Fortunately, we have legal mechanisms to compel people to testify if they have relevant information concerning a felony. It is called a grand jury, and the Connecticut state's attorney office should convene one immediately. Here is a brief list of some of the people who should be called and the questions they should be asked.

1. Ken Littleton—What did you see? What do you know?

2. Mildred Ix—What was going on in the Skakel house on October 31, 1975? Who

phoned Rush Skakel and at what time?
Who phoned Jim McKenzie and why? Did
you talk to the Kennedys? Why did Rush
collapse on January 21, 1976? Why do you
think Michael could have committed the
murder?

3. Sheila McGuire—Why were you walking
   through the Moxley yard? Did you or did
   you not know that Martha was missing? Did
   anybody tell you to look beneath the tree?

4. Jim Murphy—Tell us everything about
   the Skakel family's hiring of your firm and
   the information you collected. How did
   you get the autopsy report?

5. Jim Terrien—Did Michael go with you?
   Where were you at midnight when Dorthy
   Moxley called your house?

6. Rush Jr., John, and Julie Skakel—How
   many kids were at your house on October
   30, 1975? What exactly was going on?
   Did Michael leave for the Terriens'? What
   happened after 11:20 P.M.?

7. Helen Ix—What exactly went on between
   Thomas and Martha. Why do you think
   Thomas is innocent?

8. Tom Keegan—What happened to the golf
    club handle and shaft that Hickman and
    Jones observed at the scene?

If the Connecticut state's attorney refuses to call a
grand jury, then federal authorities should take the
next step. The Department of Justice should investigate not only the murder but the investigation as
well. I would give them everything I have, including information I did not use in this book.

I think a lot of people know something about
the murder of Martha Moxley, and that is why they
are not talking. Mildred Ix may know something.
Maybe that is why she told at least one neighbor not
to talk to me and to kick me off their property if I
ever showed up. If for no other reason, a grand jury
should be convened to compel Mildred Ix to testify.

Initially, the people of Belle Haven were very
cooperative with the police. They allowed them to
search their houses and properties and assisted them as
much as they could in the investigation. Once suspicion fixed on the Skakel house, and the police couldn't
seem to do anything to break the case, their neighbors
became afraid and disgusted. "They said, 'You know
who did it,'" Steve Carroll remembered, "'why don't
you just leave us alone.'" The good citizens of Belle
Haven knew that the killer came from the Skakel
home. They wanted their police department to take
care of it all for them. But they didn't want to get
involved. After all, that's what they pay the police for,
isn't it?

The people of Greenwich and Belle Haven have to understand that crime solving and prevention isn't like tending a prize rose garden. You can't just turn it over to your hired professionals and expect them to do everything. The police need the help and support of the community they work in. If they don't get it, they can't do their jobs. If a community doesn't even want to admit that they have crime, their police are never going to be able to solve crimes.

Belle Haven residents found the Moxley investigation "bothersome." In 1980, a *Greenwich Time* reporter wrote, "A lot of people would rather not talk about Martha Moxley anymore." They wanted the murder investigation to go away. Unfortunately, for them, it wouldn't. While he was alive, David Moxley worked hard to keep the investigation going on the right track. When he died, Dorthy and John Moxley used the media to generate public attention and pressure, and then used a great deal of their own time, energy, and money to assist the reinvestigation they had largely created.

Meanwhile, many in Belle Haven wanted people to forget about Martha Moxley and the horrible way she died. Chief among them were the Skakels and their closest friends. Some of those friends also claimed to be friends of the Moxleys, but they were secretly relieved when the Moxleys moved out of Walsh Lane and then moved away from Greenwich altogether. While they remained in Greenwich, the Moxleys were uncomfortable reminders of horror and tragedy, and the people of Belle Haven do not like to be made uncomfortable.

Unfortunately, this attitude is supported by the Greenwich police and Belle Haven security officers. They repeatedly harassed me when I was in Belle Haven. It was obvious that the Greenwich police would not have gone to such great lengths to keep me off the private property of working-class citizens. Since I was stepping onto the hallowed ground of Belle Haven, they pulled me over, checked up on my whereabouts, and questioned me five separate times. When I attempted to make a civilian complaint concerning the treatment I had received from a Belle Haven guard and Greenwich police officers, I was told by a police operator, "Well, I guess you just don't rate." Then she hung up on me.

After Steve Carroll and I were asked to leave the old Moxley property by the McAntees, Dorthy said: "I can't imagine why people wouldn't want this thing to be over with. Who are they trying to protect? Why are they acting as if nothing ever happened? It did happen, and people are fortunate it didn't happen to their children."

Since he retired, Steve Carroll makes a little side money giving people rides to the airport. One day he picked up Robert, Mildred, and Helen Ix. Helen asked Steve, "Have they finally left Tommy alone?"

"Why do you ask that?" Steve said.

"Well, I don't think he should be a suspect."

"Well, I think he should be and it's too bad we can't investigate it further," Steve said. "Your mom and dad are here, suppose the shoe was on the other foot, how do you think they should act?"

"I just think they should leave Tommy alone," Helen said.

That was the end of the conversation.

Steve's first impression was that the Ixes "were trying to brush it off and leave it alone." Then he started thinking, "They just wanted to find out what I knew and was there an ongoing investigation?" The conversation occurred right around the time the case was reopened.

When word got out that I was writing a book about the Moxley murder, John Moxley's former neighbor Wright Ferguson invited John to a party in Belle Haven. Many of their old Belle Haven friends were there. As usual, no one talked about the tragedy they had experienced together. "Nobody talked about the murder," said one person who attended the party. "It was not the type of thing that you brought up."

As the evening progressed, Helen Ix insisted that John and his wife spend the night. Helen is married now and lives with her husband in a beautiful new house at the corner of Walsh Lane and Field Point Road. Julie Skakel's soon-to-be-ex-husband also happened to be staying there, but Helen didn't find that odd. She wanted everybody to get along and forget about whatever conflicts they might have had in the past.

While some of their friends wish it would go away, the Moxleys will never let go or forget. "You just can't put it in the closet and shut the door and say it didn't happen," Dorthy said.

"There's a lot of people who are close to this who are a lot more knowledgeable about specific events who are petrified to come forward," said one Greenwich resident. "Because they know what would happen."

What would happen? I went into Greenwich and started turning over rocks. Aside from a semithreatening phone call from Sutton Associates, some silly police incidents, and a few nasty comments in the newspaper, nothing happened to me.

Yes, the Skakels are powerful. But so are many others in Greenwich, including the Moxleys themselves. Is it really the Skakel money and power that keeps Greenwich residents silent—or are they just afraid or unwilling to bring up a distasteful incident?

"The impression is you're taking on this evil empire," said one Greenwich native. "How much of that is self-created illusion and how much of that is reality, I don't know."

Dorthy Moxley doesn't understand why people are so afraid of the Skakels. "They aren't the SS or Big Brother," Dorthy said. "Who cares about this crummy family?"

Nothing is more powerful than the truth. If you are right, you have no reason to be afraid. If you have done nothing wrong, you have nothing to hide. What is Greenwich afraid of? Why don't they want this case solved?

No matter how much the Skakels, the Greenwich Police Department, and many people in Greenwich wish it would go away, the Moxley case is not over. In the opinion of one police expert who has closely observed the case, the investigation hasn't even begun. "You've got to start all over again," he said, "because it's all over the sidewalk now."

There is still hope that the killer of Martha Moxley can be brought to justice. It will take a little bit more courage and determination on the part of not just the police but everyone in the community. As far as I am concerned, the murder of an innocent young girl is the worst single crime that anyone can commit. If someone can kill a girl in the most secure neighborhood of Greenwich and go unpunished, then who is safe anywhere?

A week after Martha's murder the *Stamford Advocate* published an editorial that ended with this somber note: "Martha Moxley, bludgeoned in a heavily guarded section of Greenwich, is proof that none of us is immune from the danger of being a victim."

The people of Greenwich should understand one thing: It can happen here. It did happen here. Someone killed Martha Moxley and got away with it. And the reason he got away with it was that the Greenwich Police Department and the citizens of Greenwich didn't have the courage to go after him.

"I just know Martha's murder will be solved someday," Dorthy Moxley says. "I'm not going to give up."

Neither am I, Dorthy.

AFTERWORD

One month after the publication of this book in hard-cover, Connecticut authorities convened a one-man grand jury in the Moxley case. The target of the grand jury probe was Michael Skakel.

On June 17, 1998, a Hartford television station and the Associated Press reported that the state's attorney office would be announcing a press conference concerning the Moxley case scheduled for the morning of June 19, 1998. When word got out that the event would announce the convening of a grand jury, the authorities realized that their press conference had already lost all of its news value, and if they went ahead as scheduled, they would only have to answer more questions. The press conference was canceled.

I flew to New York on June 18. During my media tour in May, defense attorney Mickey Sherman, the only person who would publicly debate me concerning my findings in this book, had challenged me to give all the information I gathered to Frank Garr. I did have evidence to give to the authorities, but I had no intention of giving it to Frank Garr. Instead, I went over his head, contacting Connecticut state officials and offering my total cooperation with their investigation, including my interview tapes and transcripts, as well as information I was not able to include in the book.

Frank Garr was one obstacle, Don Browne was another. Although Browne had officially retired in September 1997, he had retained control of the Moxley case as special prosecutor. Shortly before my book was published, Browne suddenly gave up the Moxley case.

Browne told the press that rumors that he had been paid off by the Skakels might create a possible appearance of conflict in the case. Although these rumors, published in Tim Dumas's *Greentown*, another book about the Moxley murder, were Browne's official reason for giving up the case, in fact, Browne was forced to give up the case by state authorities who wanted to call a grand jury but felt that Browne stood in the way.

State's Attorney Jonathan Benedict took over the Moxley case and quickly applied for an investigatory grand jury. A three-judge panel sitting in New Haven granted the request, marking only the eighth time the state of Connecticut has convened a one-man grand jury since 1985.

From a pool of one hundred and sixty Superior Court Judges, Chief Court Administrator Aaron Ment selected George N. Thim, a fifty-five-year-old Trumbull resident who had been sitting as a judge for twelve years. Although most of his experience was in civil rather than criminal cases, Thim came to the Moxley case with a solid reputation.

While serving as a public defender, Thim took four cases to state appellate court and won overturned convictions on three of his appeals. The prosecutor in each of the three cases that Thim successfully appealed was Donald Browne, who was expected to be called as a witness in the Moxley grand jury. Thim was expected to investigate not only the criminal case against Michael Skakel, but the police investigation itself, exploring issues that might be brought up in a criminal trial, and determining whether any crimes were committed by the police or state's attorney office. Questioning in a grand jury has a much wider purview than examination in a criminal trial. The prosecutor and/or juror has much greater latitude in the scope of questioning during grand jury proceedings.

As grand juror, Thim will review the case file, subpoena and question witnesses, and submit a report stating whether or not Michael Skakel should be arrested. Because of the statute of limitation, prosecutors would have to charge him with felony murder, which is a reasonable charge, considering the fact that the killer left Martha battered and bleeding, but alive, for at least a half hour before returning with premeditation to cause her death. Sources close to the prosecution have told me that there will be no plea in this case.

Thim was expected to use the full eighteen months before submitting his report, but there are indications that he may wrap up the proceedings much earlier. Sources in Benedict's office are saying that they should be finished presenting their case in fall 1998. If Thim's report recommends an arrest, then a trial could begin in 1999. If he does not recommend an arrest, then the Moxley case will be considered closed.

At this writing, there has been no official report from the grand jury, but a lot has happened very quickly.

The grand jury proceedings opened on July 10, 1998. The first witnesses called to testify in Bridgeport's Fairfield County Courthouse were Dorthy Moxley, John Moxley, Sheila McGuire, Jean Walker, and Dan Hickman.

Joe Johnson of *Greenwich Time* was at the Bridgeport courthouse when Dan Hickman appeared to testify. Hickman told Joe that he expected he would be asked to describe his observations when he first saw Martha's body beneath the tree. Joe asked him if he would state that he saw the broken golf club in the victim's body. "Absolutely," Hickman said.

Though Hickman's testimony concerning the golf club shaft and handle he saw sticking out of the victim's head when he first viewed the body is central to the case, there are other questions he should have been asked. Why did he wait twenty-three years to reveal these observations? Did he tell his superiors about them at the time? Did anybody tell him to keep quiet about it? Why was he asked to attend the autopsy? Did Tom Keegan know that the golf club was present in the victim's body? If Keegan did know, when did he know it? Did Frank Garr ever contact Hickman and try to get him to recant the statements made concerning the golf club handle in 1997? What does Frank Garr know about the missing piece of the murder weapon?

Hickman's partner, Millard Jones, testified a few

weeks later. I assume he told the truth. In three tape-recorded conversations with me, Jones described in vivid detail the club shaft and handle he saw embedded in the victim's body. He also said that he had described those observations to his wife the night he returned from the crime scene, and she remembered his descriptions.

The missing golf club handle is the pivot on which the Moxley investigation turns. What happened to it? The destruction of a piece of evidence is an admission of guilt. To destroy the golf club would prove its value to the prosecution and the consciousness of guilt by the person destroying it. The only way to destroy the golf club handle completely without any chance of recovery would be to grind it into filings or to melt it in a furnace. My bet is that the golf club handle still exists. The questions remain: Who has it? Where is it? And who recovered it from the scene?

The missing golf club handle wasn't, and still isn't, necessary to catch the killer, but it explains a great deal of the behavior by the Greenwich police and the state's attorney office during the course of their investigations. Assuming the innocent explanation, that the club was lost—and not taken from the scene by a corrupt police officer—once the police realized they had lost the club, they made an error they believed they could not recover from. But they tried. From that point, the investigation had to run on two tracks. One, to continue to pursue the killer, and hope that he would somehow implicate himself or confess. Two, to cover up the loss of the golf club handle so that the police themselves did not come under scrutiny.

The golf club handle is more than just an important piece of evidence. Its absence caused all police procedure and interviews to be tainted from the onset and compromised innocent police officers, witnesses, and prosecutors. Every police officer, town, and state official who knew about the golf club handle engaged in the conspiracy, either through their actions or their silence, to cover up the fact that it was missing. The grand jury should determine who knew about the missing golf club handle, when they knew about it, and what they did to keep that information from the public.

Frank Garr and Jack Solomon reopened the case in 1991. After a review of the unredacted police report, they should have wondered why Hickman attended the autopsy and why Keegan saw fit to redact his, and only his name, from the police report. They should have interviewed Hickman and his partner, Jones. They should have asked them to describe in detail their observations and actions at the crime scene. They should have asked Hickman why he attended the autopsy and what he did there. Why didn't Garr and Solomon interview these two key police witnesses? Did they already know what the two officers would say? Did Garr and Solomon want to maintain plausible deniability concerning the missing golf club handle?

While he was on the case, Jack Solomon made countless statements to the print media and appearances on television. Since the publication of this book, he has remained silent.

Early on in my investigation of the Moxley murder, I determined that Ken Littleton had not killed Martha Moxley.

I don't know when the Connecticut authorities finally came to the conclusion that Littleton wasn't the killer. As late as November 1997, they were still calling him a suspect.

Littleton was subpoenaed and appeared before the grand jury with his new lawyer, Eugene Riccio, a Bridgeport-based criminal defense attorney who had worked closely with Thim when they were both public defenders. Littleton initially refused to testify, invoking his Fifth Amendment privilege. After negotiations with Littleton and Riccio, Jonathan Benedict asked a Superior Court Judge to compel Littleton to testify, giving him immunity from prosecution for any crime in the Moxley case except perjury in the course of his testimony.

The contents or nature of Littleton's testimony were not made public, but I hope he was asked not only about actions and movements in the Skakel house the night of October 30 and the following day, but also about his statements to the Sutton Associates, particularly his suspicion of Michael, and his belief that the murder occurred after 10:30 P.M.

Littleton testified for an hour and a half. Leaving the courtroom after his testimony, Littleton shook Jonathan Benedict's hand and said, "Thank you."

The immunity deal officially clears Littleton of

suspicion in the murder. Littleton himself wouldn't comment, but his lawyer, Riccio, said, "He's had twenty-three years of being suspected of beating a little girl to death. It certainly made life difficult for him, to say the least."

Littleton is forty-six years old. His hair is gray. He's been a murder suspect for half his life. Now that suspicion has finally lifted, I hope he can get the rest of his life back on track.

Following Littleton into the grand jury room were Detective Steve Carroll and State Chief Medical Examiner H. Wayne Carver. Carroll, no doubt, testified about the crime scene and subsequent investigation. Dr. Carver was not involved in Dr. Elliot Gross's examination of the crime scene or autopsy, but as current state medical examiner, Carver authorized Dr. Michael Baden's independent review of the Moxley autopsy. Carver probably presented testimony concerning the autopsy, and perhaps he also knows something about the missing autopsy photos.

Tom Keegan came up from South Carolina to testify and returned without commenting on the proceedings. Shortly after his return, he left a message on Joe Johnson's answering machine, calling me an "asshole" and complaining about the findings I published in the hardcover edition of this book. Why is Tom Keegan so angry at me? Joe says that Keegan is sticking to his story that he didn't see that golf club handle in the victim's body. If Keegan has stuck to this story, then a whole new line of inquiry should be followed in the grand jury proceedings to determine who knew about the missing golf club shaft and when they knew about it.

Also subpoenaed were former neighbors and friends of Michael Skakel who could testify to Michael Skakel's relationship with Martha. At least one witness reportedly saw Michael and Martha making out in the Revcon camper.

Rev. Mark Connolly testified on August 7. Connolly, a Catholic priest who used to appear on public television's *Sunday Mass*, was a friend of and adviser to the Skakel family. Connolly was with Rushton Skakel in Greenwich Hospital shortly after Rushton collapsed at the Ix residence, and arranged a meeting between the police and Rushton. Connolly also told police that he would recommend to Rushton that psychiatric and physiological tests be conducted on Thomas to prove his innocence. Those tests were conducted, with Thomas using a pseudonym, but the results were never turned over to the police. What else does Connolly know?

On August 11, 1998, a witness appeared in the courthouse—a female in her late thirties or early forties who identified herself only as Dorothy. Who was this mystery witness? Most of the locals did not know who she was, and those who did would not talk. Could Dorothy be a former girlfriend of Michael, or perhaps a fellow patient at Elan? She certainly knows something, because the prosecution was only calling very important witnesses at that stage of the proceedings.

That same day, another witness appeared whose identity was no mystery. Everyone knew Mildred Ix.

Prior to the grand jury being convened, Mildred and Helen Ix contacted Dorthy Moxley and said they would like to visit with her and John. Mildred and Helen came to Dorthy's house on a Sunday afternoon, and proceeded to say that they knew nothing of any importance in the case, and that they didn't think either one of the Skakel boys killed Martha. Mildred Ix claimed never to have been in the Skakel house the day Martha's body was found. Why, if Mildred Ix knew nothing about the murders and didn't suspect the boys were involved, would she deny being in the house? In a taped conversation, Jim McKenzie told me she was there. And Ken Littleton would certainly corroborate her presence in the house during his grand jury testimony.

After Mildred Ix, the grand jury closed in on the Skakel family. Steven Skakel has been subpoenaed to testify. Rushton Skakel has also been subpoenaed, but he refused to appear. He told the *Palm Beach Post* that he has "totally negated" the possibility of returning to Connecticut to testify. Rushton also said, "I wasn't there, personally. I was hunting when the [murder] happened, I just wasn't there and was there after the fact."

The old man is absolutely correct. He was there after the fact. But why did he not disclose that he returned at 8 P.M. the day Martha's body was found? Why did he not go directly to the police station to aid his son Thomas, who was then being interrogated? Upon his return, why did he have to talk to an attorney, Jim McKenzie, before McKenzie left the Skakel house? Why did he feel it necessary to keep his son

Michael committed in rehab centers and reform schools for twelve years following the murder of Martha Moxley? Why does he continue to refuse to cooperate with investigators?

At this writing, the court battle over whether or not Rushton Skakel can be forced to testify is still ongoing. Mickey Sherman says Rushton is claiming that acute physical ailments preclude him from appearing in the Bridgeport courthouse. If those ailments prevent Rushton from traveling to Connecticut, then what's stopping Connecticut authorities from taking the court to Rushton Skakel? He could appear by means of video link. If the subpoena is quashed, Frank Garr wants to fly down to Florida to interrogate the elder Skakel. If Rushton Skakel has refused to cooperate with investigators since January 1976, what makes Frank think that he'll talk to him?

Why doesn't Frank Garr interrogate Eleanor Stude? He has had information about her for three years, ever since she called *Unsolved Mysteries* and left her phone number and described her relationship to Rushton Skakel. If he wants leverage against Rushton, a statement from the woman with whom he spent that weekend would be very useful.

Though it has not been announced at the time of this writing, I assume that Thomas Skakel will be called in to testify. What will he do? Will he fight the subpoena? Will he appear and take the Fifth? Or will he flip and tell what he knows?

Imagine that your brother committed a murder, but you were considered the prime suspect. Imagine that suspicion followed you for your entire adult life. Thomas Skakel has lived for twenty-three years with the shadow of murder looming over him. Thomas never attempted to clear himself in the crime, except by cooperating with the Sutton Associates, and we already saw what happened as a result of all that. The Skakels use of the Sutton Associates only focused more suspicion on the Skakel family.

Still, Thomas hasn't turned on his brother, Michael. What hold did the family have over him?

I wonder what the Skakel family reunions are like these days. Thomas and Michael's sibling rivalry was already fierce and violent as boys. Did Martha's murder turn their rivalry into a silent hatred? Or was it a sin that bonded them together?

Michael Skakel has moved to Florida to be near his father. When Rushton was contacted by the *Washington Post*'s Rita Beamish, he told the reporter that both Michael and Thomas were with him, but they couldn't come to the phone. They were out golfing.

Back home in Idaho, I got a call from Mickey Sherman, who told me he had been hired to represent Michael in the Moxley case. Mickey is, by all reports, a capable lawyer. He knows most of the players in the Moxley case, having grown up with Frank Garr and defended a criminal suspect in a trial presided over by Judge Thim. The Skakels hired him as an insider, someone with connections in Greenwich and the Connecticut criminal justice system. If this case goes to trial, I don't expect Mickey Sherman to be lead defense counsel. The word around Bridgeport is that Roy Black was already on retainer. Black, who successfully defended William Kennedy Smith on rape charges, did not answer calls asking whether he had been retained by the Skakels. Since the Miami lawyer's specialty is defending rape and sexual assault suspects, he does seem an odd choice. His "blame the victim" defense won't work in the Moxley case.

I hope Judge Thim has the evidence, and the courage, to issue a true bill, and that Michael Skakel is arrested for the murder of Martha Moxley. If his report does not recommend an arrest or subsequent citizen grand jury, many observers are saying that the case will finally be closed, but no murder case is ever closed until the killer is brought to justice. For twenty-three years, the killer of Martha Moxley has gotten away with murder. If he isn't put on trial, then we will have another O.J. Simpson—a murderer who is free because of money, power, politics, and fear.

—September 14, 1998

INDEX